Alas, Jesse

By Katheryn Lynn Cameron

KATYDID PUBLICATIONS

Alas, Jesse

Copyright © 2003, Katheryn Lynn Cameron

Katydid Publications
P.O. Box 526
Point Lookout, Missouri 65726
www.katydid-publications.com

9 781879 945050

I dedicate this book to my mother-in-law,
Cora, and my daughter, Coralyn Anne.
They lived at different periods of time,
but both were able to deal with
any and all circumstances.

ACKNOWLEDGEMENTS

My grandson, Kirk, and his wife, Denise, for "dotting the I's and crossing the T's".

My son, Dr. Glen Cameron, and his wife, Kay, who said "It can be published," and then did it.

Without Anne's help I never would have been able to finish my book. I thank her and my family for their help.

Special thanks to my friend and neighbor, Carolyn Wulff, for her lovely illustrations.

Janet Miller for her time, advice and expertise

Vlady Petrova, Tanya Ganchevska, and Rezi Kerraj for for their interest and comments.

Richard Carroll for technical advice.

ABOUT THE AUTHOR

Katheryn Elizabeth Lynn was born in Marionville, Missouri. Her father passed away before she was three. The family moved to a farm nearby, and Katheryn's grandfather, Robert Fulton Bolton, a widower, came to live with them. Grandpa Bolton played an important role in Katheryn's childhood. He was the one she looked to for advice. Grandpa encouraged Katheryn to write, often dictating letters to family members for Katheryn to write for him. Katheryn penned her first poem when she was in third grade.

My name is Katheryn Lynn
I've come from where I've been.

Grandpa said, "Katheryn will be a writer, but she won't be a poet!"

Katheryn Lynn graduated from Crane High School in 1935; favorite subjects included Drama, English, History, and Chorus. She attended Harding College in Mexico, Missouri and married Virgil Cameron in 1937. Katheryn's five children all have college degrees and are successful in their careers. She has eleven grandchildren, thirteen great-grandchildren, and two great-great grandchildren.

Geography fascinated Katheryn as a child. She has been to many of the places she dreamed of going; to England several times, Mexico, Germany, Austria, Spain, Switzerland, Gibraltar, Portugal, Italy, and Egypt.

Katheryn lived in several states during the fifty years Virgil served as teacher, coach, principal, and superintendent. When Virgil retired, they returned to the family farm where Virgil's family had lived for several generations. Virgil and Katheryn had been married sixty-one years when he passed away at sunrise in 1998, a few feet from where he was born.

FOREWORD

William Kennedy and Kate Campbell were both born in County Antrim, Ireland. At the age of nine, William sailed for America with his parents, brothers and sisters. On the way his father and two brothers died from ship fever and were buried at sea. William, his mother, and his sisters landed in Canada. In 1865 William went to the Irish immigrant section of New York City.

Kate also went to America with her family as a child. They landed at Ellis Island. Kate hoped they would move on west as she had always had a desire to own land, but they settled in the Irish section of New York City.

It was surely fate that Kate and William should meet. They were from the same county in Ireland, but hadn't known each other there. Each had taken a different path in coming to New York where they met. They were married in 1870 after a long courtship. Following the birth of their first two children, Kate and William moved their family to a 360-acre farm in Missouri. They saw America prosper and change as they lived through droughts, depression, and wars. Though Kate and William changed with the times, they were always loyal to family and friends.

Their oldest son, Will, fell in love with Jessie, the prettiest girl in the community, but he was without resources to start a home. There was a Scottish-French girl, Claire, in the community, due to inherit an outstanding farm. With the Irish love of the land, Will settled for Claire and the farm, but alas, the thought of Jessie was always with him.

CONTENTS

Spring 1901

The warm May sun soothed Will Kennedy's body as he rode the old mare into Brandton. He was in need of soothing, but it would take more than a spring day to soothe his mind. He knew his very future depended on what he could accomplish today.

He would soon be twenty-one, the eldest son in a family of eight. When Will was nine his father's health had failed, and Will began doing a man's work on the farm. At the time he had been so proud to show what he could do. With younger brothers in the family, he had thought that in time one of them would take his place and he could leave home to seek his fortune. It had become obvious to Will that was not to be the case. Most families in the community let their sons leave at eighteen. Of late he could see his mother had more plans for the future of the other children than for his.

It was just a matter of time before Frank went to St. Louis to look for work. A neighbor's daughter, Ruth, had gone to St. Louis and was living with her sister and brother-in-law. The sister had written that Frank could stay at their boarding house for free until he found a job. He wasn't much help on the farm anyway. Nathan wasn't much better; he was more interested in sparking one of the girls in town. Her father owned the mill and if Nat married her he would probably work in the mill. Besides, Nat said farm life wasn't to his liking.

Will had helped in getting his older sister, Lettie, married off to Isaac Stewart. He had seen Isaac at a community baseball game on a Sunday afternoon. The minute he had seen that thoroughbred horse galloping down the road with the well-dressed young man astride he thought, "That would be an ideal match for Lettie." Will made Isaac's acquaintance and before the game was over, invited him to come for supper. It would be an opportunity for him to meet Lettie. Will had sent his youngest brother Andy home to tell his mother he was bringing Isaac home for dinner to meet Lettie. By the time they had arrived, his mother had quite a meal ready and Lettie was in her second best dress. The Kennedy's had heard of the Stewarts in the next township. They knew some of them were well to do and assumed Isaac was also, especially when he showed up in a surrey.

The romance progressed quickly and the Kennedys were impressed when Isaac mentioned his farm. After the wedding the Stewarts' gave a traditional infare dinner to welcome home the young newlyweds. It was then that Will overheard an uncle of Isaac's say "You have had the saddle horse for four years now, and you still haven't paid for it. You have until fall to at least pay the interest on all we have loaned you or we will foreclose on the mortgage."

Isaac replied quite stricken, "I thought Lettie would have some money with her dowry."

If Isaac had expected a larger dowry, the Kennedy's were disappointed too; they had gotten the impression that Isaac was comfortably fixed, if not quite wealthy. The whole family had made quite a sacrifice to provide the dowry for Lettie. Will hadn't been too pleased when his mother took his feather bed for the dowry and left him with a straw tick mattress.

Eli Cox was courting Minnie, Frank's twin sister, at the same time Lettie and Isaac were courting. The girls exchanged dresses, making their four good dresses apiece seem as if they each had eight good dresses. They were able to give the impression of having quite a wardrobe.

And there would still be Lucy and little Meggie at home if Minnie and Eli wed.

It wasn't just those things that had prompted Will to start off this warm May morning; it was standing with Jessie Randolph by her front gate in the light of a full moon the evening before. No doubt about it, Jessie was the prettiest girl in their community. She had thick dark hair with waves on top, turning to curls around her face and ringlets at her neck. She always wore a shade of sky blue that was just the color of her eyes and her necklines a little lower than the other girls. Lettie and Minnie said it wasn't proper but it surely did please him!

As he and Jessie had stood there in the moonlight she had swayed against him; he wanted her more than anything in the world and told her so. All the way home he had thought about what could be in the future for the two of them. He didn't have anything of his own. He couldn't farm with Jessie's folk after they were married. Her older brother was getting married next week and would live with the Randolph's. Another brother was sixteen and could do a man's work too. No, they wouldn't need nor want another man on their farm.

It was out of the question to even think of taking Jessie to his home for a few years. There would never be enough extra for him to save toward a place of his own. But mainly it wouldn't work because of his mother. Kate was domineering by her nature and had become even more so after his father had lost his health and she had to take over running the farm. Even before that she had 'ruled the roost.'

His parents had succeeded against great odds. Kate Campbell and William Kennedy were both born in County Antrim, Ireland. At the age of nine, William sailed for America with his parents, brothers and sisters. On the voyage his father, Malcom, and two brothers took ship fever and died. They were buried at sea. William, his mother, and two sisters landed in Montreal, Canada. A minister and his wife took them into their home until his mother could find a home for them. William became an errand boy in a printing office for which he received his room and board. At thirteen he began learning the plumbers' trade. He served an apprenticeship for six years. In 1865 he went to New York City, where he met Kate through friends living in the Irish section of the city. After a long courtship, they were married in 1870.

After Lettie and William, Jr. were born, the family moved to a 360-acre farm in Missouri. They were doing quite well until William, Sr. lost his health. Kate took over managing the farm and working in the field. Will, Jr. took a man's place in the field. His mother had come to depend on him and that worried Will. Even the little money he earned hiring out to neighbors she had taken to buy material for dresses for the girls.

Will knew there was no way he could bring Jessie to the farm, and he couldn't bear the idea of another year working for nothing. He was hoping to find an answer in Brandton. He would need cash if he found a place to rent. He didn't think the bank would loan money without a co-signer or some collateral, but he intended to talk to the banker anyway. Perhaps the banker would know someone who wanted to hire a young couple to work the year around on a farm.

Will wasn't sure about going in debt. It had been a dry winter; there was very little water in the ponds for this time of year. Rainfall had been so short this spring, and the seed they had planted wasn't coming up too well.

Will let the mare break into a trot as they came in sight of Brandton; they were both eager to have a change. Brandton was quite a thriving village.

Businesses there included three general merchandise firms, a millinery business with a dress maker, four physicians, one druggist, the bank, a harness manufacturer, a mill, a jeweler, and a real estate agency. There was also a barber shop with a photography studio in the back, two hotels, a post office, a blacksmith shop, a livery stable, an undertaker's parlor, and a tobacco manufacturer. Four churches took care of the community's spiritual needs. Besides schools for the primary and intermediate classes, Brandton had an academy for teachers. It was quite a pleasant town and Will wished he could come more often.

He decided to stop by the McCaskell's General Store before going to the bank; he might pick up some information, or better yet some courage. The young McCaskell boys, James and Eckles, ran the store while their father ran the business end. Will tied his horse at the hitching rail and went in the store. Eckles greeted him in a brisk business like way. "Hi Will, what can I get for you today?" Will hadn't intended to buy anything but didn't want to admit it. "Oh, I am just looking around. I haven't made up my mind yet."

Will was aware of the physical difference between Eckles and himself. Eckles was built like a barrel, short and wide, showing his Scottish ancestry. Will, on the other hand was tall and lean, with auburn hair and Irish blue eyes. At parties Eckles and James sat at the edge of the activities while all the girls made quite a fuss over Will. But Jessie was the only one who interested him.

The thought of Jessie brought him back to the reason for his journey to town today. He decided to look through the housewares department to get an idea of how much the necessities to start housekeeping would cost. The more he looked at the prices the more hopeless he felt his plight.

As Will continued to look through the store, he overheard a conversation between James and another customer who had come into the store. "How are things with you, John?"

"Not good. I had to mortgage 160 acres to get money for seed for ten acres of corn and forty acres of oats. Banker Jennings said that crop prospects didn't look too good this year and that if it didn't rain soon the yield would be way down. By the way, how is your Uncle Charles doing?"

"He will never get any better. I think the only thing keeping him here is his concern for Cousin Claire. I don't know what will happen to her when he is gone. He would like to see her married before he dies, but she is eighteen and has never had a beau."

"Too bad, they have a real good place out there."

Will's mind was whirling with the news he had overheard. If John Anderson had to mortgage 160 acres to get seed for this year's crop, the bank wouldn't be about to loan him money to get started. Suddenly Jessie seemed out of reach.

Will knew the Charles Lefever place, but he couldn't remember the younger daughter. He knew the mother had died years ago and an older daughter had kept house for the father until she married someone in another neighborhood. Will thought he might ride out and see the place. He had no idea what he would do when he got to the Lefever's but it wouldn't hurt to take a look.

Charles Lefever sat on the porch feeling the warm sunrays penetrate his ailing body. He could tell his health was failing day by day; the good days were getting farther apart. Dying didn't bother him, but he had one wish or prayer and that was to see Claire married before he died.

He heard a horseman coming down the lane. He wished it could be a young single man, a suitor for Claire, but he had almost given up on that happening. Then a rider came into view who was just what Charles would have asked for! He was tall, handsome, and young.

Will saw Mr. Lefever sitting on the porch and suddenly remembered what passersby did at their place when they wanted to stop and visit—-they asked for a drink of water. Will left the horse by the gate and came down the walk. "Howdy. I wonder if I could get a drink of water; this warm May sun has left me thirsty."

"Yes, yes of course, come in and sit on the porch. My daughter will bring you a drink. Claire, bring this young man a glass of water."

About the time Will sat down, Claire appeared with his drink. It was a good thing he was sitting down. She was tall and thin; she had on a plain dress like his mother worked in. Her thin blonde hair was carelessly piled on top of her head; a few strands hung down.

Charles wasn't about to let this opportunity pass. "You are one of the Kennedy boys, aren't you?"

"Yes, I'm William, Jr., the oldest son."

"Well, you must have missed your dinner by now. We were about ready to eat. Claire has made Irish stew; even the French like Irish stew."

Will said, "I wouldn't want to impose."

Charles insisted, "It wouldn't be an imposition. You really should join us for dinner." Claire excused herself, and in a few minutes, returned to tell them the meal was ready. She started to help her father but Will quickly took Charles' arm and they went in to dinner.

Will noted how neat and clean the house was and that the meal looked very inviting. Stew, yeast rolls, butter, jelly and custard pie. Charles was in such high spirits at having a young man as a guest that Claire was happy at the improvement in her father. Together they made it a most hospitable occasion.

Will gathered several pertinent bits of information. Claire's mother had died when Claire was five years old. An older sister, Aimie, had kept house for them until she married. Claire had been eleven at the time and she had been keeping house since then. Due to failing health, Charles had sold most of the livestock last fall to cut down on the chores during the winter. That accounted for the two untouched haystacks and a barn full of hay.

Will really enjoyed the meal. After they finished he said, "This Irishman says that was good Irish stew. To show my appreciation, could I bring in some wood?" Claire started to protest but Charles quickly accepted; he was going to stretch this visit out as long as he could.

Will asked Claire where the wood box was and went out to the wood pile. He filled the box and then proceeded to split a nice pile of wood for the cook stove. On a trip into the house he asked Claire if she ever went to the neighborhood parties.

Claire answered, "A few times I went with my cousins, the McCaskell's."

"I don't remember seeing you there."

"I don't wonder that you didn't see me. That Jessie Randolph was all you saw."

Will was able to laugh. "You ought to know my sisters. Why don't you come to dinner Sunday? I probably can't get the surrey but you could ride a horse, couldn't you?"

Claire said, "If Papa is feeling well, I would love to come."

As Will and the old horse made their way down the country road, Will reviewed the day. It all added up to the fact that there was no way he could strike out on his own and marry Jessie. On the other hand, anyone who married Claire would soon have a farm. Claire seemed kind and industrious; if only she wasn't so plain! If he married her he could get away from his mother and working for nothing.

As he rode up to the barn lot his mother was waiting by the gate. He could tell she was angry. She was standing with her feet spread apart, her hands on her hips, her jaw firm, and her face flushed. That could only mean one thing; she was more than annoyed, she was seething.

Kate Kennedy was a strange woman; when she was in the house everything was 'fit and proper'. Neither she, nor anyone else, dared use profanity. It was different when she was running the farm; sometimes she used the most unladylike language then.

"Will, where in the hell have you been all day? Nat and Frank have kept me prodding them constantly. You should have been here to get things done." She continued to berate him as he unsaddled the horse and turned it out to pasture. Will wisely kept his council. He decided this wasn't the time to ask for a guest at Sunday dinner!

Later, when supper was about over, he asked, "Ma, I would like to have Claire Lefever over for Sunday dinner."

"That milk sop!"

Minnie and Lucy chimed in, "What about Jessie?"

His mother said, "No, it is out of the question."

William cleared his throat, "It seems to me Will does a lot for us and this is the first time he has asked to bring a guest. I think it will be convenient for Claire to come Sunday." His father seldom disagreed with his mother but when he voiced an opinion that settled the issue.

Kate seethed inside. That was the second time today Will had gotten the best of her, first taking the mare and being gone all day and now this. She couldn't let Will leave home; he had a feel for the land that the other boys didn't. She could accept it if the others boys left the farm, but not Will; she needed him here!

Minnie and Lucy continued to titter and make remarks. Minnie whispered, "We won't have any competition with her." Lucy giggled and suggested, "Will must need glasses." Their voices were pitched just loud enough to be sure Will caught their comments, but not loud enough for their father to hear.

Will felt he was now committed to his plan. He would marry Claire as soon as he could do it without arousing suspicions. He wasn't going to stay another season on his family's farm. Jessie would be hurt. He didn't know what he would say to her or how to tell her, so until then he would just stay away from places where she might be.

17

Will's Guest for Sunday Dinner

Spring in Missouri can be fickle. Sunday the weather was cold, damp, and windy. Will was grateful he got to use the buggy to go after Claire. The weather didn't help Will's spirits, but the thought of having land to till and being able to keep the fruits of his labor, began to soothe the hurt somewhat.

He arrived at the Lefever's at ten o'clock. Claire was fussing over her father, making sure he knew where she had left his dinner.

Claire wore a white blouse with a high collar, a full black skirt, and a cape that had been her mother's. She had used a curling iron to make a few curls around her face. It was hard to make the curls on yourself but she had patiently heated the curling iron, putting it inside the globe of the oil lamp to heat. At last she was ready and she was pleased with the results.

Charles was happy Claire was going with an eligible man to meet his family, but he was disappointed she didn't look better. Her mother had been stylish, but Claire didn't seem to pick up hints on what made a woman look more attractive. Maybe it was because she wasn't around women folk often enough. Well, he would certainly give his blessing if Will Kennedy would marry her.

Since Claire was ready they all exchanged greetings on the porch. After a few pleasantries Charles wished them a good day and Claire and Will were on their way.

They hadn't gone far when the damp wind began to loosen Claire's curls. Will noticed her distress and said he knew what his sisters did when their curls drooped, they just pinned them up. He stopped the buggy, reached over and helped her catch the stray strands. While he was that close he decided to give her a kiss; maybe it would make her feel wanted if Minnie and Lucy chose to be distant.

Claire gave a gasp and blushed when he kissed her. Will said, "I hope you didn't mind."

Claire stammered, "I just wasn't expecting that."

"I will ask first from now on."

Claire gave a little laugh, "Well, all right then."

Will's parents came out on the porch to greet them. They ushered Will and Claire into the parlor where they proceeded to talk about weather, crops, and the usual things.

When Kate rose to go to the kitchen, Claire asked if she could help. Kate refused, "No, thank you, there are too many in the kitchen now."

The comment was not lost on Will. He knew his mother was giving notice that he wasn't to bring a bride here. Will was even more determined to marry Claire by fall.

Claire and Will's father got along very well. She was much more at ease with William than with Kate. Since her own father was in poor health, Claire understood how much company helped to give an ill person something else to think about. She couldn't help but feel Kate was holding her at arm's length.

At last the rest of the family came in to greet Claire. Will thought, 'if that had been Jessie, I couldn't have kept Frank and Nat out.' Five-year-old Meggie, the youngest, was the sweetest one of the family. She came and stood by Claire's chair. Where the others saw a pale, tall girl, Meggie saw a kind and loving person who asked her if she had any kittens and what their names were. Lucy and Minnie never wanted to hear anything about her pets or dolls. A friendship was cemented that morning between Claire and Meggie that was to last a lifetime.

Will was glad when it was time to take Claire home. He found just the right spot to stop the buggy. The sun had come out and warmed the day. He turned to Claire, "May I kiss you again?"

Claire smiled and said, "Since you asked, yes."

In time Will knew the answer to marriage would be 'yes' too.

As they came into view of the Lefever place he marveled at the beautiful sight. The winding driveway led up the knoll to a house ideally situated to make the most of the view. Will knew he could love the place but he wondered if he could ever love Claire. Knowing he could not manage to have Jessie left him empty, but at least through Claire he would be able to free himself. He had been feeling like a slave in bondage. He hoped he would not always feel about Jessie as he did now, but marrying Claire was the only way he could see of freeing himself.

Charles came out to greet them when they reached the house. He was pleased to see that Claire looked so happy. She even had a little color in her cheeks.

Will helped Claire to alight from the buggy. "Since I kept you so late, could I help you with your chores?"

Claire was delighted at the offer but the thought of a cow kicking milk over him prompted her to say, "I don't believe old Bossy would let a stranger milk her. But if you will come in and talk to Papa while I change my dress and do the milking I'll give you a piece of pie before you start home"

"That's quite a deal," Will said. "I'd be glad to." It was easy to talk to Charles and the time passed quickly.

When Claire finished the chores she called them in for cold chicken, potato salad, and pie. Claire hoped that the way to a man's heart was through his stomach. She didn't know that the way to this man's heart was through her farm.

When Will started home Claire followed him outside. Will asked, "I would like to come again. May I?"

"My sister Aimie and her family are coming next Sunday. They come once a month to visit Papa. Would you like to join us for dinner?"

"Yes, if you don't mind." Will thought the sooner he got into the family the better.

Will knew that Aimie had married Banker Jennings's brother, David, but that didn't mean they were rich. David was the oldest in the family; his father had died when David was fourteen. David had stayed on the farm and helped his mother raise four other children. The three sisters married neighbors' sons. David had supported his brother Wesley through college. Afterwards Wesley came back and got a job in the bank, where he quickly worked his way to the top.

Will was surprised how much he was looking forward to Sunday and going to the Lefever's. As he worked, he planned what he would do on their farm the next year. Minnie and Lucy's little remarks didn't even rile him. But the last image he saw at night was Jessie's face in the moonlight.

As he approached the Lefever's the next Sunday, Will was glad to see the Jennings' had just arrived. It would be much easier to meet everyone out on the lawn. Claire was darting from one to another of Aimie's children. Aimie was much like Claire, only older, shorter, and heavier. She had brought a cake and some St. Louis newspapers a neighbor had saved for Charles. The women took them and the Jennings' baby into the house. The older children played in the yard while the men talked. Charles sat on the porch and watched his grandchildren play. He was very contented.

David was glad to see a young man on the place. He hoped Claire would marry and free them of the responsibility of doing for them. He and Aimie did what they could for Claire and Charles, but it was becoming quite a burden trying to do as much as was increasingly needed. He understood why Aimie felt like a mother toward Claire because he felt like a father to his own sisters and even to his brother Wesley. The sisters still looked to him for help, and with his own four children it was becoming difficult, both physically and financially, to take care of everyone's needs.

At last David said, "There was some fence by the barn I didn't finish mending when I was here last time. I think I will do that before dinner."

"Let me help, too," Will offered. He was glad of the opportunity to do something.

David was pleased with Will's offer. Wesley would never have volunteered to help. He had married a girl from St. Louis, who felt Brandton was beneath her social standing and the rural Jennings' uncouth. Now it seemed that Wesley felt the same way toward the family. If any of the family needed a loan they underwent the same scrutiny as any other applicant. When they were in the bank Wesley would ask about the family, but he never said 'Come and see us.' In spite of Wesley's treatment, David wasn't bitter; the rest of the family was very loving and Aimie was the light of his life. Even so, a brother-in-law who was comfortable on the farm would be welcome.

Inside the house, Aimie put Dougie down on the bed and gave Claire a big hug. "Oh Claire, you have a beau!"

"I guess so; he took me to his home last Sunday for dinner."

"Oh, I am so glad, Claire, and he is so handsome. I hope there is a wedding in the offing."

"I am too afraid to hope."

"Well, you are going to have to make a great effort; you really need some pretty dresses. I have some material I was going to use to make Malinda a dress, but she can wait. I'll make a dress for you instead. You can go in next week and get some yardage for some more dresses. Get something bright and cheerful like pink or yellow. The clothes you have are down right drab."

"I haven't thought much about clothes; Papa says I should 'frill things up'."

Aimie grew somber, "Claire, there is something we are going to have to face. David and I notice it more than you do because we only see Papa once a month. We can see he is failing. Three months ago he wouldn't have stayed on the porch while someone fixed fence on the place. He would have been out there, if only to watch."

"I know he isn't getting better and I worry what I will do when he is gone."

"You would always be welcome to live with David and me but I would rather see you married and in your own home."

"We will work on that."

In the meantime Will and David were getting along amicably. The work went well and they found they had many things in common, although their motives were poles apart. David wanted Claire married so she would be taken care of when Charles was gone. Will wanted to marry Claire so the farm would be his when Charles died.

Charles was content to sit on the porch and contemplate his surroundings. The laughter of the children playing, the men working, the sounds of the women preparing dinner, and the comfort of his oldest grandchild, Malinda, keeping him company as they both rocked on the porch added to his enjoyment of the day. He hoped he could last long enough to see Claire married and with a family.

Everyone was in good humor at dinner. Will pleased Aimie when he commented how well behaved her children were. Aimie said, "I would be proud to take them any place for dinner, even to the banker's house!"

Everyone laughed because they knew the children were not likely to be invited to Wesley's home.

After all the guests had left, Claire asked Charles, "Papa, would it be all right if I rode into town tomorrow and got some material for dresses? I could go down to Lowes' in the morning and ask Estelle to ride with me."

Charles was delighted that Claire wanted to improve her appearance. "That would be fine. You should go to Mrs. Mason's Shop and order a summer dress for Sunday and a suit for fall. Let her choose the color and style. I am afraid you have missed having a mother to train you along those lines."

"Oh, Papa, you have always taken good care of both Aimie and me."

"It is not the same, child, but run along; you deserve some pretty clothes. Let Mrs. Mason do the choosing. This time don't be practical."

Claire was surprised at herself for being so excited about the prospect of new clothes. Early the next morning she hurried over to the Lowes' to see if Estelle could go to Brandton with her that afternoon.

"Estelle, Papa said I could have some new dresses. Can you go to town with me this afternoon to Mrs. Mason's Shop?"

"Mother, may I go to town with Claire?"

"Certainly!" Daily Lowes was glad for Estelle to accompany Claire. She didn't get a chance to go to town very often. The Lowes' were French Creoles from Louisiana. Quite a few of the neighbors held that Creole meant a person was mixed with the Negro race. The Ragain's and the Randolph's especially liked to talk about the Lowes'. They didn't invite Estelle to their homes to visit.

Claire and Estelle made a strange looking pair as they rode to town; Claire tall and thin, Estelle short and wide. They had to pass the Ragain place on the way to town. All the children ran to the front yard fence to watch them pass. Claire heard Ona, the oldest girl, call, "Here comes the elephant and the giraffe!" For Estelle's sake Claire ignored the comment.

Mrs. Ragain was sitting on the front porch; she called, "What takes you girls into town?"

Claire just nodded and on they rode. After they were out of hearing distance, Claire said, "If Mrs. Ragain couldn't hear that big mouth girl as close as she was, I couldn't hear Mrs. Ragain as far away as she was." They both laughed! Claire continued, "The reason I came over this morning is to see if you could go to town with me. I didn't want the party line to know about my new clothes."

"I am excited about going with you to see about new dresses."

Mrs. Mason's Shop was a dream world to the girls. There were fabrics, dress forms with their creations on them, patterns laid out on cutting table, and the busy seamstress.

Claire introduced herself. "I am Claire Lefever; Papa said I could order some new clothes. He said to have you pick the material, color and style."

Mrs. Mason laughed, "That is the best order I have had in a long time. Does he remember that I made your mother's wedding suit? I remember it was in January and I made a fur hat and muff for her too."

"I didn't know who made it but my sister, Aimie, has the hat and muff. She only wears it once a year, to church at Christmas."

"I enjoyed sewing for your mother. Her father, Old Doc McCaskill, let her do her own selecting. What did you have in mind?"

"Well, I need a summery dress now and Papa said to order a suit for fall. I would like a hat and muff to match. Could you have the dress by next Saturday?"

Estelle had been looking around the shop at the bolts of cloth and the dresses on the dress forms. "Claire, look at this beautiful sky blue dress!"

Mrs. Mason said, "That is for Jessie Randolph. Her mother hinted they might be ordering a wedding gown before long."

Claire's heart strings tightened; who could it be? It couldn't be Will; she couldn't lose Will.

Unaware of Claire's discomfort, Mrs. Mason began to show the girls different materials and colors, holding them up to Claire. At last she decided on a yellow, dotted Swiss. "I'll put ruffles at the throat and a sash with a big bow. I think a sapphire blue wool for your suit with a matching blue velvet muff and hat. I can have your dress by Saturday."

The girls chatted happily on the way home. Underneath Claire's gaiety was a nagging thought about Mrs. Mason's words "an order soon for Jessie's wedding dress." She had seen Will and Jessie together at the parties. Well, he was coming to see her Sunday and she would have a new dress. Claire decided she would even buy the little pot of rouge she had seen in Mrs. Mason's Shop. Claire hadn't realized until now how much she wanted Will and needed him. She just couldn't lose him!

The Letter

Will was pleased how his relationship with Claire was progressing. He spent all of his spare time at the Lefever's. He managed the farm at home and made Nat, Andy, and Frank do more of their share of the work.

Kate was pleased with their efforts but was uneasy at the way events were taking shape. She knew that any day now Frank would be leaving for St. Louis. The lure of the city and Ruth Stimson were pulling him like a magnet. Nat would be going to work at the mill for the Russell's. As soon as he had the money he would marry their daughter, Lucinda. Nat had never liked farming and never made a secret of wanting to leave. Kate could tongue lash Andy all day and not get results. Andy would stop the team at the far end of the field and rest; he thought it a great joke if she had to walk all that way to get him started again.

Will was the only one who instinctively knew how the land should be worked and she was losing him. She hadn't been concerned that he might marry Jessie. She knew the Randolphs had enough family to work their farm and Jessie didn't strike her as a person who would take second place in a household. But Claire Lefever was another matter. Will probably saw Claire as a way to get his own farm.

Will was inwardly congratulating himself at how well his plans were going as he came to the house for lunch. Lucy came running to meet him at the barn.

"Will, Will, you got a letter."

When Will saw the return address was Jessie Randolph, his heart stopped. He hoped he appeared calm as he said, "Gee, thanks Little Sister." He had known he would have to face what their relationship was and what it had become.

As Lucy ran back to the house she called, "Dinner in fifteen minutes."

Will put the horses in their stalls and quickly poured their feed. Then he opened the dreaded letter.

Dearest Will,

> *I have been so worried. What has gone wrong?*
> *After the last time you were here I had expected you*
> *back in a few days to make plans for our future. I let*
> *Joe and Martha have my room. I told them I would*
> *soon be getting married so I took the little room in the*
> *attic. I must know what your plans for us are. I can't*
> *imagine life without us together. I am waiting for you*
> *to come.*

> *Love you truly,*
> *Jessie*

Will was devastated, he knew he couldn't see Jessie again. He couldn't tell her the truth and he wouldn't lie to her. Nor could he risk Claire hearing that Jessie thought he was marrying her. He had lost Jessie but he wouldn't lose the Lefever farm too. He would decide the best way to approach the problem later. For now he would go in to lunch and try to act as if everything was all right.

Everyone was curious about the letter but no one came right out and asked. At last the meal was over and he could escape back to work.

All afternoon he tried different ideas. At last he decided the safest thing to do was to show the letter to Claire and say that he had no idea Jessie felt that way about him. He couldn't risk the Lefever's hearing gossip that he had been serious with Jessie. There was a good chance the McCaskell's might hear gossip in the store and feel it their duty to tell their Uncle Charles. They would probably think he wasn't reliable, or even worse, a philanderer and Charles would not take kindly to that.

This was Friday; he decided to show the letter to Claire on Sunday afternoon. If he handled it right Claire would believe that he was surprised by the letter, (which was true), that he didn't want to marry Jessie, (which was false), and that he wanted to marry Claire, (which was true).

He hadn't planned to ask Claire to marry him this soon but he might as well find out if this was to be his way out of working for nothing and a chance at having a farm.

Sunday afternoon came at last. Claire hurried to finish dinner so she could have extra time to experiment with the rouge. The yellow dress did seem to give more color to her hair. The ruffle at the neckline made her look not quite so flat chested ..... Oh, for a bosom like Jessie's! After she finished dressing she went to show her father.

"Claire, you look very nice. We should have given more attention to your wardrobe."

"Papa, I am happy about the dress and thank you for it. Aimie is bringing me another one when they come next Sunday."

Charles said, "I hear a horse coming; it must be Will. Go sit on the porch. I am going to lie down for awhile."

As Will came up the walk Claire stood so Will could get the full affect of her new dress and new look. Will certainly was impressed, he was also relieved to see that Charles wasn't on the porch; he would be glad to get this afternoon over. "My, don't you look nice!"

Claire blushed, "Do you really like my new dress?"

"It is a shame not to be going some place but I'll enjoy looking at it."

Claire couldn't have been more pleased. After making small talk for a few minutes, Will tackled the problem of Jessie's letter.

"Claire, something strange happened this week. I don't have any idea why or what I should do about it. I got a letter from a girl wanting to marry me. I was shocked! I hadn't asked her to marry me, but I did plan to ask you. Will awkwardly took Claire's hand and asked the question Claire had been hoping for! "Claire Lefever, will you marry me?"

Claire didn't hesitate! "Yes, yes, of course!"

"Good. That is settled," Will replied; "About the letter I got this week. I decided to let you read it but I don't intend to answer it."

When Claire had read the letter she looked at Will. "You mean I beat the prettiest girl's time for you?" It was a remark that was to haunt Will every time he heard Claire say it through the coming years.

"It was fate that brought us together."

"Yes, we will tell Papa the news after he rests awhile."

"You set the date."

Claire thought a minute. "This is the middle of July. How about the middle of October?"

"October would be good. That will give me plenty of time to finish up the crops. It has been so dry the harvest will be small."

Soon Charles decided he had rested long enough and came out on the porch. Claire was so happy she burst out, "Papa, Will has asked me to marry him in October!"

"With your approval, sir."

Charles said, "I certainly do approve! I would like for you and Claire to live here with me."

"Oh Papa, I would like that! I wouldn't want to leave you. What do you want Will?"

"We hadn't gotten that far in our discussion but that would be all right with me."

Will was jubilant as he rode home. He hadn't expected to be accepted, approved, and invited to live at the Lefever's all in the same afternoon! He could shout for joy at the thought of having land of his own. His farm would be larger than his parents! But the joy of having his own farm couldn't ease the hurt of not ever being able to have Jessie.

Will reached home as the family was ready to sit down at the evening meal. Nat had just announced he was going to start work the next day as bookkeeper and clerk for the mill in Brandton. Frank said he was leaving on Wednesday to travel over the country with a thrashing crew. The harvest was cut short because of the drought but he knew he could make enough to take him to St. Louis and keep him until he landed a job.

Will said, "Well, as long as announcements are being made I have one too. I am going to marry Claire in October."

A shocked silence went round the table, broken when Kate dropped her fork. "Now that's a pretty kettle of fish! First off, Will, I don't like the girl and second, we can't do without you now that Nat and Frank are leaving."

William came to the rescue "Katie, Will has stayed three years longer than any other son in the neighborhood has stayed with his family. We could have had to go back to New York when I got sick if it hadn't been for Will. Claire is a good girl and I hope they will be happy."

Kate could hardly hold her temper, "Well, he is not bringing her here."

"I have no intention of bringing Claire here," Will said quickly. "Mr. Lefever has asked us to live with him."

William could hardly suppress a smile as he thought to himself, "Someone outdid you this time, Katie." Kate threw down her napkin and left the table.

The mood was lightened when Meggie went to Will and said, "I like Claire, Will. I like her a whole lot." Lucy and Minnie added their good wishes with Nat and Frank making a few comments.

Andy got a laugh when he lamented, "With all you boys leaving, I'm going to drive the team to the far side of the place and hide from Ma."

Kate could hear the laughter and her resentment grew. Things had gotten out of her control. It seemed as if nothing was turning out as she had planned. Back when she was in Ireland it had been her dream to own land. She had been disappointed when her parents settled in New York. After she married William she still had thoughts of owning a farm, especially when some of their friends had left the city to buy farms in Missouri. William hadn't wanted to leave New York, but Kate had convinced him they should go to Missouri as well. They had saved enough to buy a farm, and made the move. They only had two children at the time. They liked the place they bought, but the work was different for William. He became frustrated, and as the pressures built, he developed ulcers. Kate hated to admit it, but if it hadn't been for Will, they most surely would have had to go back to New York.

Kate hated for Will to leave but there didn't seem to be anything she could do to prevent it. She would just have to make Andy shape up. He would take constant overseeing for awhile but she had overcome greater obstacles.

This had been a bad year; the drought cut short the crop; Lettie was prone to whining because she was, as the Irish say, 'in the family way.' Now Will was going to marry Claire. She wouldn't have liked Will marrying anyone for a few years, but least of all Claire Lefever. Well, she had better get back to the family before they got any more out of control.

Eli Cox was there when Kate got back to the dining room. He had dropped by to ask Minnie to go for a buggy ride. Any other time Kate would have said it was not a respectable hour for a respectable man to ask a respectable young lady to go for a ride, Kate felt she was out of favor with the family and needed to get back in their good graces she said, "Yes, a buggy ride in the moonlight would be nice."

Kate was so engrossed in the turn of events in the family that she failed to notice Minnie's flushed face and her rumpled appearance when she returned from the ride with Eli.

Nat left the next morning to work for the Russell's at the Mill.

As Will started to the field Kate called to him, "Will, take Andy with you and let him do the work. He is through playing around."

"Ma, that is the hardest job I could have; I would rather do it myself."

"I know, but Andy will be a farmer, not because he loves the land like we do, but because he loves the freedom of the outdoors. He could never live in the city. You are the only one of my children who loves the land as I do. We would both do anything to have land and I think you just did." She turned to leave, then added, "I am glad you are going to have a farm, but it will be hard to do without you. If it doesn't rain by Wednesday we will have to drive the cattle to the river. We will take the wagon and bring back barrels of water from the spring for use at the house."

It hadn't rained by Wednesday, so the family and the cattle started out early for the six-mile drive to the river. Will and Andy were on horseback so they could ride along side the cattle and keep them from turning off on another trail or road. Lucy and Meggie came along behind to keep the cattle moving. It was quite exciting for the girls, more of a picnic than a chore. Kate and Minnie followed the procession in the wagon to carry the barrels for water. They also had lunch for everyone and the laundry, which they would wash upstream from where the stock drank. The boys would fill the barrels across the river at a spring. Lucy and Meggie played in the water until time for the return trek. It was the most exciting day the little girls had ever had. The adults did not share in the girls' pleasure; they could foresee a long hot summer unless the rains came soon.

Spreading the News

On the Monday morning following Will's proposal, Claire hurried to do her work. She wanted to run over to the Lowes' to tell Estelle the good news. My, how surprised she would be!

Claire caught herself skipping down the lane and stopped short. Why, she would soon be a married lady; she must act more dignified. She wondered how it would be. She had always been sure she wanted to be married but until yesterday had despaired that she ever would be. And Will was so handsome! She would be the best little homemaker in the whole community. Will must never be sorry he hadn't married Jessie.

Mrs. Lowes was surprised to see Claire. "What brings you over on a Monday morning, child?"

"I wanted to talk to Estelle for a few minutes. Maybe she could walk me part way home."

Claire could hardly wait until they were walking along the lane to tell Estelle her news. "Estelle, you won't believe this. I hardly do myself; I keep pinching myself to see if I am awake and not dreaming. Yesterday Will Kennedy asked me to marry him! Papa approves and has asked us to live with him. Oh, Estelle, it is all too perfect."

"I am so happy for you Claire. You're my best friend. I couldn't think of you moving away."

"Estelle, you remember Mrs. Mason saying Mrs. Randolph hinted they would soon be ordering a wedding gown for Jessie?"

"Why, yes. I wonder who?"

"She wanted Will. He let me read a letter she had written. She wanted to know when he was coming over to make plans for their wedding. Will said he didn't know where she got the idea he wanted to marry her."

"I think it's time someone took her down a peg or two," Estelle added. That was the beginning of the story of how Jessie had pursued Will and Claire had beaten her time. Will hadn't wanted anyone else to know about the letter but he wasn't schooled on how one female tells something to another until everyone knows the story!

Jessie had snubbed Estelle on several occasions and made remarks behind her back that she was Creole of mixed blood. Mrs. Lowes wasn't slow in getting her evens when Estelle shared the story of how Will had proposed to Claire when Jessie had wanted him. Daily Lowes knew just how to get the story out into the community. She would call Mrs. Ragain on the party line.

Mrs. Lowes went to the telephone and cranked out the long and short rings that made the Ragain's number. She was gratified to hear other receivers on the party line come down.

"Bertha, this is Daily Lowes. How are you folks this dry Monday morning?"

"We're well considering how dusty everything is."

"I was wondering if you had the pattern to that pretty dress you wore to church yesterday?"

"Why yes, I would be glad to loan it to you."

"I'll have Walt stop by and pick it up when he goes to town Saturday. Have you heard that Will Kennedy has asked Claire Lefever to marry him?"

"Lands sakes! I don't know when I've been more surprised. I thought he and Jessie Randolph would make a match."

"Oh she tried; she even wrote Will a letter asking him to marry her but Claire beat her time."

"Well, how about that!"

"I must finish our dinner. I'll have Walt stop for the pattern Saturday."

"Pattern? Oh, yes the pattern, I'll have it ready."

Mrs. Lowes hung up the telephone receiver and laughed to herself, "I guess Bertha is calling her sister Rose right now. I'll eavesdrop in a bit."

When Mrs. Lowes lifted the receiver she heard Mrs. Ragain telling all about how Claire had taken Will away from Jessie. Mrs. Lowes was satisfied with the retelling. The Randolphs were on Rose's party line and this time of day all the women folk were in the house. It would be safe to say some of the Randolphs were listening. It was sweet revenge for the way Jessie had treated Estelle. She would have to make a dress like Bertha's but it would be worth it to take Jessie down a notch.

In the Randolph household it was a good-natured race between Martha and Jessie to see which one would get to the telephone first to listen in when it rang for someone on the party line. It was Jessie's misfortune to win that morning. Jessie couldn't believe what she heard. Will most certainly wouldn't ask Claire Lefever to marry him! Then they began talking about the letter. How could Will have let anyone read her letter? How humiliating! She couldn't grasp what had gone wrong. Why had he said he wanted her? Why hadn't he come back? And why hadn't he answered her letter? She could find no answers. Bewildered, she hung up the receiver and began to cry.

Martha saw the tears and rushed to her side. "Jessie, what is wrong?"

"Will is going to marry Claire Lefever:"

"But I thought....."

"So did I. I just can't believe he would prefer her to me."

Mrs. Randolph had overheard and came to comfort Jessie. "Just what did Will say to you?"

"He said 'I want you.'"

"And you said?"

"And I said 'you can have me'."

"That is not exactly asking you to marry him. The best thing you can do now is to act as if you don't care."

"But Mama, I do care. There's not another boy around half as handsome as Will. I know he cared for me."

"Well, it is over now. Will couldn't have taken you to the Kennedy's and we hardly have room for another hand on the farm." Suddenly the reason for Will's proposal became clear to Mrs. Randolph. "That Claire Lefever has a farm, and that's what Will wants. I am sure no one has said out loud yet he's marrying Claire because of the farm, but I will see that they do."

Indeed she did! That Saturday when she and Martha were in McCaskell's Store she made sure she was within the hearing of James when she said, "I hear Will Kennedy is marrying Claire Lefever for her farm."

Martha was so surprised her mother-in-law would make such a comment in a public place that she could only stammer, "Is that so?"

James gave no sign he had heard but he felt his face flush. The comment made him angry. How unfair of Will to take advantage of Cousin Claire, and how cruel of Mrs. Randolph to say such a thing.

His first thought was to tell Uncle Charles; then better reasoning set in. Claire needed someone, and the Kennedy's were honest people. If he broke up the marriage, then someone else who wasn't half as good as Will would probably marry Claire for the farm.

James had to admit that most of the girls he had dated were more interested in his property than in him. The more he thought about it, the more he decided it would be a fair exchange. Will would get the farm and Claire would get someone to help take care of her and her father.

James remembered that it had always been Jessie and Will together at parties. That was probably why Mrs. Randolph was spreading her story. Well, he wouldn't react in the way Mrs. Randolph thought he would. The McCaskell's would be supportive of the marriage.

The hot dry summer dragged on into September. Every day they faced the same challenge of getting enough water for their needs. Will thought the weather was affecting the people too. He even noticed the difference in Minnie and Eli.

Minnie hadn't been herself lately. He had expected some of her sharp comments about Claire after he announced his marriage plans. Instead

Minnie had been most kind of late, going out of her way to do little favors for him. He noticed Eli seemed ill at ease when he came to see Minnie, but after a short time would be his jolly self. Will decided he would ask Claire if Eli and Minnie could be their attendants when they married. Claire had said it would have to be a private affair at the parsonage since her father wasn't up to a wedding at home.

Nat had been coming home every other Sunday to help Andy take the cattle to the river. That gave Will time to go to the Lefever's.

The Lefever's were fortunate to have a spring-fed pond. They didn't have a problem for water for the stock but they were conserving water at the house. To insure that their cisterns would last longer, Will would fill barrels with water from the spring for laundry and watering the chickens. The thrifty ways of Claire's Scottish ancestry stood her in good stead. She used every drop of water more than once. Wash water and dishwater went on plants and flowers. She scrubbed the floors and porches with water from the laundry. Claire hoped the cistern would last until the rains came or they would have to haul water from Brandton.

Claire hardly noticed the scorching summer. She floated through the days thinking she would soon be Mrs. William Kennedy, Jr. They had set their wedding date for Wednesday, October 16th. She was sorry not to have a home wedding with the McCaskell's, Aimie and her family, and the Kennedy's, but that would be too much for Papa.

After she and Will were married she would have everyone for Sunday dinner. She wondered how much visiting they would do between the relatives. She planned to have them all over at least once. Claire had her mother's linens and she felt she could set as fine a table as any of them. Will would be proud of her.

Claire had no clear idea what marriage would be like. She knew she could keep a house, weed a garden, and fill a cellar with produce as well as any married neighbor could. Having a husband and family alarmed her and Claire was afraid she wouldn't please Will. She thought if she could get past the marriage ceremony then she would know it was real and not a dream. She could handle reality after she was sure she was married. She would never complain; she was grateful she wouldn't be an old maid.

Claire had hoped to have a romantic courtship like her parents had. She remembered hearing her father tell how he had come by the McCaskell place to look at some livestock. Nora's father, who was a country doctor, had been away at the time but Nora had invited Charles into the parlor. He had been immediately attracted to Nora but hadn't realized she was only fourteen years old. When Dr. McCaskell came home, Charles had asked permission to court his daughter. The Doctor became very angry and ordered Charles not to come back for two years.

Charles had said he would honor Dr. McCaskell's wishes but that he would be back in two years to court Nora and try to win her hand in marriage.

Nora had been so swept off her feet by the tall, handsome Frenchman that she refused to keep company with the many young swains who came to call on her. Charles had returned two years to the day after he had been sent away. Dr. McCaskell had been so disgusted with Nora's stubbornness in not seeing anyone else during the two years that he had given them his blessing for their marriage.

They had been very happy together. Charles had never gotten over her death. Claire had been only five at the time, but she could remember how they had adored each other. Many a matron had set her cap for Charles since then, but Nora was the only one in his life. Claire thought it would be wonderful to have such a marriage. It bothered her that Will had seldom even held her hand, and when he did it seemed an afterthought. She assured herself it would be different after they were married.

Estelle came to spend the afternoon with Claire a few days before the wedding. She brought a wedding gift of a blue milk crystal pitcher and glasses. Claire was delighted. "Oh, Estelle, you are such a jewel! I will keep it in the china cabinet Grandpa McCaskell had made for Mama's wedding gift."

"I have some good news." said Estelle. "I passed the Teachers Examination given by the County School Superintendent. I've been hired to teach at Oak Grove. They had a teacher but she married last week and is moving to Kansas. I will start next week."

"That is wonderful news. Can you stay at home?"

"I will go horseback until cold weather, and then I'll board with one of the school board members."

"I am glad you have a school. You have always wanted to teach."

"If I am rehired at the end of the term I will go to the Teachers Academy next summer. Now, I want to see how you look in your new suit. I just know you'll be so stylish in it."

Claire smiled, "I hope Will thinks so!"

October 16, 1901

October sixteenth finally crept around for Claire. She had been apprehensive that something would happen to prevent the wedding. She even had nightmares that Will had eloped with Jessie. She kept busy through the day seeing that the house was in apple pie order.

Will had been over on Sunday to tell her Eli had offered to drive them to the parsonage on Wednesday. He and Minnie would stand up with them. After the ceremony Eli was taking them to the Star Hotel for dinner. That made Claire feel good; it was as if he felt something special should mark the day. She was glad Papa had insisted she get the new suit. Claire had looked forward to wearing it, but had saved it for this special day. Besides the suit, the McCaskell cousins had Mrs. Mason make a complete trousseau. All these things seemed so wonderful to Claire when only a few months ago she didn't even have a prospect of a beau. Then she had resigned herself to the fact that she would be an old maid; now she was afraid she would wake up and it would be a dream.

The curling iron seemed to take forever to heat and then even longer to get the curls just right. Next she painstakingly smoothed a tiny bit of blush on each cheek and smiled at the reflection in the old mirror. She was pleased with the results. Mrs. Mason had outdone herself on the suit. Claire remembered what the seamstress had said about making her mother's wedding suit. She went in to tell Charles that she was ready.

"You look lovely, Claire. Mrs. Mason did you proud on the suit."

"Papa, Mrs. Mason told me that she had made mother's wedding suit too. It is so special to me that she made mine too."

"Yes, I remember that suit, and the hat and muff she made for my Nora. I wish your mother could have lived to see you all grown up and to see how happy you are today. She would be so proud of you, Claire. I am happy for you; I am glad you are marrying such a good man. I hope you and Will have a happy marriage."

Charles was almost as nervous as Claire was that there would be a delay to the marriage. They both had a sense of relief when they heard Eli, Minnie, and Will coming down the lane.

"Now, Claire," said Charles, "let Will come in after you."

"Oh, Papa! I wasn't going to run out!"

They both laughed. Claire gave her father a hug. "Thank you for everything, Papa."

Will came in for Claire. He was surprised how dignified and serene she looked. He had expected her to be nervous, or blushing, or excited. He complimented her on how nice she looked in her fine suit and said, "I declare, Minnie is more nervous than you are."

Charles thought a little speech by way of a send off was in order. "Will, Claire has been hostess here for seven years; keeping a house will be nothing new for her. Now you are the head of the household. My daughters are the dearest things left on earth to me. I hope they both have married men who will take good care of them."

Will said, "Thank you, sir. I will certainly try."

Claire was close to tears so she just hugged and kissed her father.

Will held out his hand to Claire. "We must go now. Eli has the surrey."

Eli tipped his hat when he saw Claire. "My, you are looking mighty fine."

Minnie chimed in, "Claire, you do look lovely. Your suit is so stylish."

"Thank you, Minnie. Mrs. Mason made it for me. She made my mother's wedding suit too."

"I know that makes it even more special for you! I am glad this is such a grand day. Eli has already ordered our dinner to be ready when the ceremony is over."

Claire was happy to hear this. She had never eaten in a public place before and had heard the Star Hotel was the finest place around.

As they drove down Main Street of Brandton, Claire was pleased to see her cousin James out in front of their store. She gave him a little wave, which James returned. He felt a sense of relief that Will was now committed to care for both Claire and her father. He had wondered if in the passing of Uncle Charles, Claire might have to live with him and his family. They would have taken her in, of course, but he was glad to know she would have a husband instead.

Claire and Will had decided on the Methodist Parsonage for their wedding. The Kennedy's were Episcopalians, but there wasn't an Episcopalian Church in Brandton. Claire's mother's family was Primitive Baptist but her father thought they were too narrow in their beliefs so he and Claire attended the Methodist Church.

The Reverend Jordon cordially welcomed them into the parsonage parlor. He thought Minnie and Eli were the bride and groom. Minnie blushed and said, "I am the sister of the groom, but I hope to be a bride someday." Will thought Eli blushed at that remark.

Reverend Jordon was anticipating a new family for his congregation so he performed his special ceremony.

Claire heard Will's promise to "love, honor, and cherish" her. Then she heard Reverend Jordan ask if she promised to "love, honor, and obey" William Kennedy, Jr. With every fiber of her being Claire said, "I do."

The ceremony was very meaningful to Claire, who that morning had made a vow to herself that she would never leave anything undone if it could help them have a good marriage.

As the four walked out into the lovely autumn sunshine, Minnie said, "It couldn't have been a nicer day. I am happy for both of you. Welcome to the family Mrs. William Kennedy, Jr."

Claire smiled, "I am very pleased to be part of your family."

Eli laughed and grabbed Claire, "Hey, the bride should be kissed." Then he kissed Claire so hard she almost lost her hat.

Will put his arm around her and gave her a quick kiss on the cheek, "I will take care of that."

As they got into the surrey, Will looked up at the clear October sky and saw it was Jessie's favorite sky blue color and his heart ached. He was brought back to reality by the shouts of James and Eckles.

No one in the wedding party had noticed the boys behind the trees until they stepped out and showered them with wheat, calling, "We wish you many years of happiness." Claire was pleased they had thought to add to her day.

At the Star Hotel, luxurious dark red carpet made Claire feel as if she were stepping on a feather bed. Mirrors on every wall were flanked by lighted candles on each side. Claire was startled when she saw her reflection. Her cheeks were flushed; why, she was even glowing! It was all so exciting. Claire marveled at the splendor of the dining room. The draperies were of deep red velvet; the tables were prepared with white linen table cloths and gleaming silverware.

A waiter stepped up to Eli and said "Sir, your table is ready." He led them to a beautifully appointed table with a lovely centerpiece of chrysanthemums. Champagne was waiting at the table. Eli pulled Minnie's chair out and seated her. Claire was thrilled when Will assisted her too.

As soon as they were seated Eli poured the champagne and offered a toast. "To the health and happiness of Mr. and Mrs. William Kennedy, Jr."

Will responded, "Claire and I would like to thank both of you for making this day so special. Eli, you outdid yourself on all the arrangements. Thank you again." The champagne left Claire light headed; her happiness knew no bounds.

The meal was beyond belief to Will and Claire. The first course was soup, made from fresh oysters shipped in ice from the East Coast. That was followed by steaks, mashed potatoes, green beans, and the crowning touch, ice cream! When the steaks were served Will looked at Minnie and said, "Ma would make one of these steaks do for the whole family." Minnie laughingly agreed. Despite their protests, everyone managed to eat the entire meal. Eli was delighted to see them enjoying the dinner so much. It was all too wonderful when the proprietor insisted Claire take the chrysanthemums with her.

It seemed like a short ride back to the Lefever place. Eli and Minnie declined Will's invitation to come in but agreed to come to dinner in two weeks. "It won't be anything like today though; how can we ever thank you, Eli?"

"Just be happy Claire. Don't let the Kennedys run over you." Eli said it good-naturedly but he could foresee Claire would have to stand up for herself or Kate would run her household too.

More Kennedys Leave the Nest

Nat had adjusted quickly to life in Brandton. He was good at his job and got along well with customers. He had hoped his romance with Lucinda would have developed but there had been little progress. She was friendly, having invited him a few times to go to Church with her and her family and have dinner afterwards. Sometimes she would see Nat as she was walking home and ask him to come on home for supper. But lately he hadn't seen her except in Church.

Nat had been surprised this morning when Mr. Russell had said, "You don't look sleepy this morning but try to get Lucinda home a little earlier after this." He didn't know why Mr. Russell would make such a comment, but something had prompted Nat to respond, "Yes, sir," without asking for an explanation.

Nat was puzzling about that remark when he reached his boarding house. He was surprised to find Lucinda waiting for him in the parlor.

"Let's go for a walk Nat."

"Fine," he agreed, "but why the furrowed brow?"

"I will tell you as we walk."

They walked along a pleasant shady street to the town's park and picnic grounds where they found a bench and sat down. "Now, I want to hear what has caused your long face."

"Oh Nat, I hope you won't hate me for what I've done."

"Come now, you know I won't hate you."

"Wait until you hear what I have to say."

Nat could see Lucinda was truly upset about something. "Just stop crying and tell me."

"Well," she said slowly, "I've been going out to see Bob Burtrum."

"Say, isn't he a little wild for you?"

"I thought I could handle him. It was all so intriguing and he can be charming."

Nat was beginning to suspect the reason behind Mr. Russell's remark earlier in the day. "How did you persuade your folks to let you go out with him?"

"I told them I was going with you," she admitted.

"Now I see. Well, that's not anything to cry about."

"That isn't the worst of it. I...I am in trouble; I told Bob last night and he left for California today."

"Do you want me to go after him?" asked Nat.

"No," said Lucinda fiercely. "I hate him now. I will never forget or forgive the way he laughed at me. I have some money; I will go some place for a while until I can decide what to do. I am so sorry I used you though. Papa will think you are to blame. That is why I had to tell you first."

Nat thought for a minute. Lucinda's deception had put him in a difficult position. "Well, since I would get the blame and get fired if you did that, why don't we get married and go to St. Louis instead?"

Lucinda looked at him in amazement. "Oh Nat, you are a good man. I can't believe anyone would do so much for someone in my condition."

"Saturday we will go to the County Seat and get married. After a few days we will tell everyone that we have been secretly married for a while."

Lucinda was beginning to think she had some options after all. "The folks have a place at the edge of town I am sure they will give us. If you do this for me, I will try to make it worth your sacrifice. My how my life has been turned around. I even thought of suicide but I felt you should know what I had done first."

Nat patted her shoulder. "You dry your eyes and I'll walk you home. And try to look happy for the next few days. We can't have your folks thinking something is wrong." He laughed as they stood up from the bench. "Here old Will just got married and upset Ma. If she knew about this she would be speechless!"

His attitude cheered Lucinda. "You had better stay for supper tonight, and Sunday we'll go to Church together. I am beginning to hope there is a future for us."

In the years to come Nat was to ponder many times why he had been so rash as to take on another man's responsibility, but at the time it seemed the right thing to do.

At supper that evening Lucinda was attentive to the point that Nat was slightly embarrassed but her parents were delighted. They were glad to have Nat around; he was such a polite young man. Lucinda was head-strong and given to sarcastic remarks. They would be glad when she settled down. After supper they all sat on the porch for awhile, then Lucinda walked with Nat to the gate to say goodnight.

"If Bob came back what would you do?" Nat asked.

In a voice as hard as nails Lucinda replied, "I would take a gun and kill him!"

"We can't have anything like that so you better get ready for Saturday. I'll rent a buggy and we'll make a day of it. In a few days we will tell everyone we have been married awhile and decided to tell it since Will and Claire got married."

The Russell's had enough pride that they went along with the face-saving story. True to Lucinda's prediction, her parents gave them the house at the edge of town. They also gave a reception to announce the marriage. Lucinda had a lovely rose-colored gown and Nat spent a month's wages on a suit; they made a handsome couple. The Russell's were proud and relieved to have Nat in their family.

There were three pregnant Kennedy women at the reception that day. Lucinda and Minnie knew they were pregnant; the third, Claire, did not.

As Eli drove Minnie from the reception, Minnie knew she had to find out what Eli intended to do about her 'delicate condition'. Just the thought of how desperate she was brought tears to her eyes. "Eli, I can't hide the truth from Ma much longer."

"You won't have to. I am closing a deal for the Simpson place tomorrow. I'll come over and take you there as soon as it is mine, then in a few weeks we will go to Springfield and get married."

"In a few weeks! But Eli, that would be——-"

"Living in sin? What do you call what we have been doing?"

Minnie's face flushed. "I will have you to know I am a proper lady."

"You are a proper lady all right. I'll even buy you a fur coat when we go to Springfield. That's what they do for their ladies in the Big City."

The meaning of Eli's remark was lost on Minnie. She was just happy to be getting away from home before Ma found out what she had done. It would be wonderful to live in the Simpson place and have a fur coat. Oh, she would be a grand lady. Lettie would whine and complain of her meager lot and be so envious of her.

While Minnie looked forward to life in the Simpson place, Frank was enjoying his life in St. Louis. He hadn't known the world could have as much excitement as he found there. The Farrell's lifestyle was very different than the folks back home. Bohemian would best describe their free and easy ways. Among their boarders were an artist, a writer, and several actors and actresses. Through them Ruth had obtained a job in a burlesque theatre. Frank thought that wouldn't do to tell back home!

Frank had no difficulty getting a job in the city. His first was as an ice delivery man. When he applied for the job he noticed that one open route paid more than the others. He asked why.

"We had to fire the driver, a big black named Sam King," the supervisor explained. "He was messin' around with the women folk on the route instead of delivering ice. Every driver we have had since has been beaten up by Sam."

Frank loved a good fight; back home he had been the cock of the walk. Folks there admired and respected the handsome Irishman. He turned aside from no fight and no one had ever really hurt him. Will was the only one to ever make him say 'enough'.

Frank told them he could handle Sam, and the ice company agreed to give him a try.

Frank was eager for the first day on the job. He had his strategy all mapped out when he reported for work. Very confidently he climbed up on the delivery wagon. Frank had made a few deliveries and was looking into the ice wagon getting ready for the next one when he heard a deep bass voice behind him. "What you doin' in my territory, White Boy?"

Turning quickly, Frank threw the heavy ice tongs directly into Sam's face. "No one calls me White Boy," he said as he turned. Sam fell to the brick street, out cold and minus his front teeth. Frank strode forward and retrieved the tongs. "Anyone else like to mix it up with me?" The gathering crowd faded away.

From that day on, no one crossed Frank. He enjoyed giving piercing stares and seeing the crowd give way. The Ice Company even gave him a bonus for getting the route running again. He was having the time of his life.

Back home Andy and Nat were feeling sorry for Frank, stuck among

all those buildings, driving on brick streets, with just a room at night. Andy and Nat knew they would feel as if they were in jail. But Frank was enjoying every minute. Even as he hoisted the big cakes of ice on his back he was conscious of the admiring glances he received. It was certainly better than plowing corn all day behind an old mule and then having Ma berate him for not getting more done. He felt sorry for the folks back home in their humdrum life—looking at the clouds, hoping for rain; looking at the crops, hoping for a good harvest; hoping to make enough to pay taxes and have enough left over to buy seed for next year's crop. That life wasn't for Frank.

Frank and Ruth were a fine pair. Neither of them wanted to marry. They both liked their freedom and space. They were enjoying what they were doing and wanted no ties to hold them. Things back home seemed so dull; St. Louis was the place to be for them.

Ruth sometimes went on the road with the Chautauqua Society Theatre Company for a few weeks. At such times Frank never lacked for the companionship of the fairer sex. The ladies adored the tall auburn-haired Irishman. He made no commitment to Ruth nor did she to him, and that was the way they wanted it. Things just couldn't be better for Frank.

Will was beginning to feel comfortable at his new home. He had to admit that Claire was a good cook and conversation was much more tranquil than he had ever known with his own family. With his family, Lettie was usually whining, Minnie was giving advice, while Kate was taking sides and giving orders. Lucy and Andy constantly had a dispute going even though they were careful not to let their controversy reach the ears of their father. If Kate heard them she most likely would join in the fray.

Claire was so happy at being Mrs. William Kennedy, Jr. that she didn't notice Will's strategy to spend very little time alone with her. The first sound she heard in the morning was Will starting the fire in the kitchen range; she would quickly come in to get breakfast. Will would head outside to start the morning chores. He spent most of his time outdoors tending to the farm while Claire took care of the house and her father's needs. Will drew most of the water and kept the wood box filled, so Claire's only outside chore now was taking care of the chickens. Charles joined them for meals, and most evenings after supper the two men would adjourn to the parlor while Claire cleared the kitchen. Of course, neither man even thought about helping to clear the table.

Claire hated to miss any of her Papa's stories so she hurried to clean the kitchen so she could join them. Naturally, all of Charles' stories were new to Will, and Claire never got tired of hearing them time and time again. Charles was thrilled to have a new audience. Claire especially enjoyed hearing him tell about his family.

One evening in late October as Claire came into the parlor, Papa was talking and Will was listening intently. Neither man really noticed that she had joined them. Charles told Will that the Lefever family was originally from France. "Some of my family was in each of the three regiments of Huguenots. They tell me that each regiment had seven hundred and fifty effective men who were fighting with William of Orange's army that numbered eleven thousand. They sailed from Holland to aid King William in obtaining the Crown of England. They were in sympathy with their suffering brethren who were driven violently from their homes and native country simply for their religion! King William was so grateful to these zealous and loyal supporters that he invited them to make their home in his new dominion in America.

My people were in with a large group of these Huguenots who sought homes in Virginia. They settled along the Potomac, Rappahannock, and James Rivers. They even had freedom from taxes for seven years. After that seven years they came into Court to prove their importation, claim their headrights, and take out their land patents. When we Lefever's were in France, they spelled our name Lefevre. After we came to America, somebody started writing our name with the 'e-r' ending which is more English."

Charles yawned, "It is getting late and I'm afraid I'm growing weary. We'll have time for more stories another evening."

Will said honestly, "I have really enjoyed hearing about your family and I'll look forward to the next time."

"Goodnight, Papa; I hope you sleep well."

Claire's days were busy, seeing to the chores and making sure that Papa was comfortable. She hoped and prayed she would be expecting a baby before long. Papa seemed to be failing fast, and she wanted him to live long enough to see a baby that would carry on the family.

Will worked hard every day from sunup to sundown. He mended the harness, repaired the farm machinery, kept the wood pile well stocked, and occasionally went hunting for wild game. Charles could find no fault with Will's work and was pleased that he seemed to enjoy working on the farm. However, it did bother Charles that his new son-in-law didn't seem as affectionate with Claire as Charles had thought he would be. They got along well enough, but something just seemed to be missing. It wasn't at all like he and his Nora had been. Charles rationalized that it was probably because he was living there with them.

One evening in early November, Charles continued his story about the family. "About 1810 Elisha Lefever, his brother Peter, and their families left Buckingham County in Virginia and headed west. They settled in Knox County, Tennessee. Elisha had six sons; the youngest one was my father, Henry. About 1836, my Pa and Ma decided to move on. They traveled the Warriors' Path, and settled first in Jackson County, Alabama. They had friends, who had gone to Kentucky, so in 1852 Pa and Ma took me, my brother Johnnie, and my sister Hallie and moved to Kentucky too. They only stayed there two years before moving further west. By then we had lost Hallie to yellow fever and conditions were building up to the Civil War."

"Papa," Claire said, "tell Will about the time you met Uncle Johnnie in the woods at Vicksburg and almost shot each other."

Charles explained, "John had married and gone back to Alabama as a young man. During the war, he fought for the Confederacy, while I fought for the Union. We were both assigned scouting duties for our units. I had just topped a ridge at the edge of a thicket when I saw a figure of a man in a Confederate uniform a short distance away. We both reacted as any good soldier would; we each had the other in our sights. It could have been one of the terrible tragedies of that bloody war, but at the same instant we recognized each other and dodged behind the nearest trees. I heard Johnnie call, 'Charles, is that you?' I answered,

'Yes, Johnnie, it is me'."

Charles shook his head. "Thank goodness we recognized each other in time. I asked Johnnie how he'd left his family. 'Doing pretty good,' he said. 'Sally's cured one tobacco crop and is taking care of our two tykes. You married yet?' I said no, but that I had a good piece of land and was building the nest. He asked me how the folks were when I left. I told him they were fine and said 'Come and see us when this bloody war is over.' He said he hoped we both made it through the war. Then he said to me, 'I'm going to go back to my lines now. Wait a few minutes until I'm gone, and then come out to this tree. I'll leave some of Sally's tobacco for you.'

"When I got back I told my buddies I had found the tobacco pouch on the trail. When they wanted some I told them 'No, it isn't every day I have such good luck.' "

Will exclaimed, "I'm glad you recognized each other in time. It would have been awful if one of you had killed the other and realized it too late!"

Claire didn't mind the evenings of the men's conversations. It seemed to help Papa to talk about the past; it was as if he was living it one last time. She knew she must tell Will and Papa soon that she was in the 'family way', as the Irish tell it. She wanted a boy because she knew she wasn't good at ribbons and frills, but a girl in the house to talk to would be nice. It surprised her how lonely she felt even when the men folk were around. She hoped Papa would live to see her child.

Dr. Holmes stopped in to see Charles every time he was in the neighborhood. As time went on, the only medication he could leave was laudanum for pain. After one such visit Charles told Claire and Will he was putting his affairs in order. He had sent for Lawyer Webb to come out. He was leaving Claire the place, stock, equipment, and furniture. He would give Will seed money for the coming year. To Aimie he would leave all of the money after his expenses were paid. Since it looked like another dry year he advised Will to plant oats since it was an early crop, and no corn because it was a late crop.

Claire cried, but Will was glad to get it settled while Charles was still able to care for business. The end seemed more inviting to Charles than ever.

On a lovely spring afternoon in March, Kate and Lettie drove over to show off the Stewart's new son, William Isaac. Kate made much of the name. "All the first sons in the Kennedy family for generations have been named William'," she told Claire pointedly.

Lettie said she had been so poorly since little Willie came that Isaac had been doing most of the caring for Willie. "Isaac is such a dear."

Lettie fell silent as Kate changed the subject and began to speak in glowing terms of Minnie's home and activities. "Minnie has been busy furnishing her home, and they have taken several trips. Eli is so generous with her. Why, he even bought her a fur coat when they were in Springfield."

The little gathering was disrupted by Andy dashing up on horseback. He had hardly said hello before he blurted out his news. "Ma, Ma, Eli called. Minnie just had a baby boy!"

Kate was stunned and speechless! She began to hurriedly gather up their things, saying she must go see Minnie. When Claire told Will about it later she said, "Why your Ma was so rattled she had her hat on backwards when they left."

Kate fumed to herself on the drive home. She was disappointed Lettie was in such poor circumstances, but she had wanted to tell how well one of her daughters was doing. That had been the main reason for the visit to Claire's today. Minnie certainly had deceived her; if only she hadn't been bragging about Minnie at the time. Andy's unexpected announcement had made her look foolish in front of Claire. Imagine, Minnie not telling her own mother she was expecting! How could she have done such a thing?

Lettie was quiet on the drive back; she was relieved she wouldn't be hearing about Minnie's wonderful good fortune anymore. "Ma," she asked, "do you suppose they will name the baby William?" For a reply Kate lashed the buggy whip across the back of the already galloping horse.

Kate deposited Lettie at her home, put a few clothes in her grip, gave some instructions to Lucy and Meggie, and then drove on to the Cox's. Minnie was surprised to see her.

"Why Ma, we're glad you came to see the baby, but Eli asked Mrs. Dyer to come for awhile. You don't need to stay."

Kate had been humiliated again. She would have to take her little bag back home and everyone would know she hadn't been needed or wanted.

Claire Gets A Letter

Estelle was often over at Claire's that spring. She had been rehired to teach at Oak Grove. They were so pleased with her teaching that they were going to extend the school year to seven months instead of six. Estelle planned to attend the Springfield Teachers College for the spring and summer terms. She was good company for Claire; Estelle talked so much about her pupils that Claire felt as if she knew them. Estelle told her about Luke. "When I accepted the position, they warned me about one of the older boys, who had been very disruptive in school for the other teachers. Before the opening of school my father went with me to see the school and check the books. Luke was there doing repair work for the school district. Dad complimented Luke on his work and asked him if he had ever thought about making his best girl a cedar chest. Luke said he would if he had the lumber and tools. Dad told Luke he would give him some fine cedar lumber if he would keep the woodbox filled. Dad suggested that Luke work in the wood shed in his spare time and offered to loan him the tools. My biggest potential discipline problem was solved!"

"That worked out very nicely. I know you are happy being a teacher."

When the weather was too bad to play outside Estelle taught the girls to embroider, crochet, or knit. The boys did woodcarving. On Friday afternoons, if all lessons were done, they had spelling bees, ciphering, even debates sometimes. She found the students eager and very bright; they just needed a teacher who cared.

They found a way to show their appreciation at the annual school pie supper. After a program by the students, the pies the ladies brought were auctioned off to the highest bidders. Then came nominating the man with the dirtiest feet, the most lovesick couple, and the most henpecked husband.

But the highlight of the evening was choosing the prettiest girl. Votes for the person of your choice were a penny a vote. Estelle's students nominated her. Jessie Randolph and another girl were also nominated.

Jessie had come with Gus Schmidt, a wealthy German farmer. She had been nominated first and had looked confident that she would win. She thought the other girls posed no threat. When Estelle was nominated Jessie rolled her eyes heavenward as much as to say, "How ridiculous can they get?"

It wasn't long before Jessie was most distressed. Gus only gave a dollar and felt that was being a spendthrift. Jessie was so angry she was close to tears. Her total was $1.35; the second girl's was $4.20. Estelle had $6.39! The students cheered and cheered.

The next day Estelle told Claire, "I was so embarrassed when the students nominated me, I could have spanked them all. But after I won I could have kissed them all. I have never been so happy."

"You have done so much for them, Estelle. And how sweet the victory over Jessie!"

"That is what Ma said. I love teaching, I hope I have a family someday but I will always want to teach."

"I am looking forward to raising a family too," said Claire. "I hope you can teach them when they go to school." They continued chatting as they walked to the gate. They saw Will coming from town where he had gone for supplies.

"Hello, ladies. How is the school teacher?"

"Fine, I just had to come and tell Claire the latest about my students."

"Well, you are in time to hear the latest Kennedy news. Nat and Lucinda have a baby boy."

"Well, well, and what did they name him?" asked Estelle.

"John Russell Kennedy."

Claire ventured to say, "You mean they didn't name him William?"

Will laughed, "No, and Ma will sure be upset over that."

"Looks as if you Kennedy's are going to keep me in a job," Estelle said.

Claire had enjoyed the afternoon and was sorry to see Estelle leave. When someone was there Claire could think of other things and forget her worries for awhile. When alone she was constantly nagged by the worry of how she could take care of a new baby with her father requiring more help each day. On top of her garden and the summer canning season, it seemed a crushing load.

The thought of her garden took Claire back to an episode with Kate. Claire had been making a garden almost as long as she could remember and considered herself quite successful. Will plowed and worked the soil down for her. She always planted in rows, measuring carefully between them. She used heavy twine stretched between two stakes to mark each row as she planted it. That day, she had just finished planting when Kate had stopped by.

Kate saw the rows across the garden and began to expound on how that was completely the wrong way to lay out a garden. She insisted it was better to plant the garden in beds instead of rows. She said that way it could be weeded with less moving around and little or no plowing. Kate went so far as to say Claire should have sent for her to help. Claire had listened quietly then had said, 'I've always done it this way.'

Kate had snorted and replied, 'You are just an Ozarkian! Will shouldn't have to take time out of the field to plow the garden for you.'

Claire had calmly told Kate that they would manage.

Kate's domineering ways were especially frustrating because Claire was becoming more and more anxious over Charles' condition. He spent most of the days in bed now. Will helped him to the table for meals. After supper he stayed up for a while for some visiting. If Aimie came for Sunday he would try to stay up in the afternoon but each day was taking its toll of his strength. They could all see the changes. The day finally came when he didn't leave his bed. Claire fed him his meals.

The worst time came when Charles was restless at night and Claire was up with him so many times she was on the verge of collapse. She was going to send for Aimie to help out when Kate showed up and said she would sit up at nights. Claire was so grateful for the help that she began to think of what she had missed by not having a mother all these years.

Charles made a valiant effort to live until Claire's child was born but on June 1, 1902 he passed away. Will laid Charles out and Walt Lowes made the coffin out of some of his prize lumber. The funeral was at the house on a balmy June day. Family, friends and neighbors overflowed onto the lawn. Claire wasn't able to go to the cemetery so Kate and Estelle stayed with her.

Claire tried to thank Kate for her help in caring for Charles, but Kate brushed her thanks aside. "When the wee one comes I will come and help again."

Aimie stayed a week with Claire to give her some rest. The two sisters carried out their father's wishes amicably. Aimie had given Claire all of the baby clothes she had and the two of them hemmed squares of muslin material for additional baby diapers.

After Aimie went back to her home Claire had never felt lonelier. The house seemed empty without her father. Will was in the field all day. After supper they would sit on the front porch for a while before bedtime, but it seemed to Claire that Will was always preoccupied with things he wanted to do for the farm. More and more she looked forward to the arrival of the baby. Then she would have something all her own, to be with her all day.

A few days after Aimie had returned home, Claire decided to walk to the crossroads to the mailbox and pick up their mail. It was a lovely day, and she thought the walk would be good for her. She put on her sunbonnet and set off. The fresh morning air raised her spirits. She was feeling almost jaunty by the time she covered the half-mile to the mailbox. It had been a long time since she felt free to leave the house. They didn't receive a great amount of mail so they didn't go too often to check their box.

Claire was pleased to see a letter with the return address "Mrs. William Kennedy, Sr." Eager to see what Kate had to say, Claire quickly opened the letter. She was stunned by the message on the enclosed page:

Nursing services for Charles Lefever — $40.00

Claire stared in disbelief. When she grasped the contents, she was more hurt and angry than she had ever been before. It was especially distressing because she had begun to think maybe Kate could make up for some of what she missed by not having her own mother, especially with the baby on the way. Then for her to do something like this!

Claire was so angry she didn't take the road back to the house, but cut across the field to where Will was working. Will saw her coming; he couldn't imagine what would bring her to the field. Her sunbonnet was off, her face was flushed and she was crying. For the first time he was concerned for her. "Claire, what on earth is wrong?"

"You tell me!" She thrust the letter into his hands.

He frowned in disbelief when he read what she had given him. "Claire, I don't know what to say. I don't know why Ma would do something like this."

"She just came. I didn't ask her to help!" Claire protested. "I thought her coming was like having a second mother. I feel deceived. I have never been so hurt and angry in my life. Aimie would have come and stayed at the last but when your Ma showed up I didn't even send for Aimie. I wish I had now. Even worse, we don't have forty dollars, but I wouldn't tell your mother that for anything."

"You are right about that!" Will agreed. "I would like to cram this down Ma's throat. And I would be ashamed for Aimie to know about this. How can we raise the money?"

Claire thought for a minute. "We can sell the Jersey cow. She is dry now anyway, and Mr. Winningham asked to buy her last summer. She's a good cow I hate to see her go, but I am not about to be beholden to your Ma. And another thing, when it is time for the baby, don't send for her! Mrs. Lowes will come help Dr. Holmes."

Will was taken aback by Claire's outburst, but he could see why she would feel that way. "Claire, I am truly sorry, but we will manage. Now you go on back to the house and rest."

Will pondered all morning on why Ma would do such a thing. He decided she must think Claire had inherited money. Ma had mentioned again last week that Lettie was feeling poorly and had said she was sorry that Lettie was having a skimpy time of it. That was the way it had always been with Ma, taking from him to give to the girls. He suspected she would never change.

Mrs. Lowes was surprised when Claire asked if she would come when the baby was due. "Of course I'll come Claire, but I would have thought Mrs. Kennedy would have wanted to be there." Claire had to tell her the reason she didn't want Kate.

"Don't you worry," Mrs. Lowes assured her. "I'll be there for you, and one day I hope I can do the same for my own daughter."

Claire thanked her and said, "I hope the baby is a boy. Will has never said but I think he would rather have a son, especially since the others have had boys. I know one thing, even if I have a dozen sons I will never name any of them 'William'. Kate can't tell me what how to plant my garden, or what to name my children!"

Mrs. Lowes laughed, "Claire, that is the longest speech I have ever heard you make."

Claire replied, "Well, I feel better now that I have made it. I am getting anxious to have someone in the house during the days. I do miss Papa so much. I'm going to name the baby Charles Arthur."

"That would be a silly name for a girl so I hope it is a boy." Mrs. Lowes said. "You run on home and get ready for Charles Arthur."

Claire and Aimie had readied the big bedroom for the new arrival. Will could manage for a few days until she was up and around again. Claire was determined she wouldn't be like Lettie, whining about how poorly she was. She would show the Kennedy's that she and Will could take care of themselves and the new baby!

It could well be that Kate making Claire angry was the stimulus Claire needed to give her the resolve to handle her own life and take charge of her affairs.

July 18, 1902

July 18, 1902 was a hot summer day. Claire knew when she awakened that morning that her waiting to be a mother would soon be over! For weeks now she had been getting the house in order. Claire had kept extra bread made, and that morning she made both a cake and pie and quickly prepared Will's favorite dinner. She set everything on the back of the wood stove to keep warm. Then she called Mrs. Lowes. "Can you come over this afternoon? Today is the big day! I, we, will be needing you!"

When Will came from the field for lunch, he called Dr. Holmes. Dishes were washed and put away by the time Mrs. Lowes and the doctor arrived. Will did what was expected of him; he had a good fire going in the kitchen stove and several kettles of water boiling.

When Dr. Holmes arrived he said, "I can see we aren't going to waste any time getting down to business." Claire never uttered a sound during delivery even though Dr. Holmes told her she was entitled to yell as loud as she wanted to. Afterwards he told Will, "She was the best, most cooperative patient I ever had. I had my worst one this morning. I had to set Jessie Schmidt's arm after she fell off of a hay wagon she was loading. I never heard such carrying on. I think she was mad at the Schmidt's because she had to work."

Will thought,"Poor Jessie, having to work in the fields. I never would have permitted that."

He was jerked back to reality by Dr. Holmes' question. "What are you going to name the boy, Will, another William?"

Before Will could answer, Claire spoke up. "I have decided on Charles Arthur after Papa. We can call him C.A. for short."

"'But I thought...," Will's voice trailed off. "C.A. sounds just fine." Will had assumed they would name the baby William, but he knew why Claire thought differently.

Dr. Holmes filled out his records, checked Claire and C.A. again, and started back to town. Before he got to the Ragain place he heard the children calling, "Here he comes, Ma!" By the time he got to their place, Mrs. Ragain was out by the gate.

"Good afternoon, Doctor. What brings you out this way?"

Dr. Holmes knew Mrs. Ragain loved to gossip and took pleasure in not giving her any news to pass along. "Oh, just taking the long way home. Do you think we might have rain by the weekend?"

He smiled when he heard her say, "The old fool didn't tell me a thing."

Lettie heard about the birth before Kate did. She called Ma to see what they had named the baby and was most surprised that Ma didn't even know the baby had arrived. Kate had expected them to call on her in spite of the bill she had sent. Who else knew as much about having babies? Besides, who else could they call? She and Lucy would drive over and see how big a mess they were in.

Will was in the field when Lucy and Kate arrived. Will saw them come but he wasn't about to go to the house. He was sure Claire could handle Kate better than he could.

Kate came up the walk all smiles but inside she was unsure of herself. Claire had the house spick and span. C.A. had just been fed and was asleep in the cradle that Aimie had loaned them. Claire was pleased everything was orderly.

Lucy was genuinely interested in her nephew. "Oh Claire, how are you? I am so anxious to see the baby."

"He is sleeping now but you can have a look." Claire was glad Lucy was along to make things easier with Kate.

"Oh, he is darling. What is his name?"

"Charles Arthur, after Papa, but we will call him C.A."

Kate could contain herself no longer, "Why, it is a Kennedy family tradition. All first sons in the family are named William."

Claire replied evenly, "I guess you can say 'tradition' has been broken. We now have John Russell Kennedy and Charles Arthur Kennedy."

Lucy almost collapsed with glee that someone didn't follow Kate's wishes. She said, "That's a pretty name and he is a pretty baby. I love that dimple in his chin."

Kate could have strangled them both. That slip of a girl had bested her again.

Lucy added, "Lettie has such an ugly baby. He whines just like Lettie."

"Lucy, how could you say such a thing about your sister's baby?" Kate admonished.

"You yourself said Lettie cries as much as little Willie."

Claire felt invigorated by Lucy's support, "Would you like a cup of tea and a slice of crème cake or would you prefer fresh blackberry pie?"

Before Kate could answer Lucy said, "They both sound so good, I would like a little of each."

The visit didn't last much longer after teatime. Kate stood up, smoothed her dress, and said, "We will tell the rest of the family the baby is here." With a curt nod she continued, "Come Lucy, we must hurry home to fix your father's dinner."

Kate put her arm in Lucy's to hurry her out the door. As she was leaving, Lucy said over her shoulder, "Claire, you do have a pretty baby! I look forward to playing with him."

It was a happy Claire who recounted the visit to Will later.

At home that night, Lucy shared her excitement about her new nephew. "Papa, he is so pretty. He has a dimple in his chin like yours! He didn't cry at all while we were there."

"I wonder why they didn't send for your mother when the wee one came," William said.

"I guess because Ma charged them for sitting up with Mr. Lefever," Lucy replied.

"What's that? Katie come in here!" William said sternly.

Kate knew reckoning had come.

"Katie, is this true? Why would you do such a thing?"

Kate tried to justify her actions. "Lettie needed some money. I thought since I had taken Aimie's place by staying at the last that she would pay the bill."

William sighed and shook his head. "It's too late to undo what you've done, but things will never be the same between the families. It's about time Lettie buckled down in the harness and helped Isaac. The only thing wrong with her is she wants the same things as Minnie. You stay out of it from now on, and do anything you can for Will and Claire."

Kate knew she had not acted wisely and had lost again. William had always been for Will anyway. No one had questioned her authority until Will got interested in Claire.

William broke into her thoughts when he asked, "What did Will name the baby?"

"Oh," Kate replied curtly, "Claire said they named him Charles Arthur after her father. They will call him C.A."

William just said, "humph."

Loss of a Loved One

Claire was resting on the front porch for a few minutes one September afternoon. She had been canning late peaches. C.A. was asleep so she could enjoy some rest before starting supper. She had just started into the house when she saw Andy coming on horseback at a full gallop. He continued past the house without pausing, on to where Will was working in the field.

Will saw him coming and stopped to wait. Claire saw them quickly unhitch the team and run to the barn. Will called to Claire, "Hurry and get me a clean shirt." The two men slid the harness off the team and let it drop. Claire knew something catastrophic must have happened for them to be in such a rush; Will was always careful to hang up the harness.

"Will, what is wrong?" she asked, handing him a shirt.

"Lucy is dying; the doctor said it was appendicitis and the appendix ruptured. There is nothing they can do. I don't know when I will be home."

Claire was stunned. Lucy had been over often since C.A. had come and Claire had enjoyed her company. The day seemed to drag on forever as Claire waited for Will to return. Why Lucy? Things like this weren't supposed to happen! The young are supposed to bury the old.

Will came home early the next morning. Lucy had passed away at sunrise. It had all happened so quickly; the family felt helpless that they hadn't been able to do anything for her. Lucy had complained of her side hurting when she came from school. She had gone to bed and seemed to feel better, but in the night she developed a high fever. They had sent for the doctor, but by then it had been too late.

Her passing would be felt deeply by all the family. Friends and family gathered two days later for her service. It was a sad homecoming for Frank. The service was held in the afternoon on the Kennedy front lawn. Meggie had gathered huge bouquets of wild flowers to bank around the casket. She couldn't imagine Lucy not being with them. All were deeply touched by one so young being taken from them.

When Will, Claire and C.A. came, Meggie never left Claire's side. The two of them and Lucinda tended the babies so Lettie and Minnie could be with their mother. They spread a quilt under a shade tree and put the children on it. It was the first time the four babies had been together.

"Four babies," said Claire. "That's quite an addition to the family in one year."

"Yes," said Lucinda. "And four marriages, too. Claire, we should be special friends since we're both the outsiders to the Kennedy's."

"I'd like that," said Claire. "I'm afraid Kate thinks of me as an outlaw."

"Oh, Claire," Lucinda protested, "not an outlaw. But this has been a hard year for Kate. Frank moving to St. Louis, four of her children getting married, four new babies...and now the loss of Lucy."

"It is hard to imagine she could go so quickly. She was so healthy; Lettie is always the puny one."

"Yes, and speaking of Lettie, have you noticed how happy Willie has been with us?"

"He does seem to be happy. Lettie's complaining may make him cross. She will be disappointed he hasn't cried the whole time she's been gone. Lucinda, how come you didn't name John Russell 'William'?" asked Claire.

"Well, I have been a Russell longer than I have a Kennedy," replied Lucinda. "It seemed to me that made it appropriate to name him John Russell Kennedy. Why didn't you name C.A. 'William'?"

"I had planned to," answered Claire, "until Kate did something that hurt me very much. Since we're going to be special friends, I'll tell you about it sometime, but not today."

"Come by when you come to town. John and C.A. could grow up as special cousins too."

"I would like that," said Claire. "All the boys should have fun together as they grow up. I am glad they were all boys."

"Claire, a week from Tuesday Mother is having the church ladies' organization, The Ladies Aid, for the afternoon. We would love to have you and little C.A. come. You need a change."

Actually Lucinda needed to show the ladies that the Kennedy's accepted her. Several had daughters her age and suspected how she had felt about Bob. They found the timing a little off between that affair and her sudden marriage to Nat.

It would be just the right touch to have sweet, innocent Claire included in the gathering. Claire was so good with the babies. If John Russell fussed, Claire would be sure to pick him up and rock him as quickly as she would her own. Yes, it would make a perfect picture.

Claire was pleased with the invitation. "Yes, I do need to get out. Thank you for inviting us. Sometimes I find myself wanting to wake C.A. to have someone to talk to during the day. I do miss Papa so much."

"I'm glad you will come," said Lucinda. "I see the family coming. The first thing Lettie is going to say is 'did little Willie cry after me?'"

Lucinda's prediction was right. As soon as Lettie got out of the buggy she asked, "Did Willie cry after me?" She seemed disappointed when they assured her he had been quite happy to sit on Lucinda's lap and play.

When Kate returned from the cemetery, she didn't go into the house with the rest of the family. She needed some time alone with her thoughts. She felt as though everything was against her. She had always thought Lucy was more like herself than the other girls; Lucy had been the only one to speak up to William. And now she was gone. Kate was coming to realize that the family no longer respected her authority; instead she thought they saw her as rather bossy.

She had wanted the girls to marry well and for the boys to have adjoining farms and all work together, but nothing was working out as she had planned.

She thought Lettie had made a good marriage but it certainly was very meager at present. Perhaps William was right about Lettie complaining too much. She would speak to Lettie about that. If Isaac got tired of her complaining and brought her back home, it would be another blow. Kate thought that she might have held the boys on the farm if Will hadn't left when he did. Now it seemed they were all leaving.

But the cruelest blow of all was losing Lucy. Kate was devastated by Lucy's death. She didn't think she could go on. She walked until she came to the haystack; then she lay back against the soft hay and began to weep. It was there that William found her.

"Crying won't change anything, Katie. We have to go on. Come on back to the house. The girls have supper on the table and the babies are asleep. Everyone is feeling pretty well spent. We could all use some nourishment."

Kate was glad William had come for her. She felt very weak after her round of tears, and she couldn't remember the last time she had eaten. The family was gathered at the table when they got back to the house.

Frank tried to lighten the mood by telling stories about his experiences in the city. He told them of the plays Ruth had been in but he didn't tell them that she also worked in the burlesque houses. His accounts of life in St. Louis helped to take their minds off the sad circumstances for the gathering.

Minnie asked, "I would have thought you and Ruth would have been married before now."

Without thinking, Kate said, "We don't need an actress in the family." As soon as the words were out, she could have bitten her tongue for saying them. The family was right in thinking her domineering and too outspoken.

Frank laughed, "Ma, she likes what she is doing and doesn't have time for homemaking right now. And I am making up for lost time. I will try to see you folks more often from now on."

As they began to gather up their things to return home Will overheard

Minnie comment to Lettie, "I hear the Schmidt's sent Jessie back to her folks until her arm heals. I guess if she can't work they don't want her."

"What good are her low cut gowns now?" asked Lettie. "She is no better off than we are."

"Gus knows his livestock but not his women," replied Minnie. "The doctor said she used her arm too soon after she broke it and that was why it hadn't healed. Maybe Gus needs two wives—a big strong German, like his mother, for the farm and a pretty one for when he goes out in society."

Will's heart sank; he had already been depressed over Lucy's death and now to hear such bad news about Jessie. How he wished things could have been different for them.

Going home in the buggy Claire noticed how forlorn he was. She thought he grieved for Lucy. Claire was so gentle and caring that Will felt even more depressed. He didn't know anyone could be as miserable as he was.

Will was a little suspicious of Lucinda's invitation for Claire to attend the Ladies Aid meeting. But, he reasoned, it would give him some time alone. And since the invitation gave Claire something else to think about, perhaps she wouldn't notice how deep in his own thoughts he was.

Claire was excited over the invitation to the Russell's. She planned to wear the suit Mrs. Mason had made for her wedding since she had only worn it twice. It was pretty without the coat so she would be comfortable in the house. She had little C.A.'s outfit planned and ready too. Aimie had made two lovely long baby dresses that she had loaned Claire. They had hours of handwork on the tucks, lace, embroidery, and ribbons; and the slips were just as fancy.

It would be nice to go out in society. The word 'society' made Claire smile. She hadn't had a change from her everyday chores since she married. She had to admit that she had never taken much time for socializing.

On the day of the Ladies' Aid meeting, Will hitched the horse to the buggy and loaded the things Claire wanted to take with her for Mrs. Russell. She had a basket with fresh eggs, a jar of sweet cream, and a pound of butter shaped by her mother's wooden butter mold. City folk were always glad to get fresh farm things.

Claire had padded a box for C.A. so she wouldn't have to hold him and drive. She called Will to look at C.A. in his outfit before she wrapped him up. Will said, "You two look as fine as city people. You will impress them today."

Claire was pleased with his compliment. "Why thank you, Will. I am looking forward to going. I wish you would go along; you could go on downtown and visit with Nat. You need a change as much as I do."

"No, you run along; I'll be busy here." Will was only too glad to have some time alone. After Claire left he did something he had never done during the day on a weekday; he went out on the front porch and sat down.

As he looked out across the land, he reflected on the problems of his life and Jessie's. He had been over it so many times, pondering what he could have done. The results were always the same—he had made the best decision under the circumstances.

He told himself that Jessie's situation now wasn't his fault. She had had several options besides marrying Gus. Her family must have had their eye on the Schmidt's money. With Gus, Jessie might have money but she would never be allowed to spend it on frills. He knew he shouldn't feel guilty about Jessie's hardships, but he did.

His heart ached at the thought of what lay ahead for them both. He told himself that nothing he could have done differently would have been any better. This way he had the land he wanted and in a few years he would be making money on the farm. This hadn't been a good crop year but he wasn't in debt. He was better off than his neighbors.

He could find no fault with Claire; he might have felt better if he could have. She tried to do everything the way he liked; if he said he liked something a certain way, that was the way she fixed it. It wasn't anything she did or something she didn't do. It was simply the fact that she wasn't Jessie. He knew life with Jessie would have been different. With Jessie he would have had to do things her way, but the knowledge of that didn't stop the longing.

Claire had arrived early at the Russell's. Mr. Russell had sent an employee to help take care of the horses and buggies. Claire was glad to have help getting things into the house.

Lucinda and Mrs. Russell were delighted with the eggs, cream, and butter. They put the babies in the back bedroom. Little John was already asleep and the fresh air had made C.A. sleepy too. The young mothers were glad to have a good start on the afternoon.

Wesley Jennings' wife, Cordelia, was the first to arrive. Lucinda introduced Claire as, "my favorite sister-in-law". She made it a point to mention that Claire was David's sister-in-law because she and Aimie were sisters.

Cordelia said, "I just must have a peek at the babies before the others arrive." She made the usual compliments one says about new babies, and then exclaimed, "What lovely handwork on C.A.'s dress. I know a shop in St. Louis that would pay handsomely for work like this."

"My sister, Aimie, made it," Claire replied. "She only sews for family members." Claire was delighted with the way the afternoon was going; she could hardly wait to tell Aimie about Cordelia and her hand-made baby dress. Claire was sure Aimie would be pleased with her reply!

Claire enjoyed the afternoon immensely. The babies slept all through the meeting. Just as Mrs. Russell was ready to serve refreshments little John woke up. Claire offered to take care of him so Lucinda could help her mother with the refreshments. She brought John out for the ladies to see. They exclaimed "What a darling baby."

Claire said, "The Kennedy's are so pleased to have four grandsons in one year. The children should enjoy each other very much in growing up."

Lucinda was pleased with the way the afternoon had gone. Claire had done just what Lucinda had hoped she would to show how she and John belonged in the Kennedy family. Lucinda knew some of the 'old biddies' had doubts that John was really a Kennedy, but after Claire's performance today they couldn't very well express that to others.

After the ladies left, Claire began to get ready to leave. Mrs. Russell filled Claire's basket with little cakes, dainty sandwiches and a tin of English tea. "Thank you, Mrs. Russell," said Claire, "it was a lovely afternoon."

"We are glad you came. Lucinda is lucky to have you for a friend, and I hope your boys have good times growing up together."

Lucinda hugged her warmly and carried C.A. to the buggy. "Thank you for inviting me to come today, Lucinda. It is the happiest I've been since Papa and Lucy passed away."

As soon as Claire got out of town she picked C.A. up and nursed him; he seemed quite content. After she put him back in the box she treated herself to one of Mrs. Russell's little cakes. She, too, was quite content.

When she arrived home, Will came out to help her get things into the house where he already had a brisk fire started in the kitchen cook stove. C.A. stayed asleep so Claire quickly changed clothes and put on the dressing gown that had been part of her trousseau. She had only worn it a few times and it gave her a pleasant feeling. She made a pot of tea and set out Mrs. Russell's sandwiches and cakes. She had so much to tell Will about the afternoon that she didn't notice how silent he was.

The Family Starts to Mend

Minnie felt the family ties were slipping and wanted all of the Kennedy family to get together for Thanksgiving. She knew Kate didn't feel like having the family this year, so Minnie invited everyone to her home.

Claire was glad for the invitation because she didn't feel she was ready to make it the occasion it should be. Maybe next year she would have the family. She missed Papa so much! She missed his stories and their conversations; she even missed the scent of his pipe smoke. Will didn't smoke and their conversation was mostly what he was doing on the farm.

Kate was relieved that Minnie was having the family for Thanksgiving. She just didn't feel she could get a holiday meal and have the chatter of the family during the day. It was time the families were entertained in Minnie's nice home. Of course Lettie would be envious and in the doldrums afterwards but maybe it would help snap her into making her own situation better.

Lettie had mixed feelings about Minnie's invitation. As the oldest daughter, she should have invited the family for Thanksgiving since her mother wasn't up to having them, but she was glad she wouldn't have to have them this year. On the other hand, it would be hard to be in Minnie's grand home and look pleasant.

Lucinda was delighted with the holiday plans. She told Nat she would like to invite all of them for Christmas. Nat was pleased she wanted to have his family, but what pleased him more was that Lucinda also said she wanted a child of their own before too much longer.

Frank and Ruth were glad to be going to Eli and Minnie's for the holiday. Ruth had a few days off before she joined her company in Chicago; Frank had to be back in St. Louis on Monday. Spending Thanksgiving at the Cox's made it more of a social occasion than if they had been at one of their parents' homes.

William saw the gathering as a chance to help bind up the wounds the family had suffered the past year. He was careful to adhere to his diet of buttermilk so he would feel like going. He doubted Claire and Will would have come to their home this year. Claire could have given several excuses and he wouldn't have blamed her for any one of them. Ruth and Frank would probably have gone to the Stimson's instead.

Meggie looked forward to playing with the babies. Things had been very bleak for her since Lucy had died. She hadn't realized how much Lucy had done to let her play. Lately it seemed the chores were endless; she was always washing dishes, peeling vegetables, sweeping, dusting, making beds, getting wood and water. It would be so good to get away.

Andy and his mother had never gotten along very well; now he was finding it almost impossible to do any job to please her. For weeks now, he had been working on a plan that would give him some freedom. He was secretly doing small jobs for the neighbors to get enough money to buy a saddle horse. He had almost enough saved and Eli had said he would loan him the rest. Eli had promised to give him the money when they went over on Thanksgiving. A horse would mean he could go someplace on Saturday night without having to ask Ma's permission to use one of the family's horses. If Frank could raise hell in St. Louis, surely Andy could liven things up in Brandton!

Minnie saw to every little detail that would make the whole day perfect. Eli was more than proud of the special touches she gave their home. He wanted it to be a show place. Although he strayed from the marital path through the years, Minnie, their family and his home were his pride and joy.

The family had all arrived by mid morning on Thanksgiving Day. The men were visiting in the parlor, the women were in the sitting room, and the babies were in the bedrooms. Minnie had a neighbor woman and her two teenage daughters to serve the meal and clean up afterwards. One of the girls worked every day for Minnie so Minnie was sure everything would go smoothly.

Kate's spirits brightened quite noticeably at how well Minnie managed. Lettie's reaction was quite different. In a low voice Kate said to her, "Now don't spoil the day for all of us by getting one of your vapor spells. You should be doing better with what you have than you are doing."

"It's so hard, Ma. I really thought Isaac and I would live like this. I am just so downhearted."

"Let's be gracious. Today is quite a treat. I almost didn't come because I was too downhearted, but it is not my nature to sit and complain. I plan to enjoy the day."

Ruth was regaling Lucinda and Claire with the latest fashions in St. Louis. Bicycle Clubs were the 'in' thing and had a lot to do with getting rid of the bustle. Skirts were not so full and most of the men were wearing velvet knickers. Ruth was using henna on her hair, mainly to make herself stand out on the stage. She told Kate that henna would 'liven up' her hair and Claire that it would 'give more body' to her hair. To both suggestions Kate gave a "humph."

What Ruth did not tell them was that at the theatre where she worked they were prepared to give two programs. If they knew police were present they did vaudeville; otherwise they did burlesque. She got twenty dollars a week, fifteen dollars when on the road. It was a very good salary considering a plumber was paid only twelve dollars a week.

When William went into the bedroom to rest, Frank showed the men his breast pocket flask and offered them a drink. Andy, Isaac, and Eli accepted eagerly but Nat and Will hesitated. Then Nat laughed, "Come on Will, I guess we shouldn't pass up a chance to be like a city dude; let's have a nip. We only live until our wives get a hold of us!"

Frank passed out cigars. When Isaac started to trim the end by biting it off, Frank said, "Wait, I have something special for that. Look at these cigar cutters."

Isaac said, "Frank, you are really doing all right by yourself. You will have to come home more often to show us country folks what is new in the city."

Will was enjoying the warm glow from the whiskey. "Andy can have my cigar. I don't think I could handle a nip of whiskey and a cigar at the same sitting. My stomach is not as strong as Frank's; it's more like Pa's."

Isaac said, "Eli, you are going to have new neighbors. Schmidt's have bought the Wallace farm. Old Henry said Jessie wasn't doing her fair share of the work, and that Gus would have to get along with what they could make on their own. Henry will set them up but they will have to pay him back."

"And with interest you can bet. I saw Jessie in the store the other day and she looked as old as her mother-in-law," was Eli's comment. The whiskey glow went out of Will and he was left with a cold, dark feeling.

Lettie pulled Kate aside and whispered, "Ma, I saw Eli pat Alice on her behind as she went into the pantry. Do you think I should tell Minnie?"

"Lettie, you would ruin Minnie's home and spoil this day for all of us," Kate scolded. "Eli was just being friendly. I knew you were jealous of what they had but I didn't think you were this jealous. Now you brace up and tend to your own affairs."

Poor Lettie, she had expected some satisfaction out of seeing Minnie brought down a notch or two. All at once she realized Willie hadn't cried all day. Everyone was happy to be at Minnie's except her!

William felt rested after his nap. "I guess it is time to think of heading home, Katie. It has been a fine day in your home Eli. You and Minnie did us proud."

"Nothing in St. Louis would have been better," Frank agreed.

"Well, I appreciate you saying so. We are glad you all could come," said Eli.

The ladies had joined the men by then and all were talking at once. "Lucinda and I would like for you all to come to our home Christmas," Nat invited.

"See you at Nat and Lucinda's on Christmas Day!" was echoed again and again as everyone prepared to leave.

Claire chatted merrily on the way home; it had been an exhilarating day, so out of the ordinary. She was looking forward to going to Nat's and Lucinda's for Christmas.

After seeing Minnie's fine home, Claire wanted to do some sprucing up. It had been a long time since there had been new curtains in the parlor. The groceries usually took most of the money from selling eggs, but she had managed to save a little. After she got C.A. to sleep she would study the national 'wish book', the Sears Roebuck Catalog.

After pondering for two days she decided on three pair of medallion Brussels net ruffled lace curtains. Their description set Claire to day dreaming, "It has the effect of a real imported French Brussels net curtains that would ordinarily sell at $13.00 to $15.00 a pair, Sears price $3.35 a pair." With the postage at 14¢ a pair that would be $10.47 and Claire had $14.12. After supper she would tell Will she was sending for them.

While Claire washed the supper dishes, Will looked at the Sears Roebuck Catalog. He found an item described as "the most durable, best finished, and most perfect lever motion forge on the market," for $10.90. When Claire came from the kitchen Will asked her, "How much money is in the egg fund?"

"$14.12." said Claire.

"Tomorrow I want you to order this forge for me. I can do lots of repairs on machinery and shoe the horses using it. It will save time going in to the blacksmith shop, besides saving money."

"Oh, Will," Claire protested, "I was going to use the egg money for some new curtains for the parlor. I found some lace ones for only $3.35 a pair."

"Curtains won't save money," Will replied. "Don't try to keep up with Minnie and Lucinda."

Claire's eyes smarted with tears; she was so surprised she didn't know how to reply. Will had been so moody lately she thought it best to remain silent. How she missed Papa! She had seldom asked him for anything but he had always seemed glad to get what she wanted. If she picked something plain or less expensive he would say, "I believe you had better get the other one." Will certainly was not like Papa.

Claire was a likely customer when the itinerant photographer knocked at the door the next afternoon and asked, "Do you have any children you would like to have a picture taken of? They will be ready by Christmas."

"Oh, I would like to," Claire said, "but I am very short of money right now."

"You can have a 16x20 with a frame, and five 4x6's for $5."

"I would love to, but I only have $2."

"You have chickens, eggs, and maybe butter, don't you?"

"Yes, but——"

"I'll take the $2, two chickens, three dozen eggs and a pound of butter."

"All right, I will do it. Get your things set up and I will dress the baby. He hasn't gone to sleep yet." Claire thought she wouldn't have to tell Will until the pictures came. It would be a Christmas surprise. She got out the long dress with the tucks, ruffles and lace that Aimie had made. C.A. was getting so fat the dress wouldn't fasten in the back but that wouldn't show in the picture.

C.A. was delighted and puzzled by all the activity. The photographer said, "He is the best subject I have had all day. It won't take long to get this over."

As soon as the picture was taken, Claire took the dress off of C.A. and put him to bed. Then she got the money, butter, and eggs before going to the hen house for the chickens. She had two hens that had quit laying; she wouldn't miss them, but she would be short on egg money next week.

The photographer promised to bring the pictures in two weeks.

"That will be fine," said Claire. "Try to come in the afternoon. I would like for the pictures to be a surprise for my husband."

Thinking about the pictures lifted Claire's spirits. Five extra pictures would be enough to give one each to Aimie, Lucinda, Minnie, Lettie, and Kate. She didn't really care about giving one to Kate but William had always been kind to her.

Christmas, 1902
The Family's First Auto Ride

Claire set about getting things ready to go to Christmas dinner at Nat and Lucinda's. She aired and brushed all their wool clothes. She would take Lucinda some cream, butter, and eggs. She would have to use them sparingly at home to have the extra but she didn't intend to look like they had to skimp. She was still upset that Will hadn't let her get the lace curtains. She hadn't had anything new since she married, and she was beginning to see what their home would look like if left to Will. She had decided to keep two nest eggs, one Will could share and one for the house. She had been a Lefever longer than she had been a Kennedy and she wasn't about to look like a poor relation.

Will approached the coming holidays reluctantly by trying to ignore them entirely. Claire spent more and more time talking and playing with C.A. of late; they seemed so happy, but Will just couldn't share their sentiments. His thoughts were often of Jessie and how miserable she must be; depression would set in on him again. Since Claire had spent so much time preparing for the day, he couldn't bring himself to say they should just stay home, but that was what he would like to do. Maybe they would have a snow storm and not be able to go.

The day before Christmas Claire had everything ready to go to Nat's.

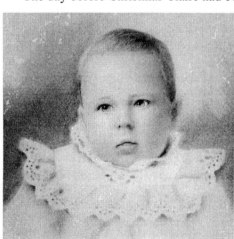

She hoped Ruth would be there to tell about the latest in St. Louis. Claire was especially proud of C.A's pictures. She had wrapped each of the small ones in red tissue paper, and slid the large one under the bed to bring out on Christmas morning.

When Will came in from doing the chores Christmas morning, Claire gave him C.A.'s picture. To say Will was surprised and pleased would be to put it mildly. He was dumbfounded! He couldn't imagine Claire taking all of the steps necessary to get the picture and not talking about it; perhaps she had more depth than appeared on the surface. "Why, Claire, that is a splendid picture. I hadn't realized little C.A. was such a handsome child." Truthfully Will had never thought much about C.A. as a person who was a part of his life at all. Instead he had let his disappointment crowd out his own family.

"I am glad you like it. I got C.A. some soft kid shoes with little straps that go up as high as button shoes would. I think he will look darling in them. When you go back out, please bring in some sprigs of cedar. I want to stick them around in the basket I am taking to Lucinda."

Will brought the cedar and was pleased at what a merry looking basket Claire had fixed. The little red packages in the split stave woven basket filled with farm produce looked quite festive. They would make a good appearance at the family gathering. He should be glad that Claire didn't whine because of the things she didn't have like Lettie did. Will began to hurry so they could get started; suddenly he wanted to be with the rest of the family.

Nat was eager for the family to arrive. Mrs. Russell had let her maid help Lucinda for a week and together they had decorated the house and cooked all of the traditional Christmas dishes. But what Nat was most excited about was that Mr. Russell had loaned them their new Oldsmobile to give the family rides around town. It was the first automobile in Brandton. Mr. Russell was going to wait until spring to learn to drive it, so until then Nat was to be the chauffeur. He planned to take each couple for a drive, and he was pleased that he would be the one to give them their first ride in an automobile.

They all arrived at almost the same time. After their joyous greetings Nat told them his plan. A hubbub of excitement followed his announcement. Nat told Kate and William not to take their coats off, that they would be first to go for a ride.

Kate's heart swelled with pride as they rode down Main Street and back around the park. It was good to see the people on the street stop and stare; others in their homes ran to their windows to watch them go by. "Why, I didn't know I could feel so grand," she said.

William said, "I never expected to ride in an automobile."

Nat was pleased with their enjoyment. "I am glad I could do it for you folks. This should be a day to remember. Even Banker Jennings doesn't have a horseless carriage yet."

Eli and Minnie were next, then Lettie and Isaac, then Andy and Meggie.

When it was Will and Claire's turn, Claire ran to get C.A. "I want him to go too. Someday I will tell him about his 'First Christmas' and his first ride in an automobile.

Meggie said, "Claire, you are such a good mother. Lettie never thought to take Willie."

Ruth wasn't coming until later so Nat planned to take her and Frank for a ride when she arrived.

It took all of them some time to settle down after the thrilling ride. When things calmed down, Lucinda thanked Claire for the basket of produce. "I opened the red package with our name on it. C.A. is adorable! Here are the other packages if you want to hand them out."

Claire relished all of the compliments, especially Meggie's. "Claire, he is such a handsome baby and his new shoes today are just what a little fellow should have." The photographer had not gone to any of the other homes; that made C.A.'s picture even more special.

Ruth arrived just before dinner, and Nat took her and Frank for a ride. Then everyone sat down to enjoy the sumptuous dinner. Conversation was lively and before they knew it they all had eaten too much. The women were grateful Lucinda had her mother's maid so they could go into the sitting room while the men went into the parlor. William went into the bedroom to rest awhile.

As the men went into the parlor Frank asked, "Does Lucinda allow smoking in here?"

Nat laughed, "It's all right on special occasions. She is just glad I don't smoke all the time. Her Dad always has a cigar in his mouth, whether he is smoking it or not."

Andy and Eli accepted a cigar from Frank but Will declined, "I will pass on the cigar; later I will have a nip of Frank's Christmas cheer."

Their main topic of conversation was the automobile. Eli said, "I read there are 8,000 automobiles in America now. When the roads get better we will get one; until then I will rely on good horses."

"You had better start looking for some that are not easy to scare," Isaac commented. "Mine shy at a piece of paper in the road. I hate to think what they will do when they meet an automobile."

"It is hard to get the people interested in working on the roads," Andy said. "If the whole community would work together we could get roads good enough for automobiles."

In the sitting room the ladies made themselves comfortable. "When I came to Missouri I thought things would be better," Kate mused. "But I never dreamed of a day like today. There have been hardships but there have been many more blessings."

"Kate does have a soft spot under that hard exterior," Lucinda thought to herself. Aloud she said, "Ruth, what is new in St. Louis?"

"A member of our company just came back from Paris. She said clothes there are very elaborate, with ruffles and frills and lace. A ball gown would have a train, a low-cut neckline, and be lavish with pleated lace and bows and embroidery. Lace-flounced petticoats are most important since a lady would gracefully lift her train when she waltzes. My friend said we didn't have anything as fancy as in Paris."

"What about their hair and hats?" asked Lucinda.

"The style is for upswept hair with a hat sitting lightly on top. My friend purchased a feathered hat for this winter, and for next summer she got a knee-length bathing dress and bloomers!"

Ruth's audience was fascinated, except for Kate. She snorted, "What's this generation coming to? Wherever men go astray, there will be a woman with bare legs leading them!"

"Oh, the ladies wear stockings and rubber bathing slippers. It is the men that have bare legs," Ruth laughed. "We'll have some time between plays in the spring, and five of us girls are going to Coney Island in New York. I already have my suit. It is all wool and is it scratchy!"

"My! You will have to tell us all about your trip when you get back," said Minnie. "We'll tell you about wading in the river at the family 4th of July picnic. The only way we'll get wet all over will be to slip on a slick rock and fall in!"

Even Kate laughed at that. "If that happens we will know you did it on purpose!"

Ruth said she and Frank must leave as her family was gathering in the evening. The others began to get their things ready to leave too. The young mothers thanked Meggie for playing nursemaid. It had been the best day for Meggie in a long time.

In the parlor Frank passed his flask around again. Andy took a second drink and thought he wouldn't mind his mother's chatter on the way home now.

As Isaac listened to Lettie's whining about the things Minnie and Lucinda had that she didn't, he wished he had taken another drink from Frank's flask too. Finally he said, "Lucinda's family gave them those nice things. Nat couldn't have afforded most of them."

"Now you are putting my family down," Lettie protested.

"No, but everyone should do the best they can with what they have. We could do better if you took care of the house so I could spend more time in the field." Isaac had never spoken to Lettie like that before.

"But the rest of the family is doing well."

"Are they? There are a few things you might not realize. Do you know why the Russell's do so much for Nat?" asked Isaac.

Lettie was surprised. "Because he is so good to Lucinda?"

"Well, that's true. But the main reason is because he married Lucinda after Bob Burtrum ran off and left her in the family way!"

"Isaac! Are you sure?"

"I wouldn't say it if I weren't. And almost everyone else is too. And as far as Minnie's fine home and maids, Eli takes many liberties with those maids. You saw how familiar he was with one of them on Thanksgiving. Minnie will have to look the other way all of her life or lose her grand home."

Lettie had never thought of it that way, "How awful for her."

"And you should remember how there was no one for Will but Jessie until he heard of Claire's farm. He sure loves that farm."

"Now that you have mentioned it he doesn't pay much attention to Claire."

"Are they all doing so well? Would you trade lives with any of them? At least you have a husband who loves you and helps you."

Lettie answered sincerely, "No, I would rather have you as a husband, Isaac. I know I have complained a lot that we don't have nice things, but I have to admit that you mean more to me than any fancy things we could have. Maybe I can stop being so jealous. I am going to try. I'll bet all those things don't make Minnie happy. Even Ma told me I could do better."

"You know how it is with a team of horses. If they pull in opposite directions, they don't get anywhere. If we could just work together with both of us pulling in the same direction, we could be a good team. We seem to be the only ones in the family who are really man and wife."

"You're right, and I will try, but I have been jealous of Minnie all my life."

"Yes, and being sick was the way you got attention."

"I did have the first grandson named 'William'."

"Well, look at Willie, he's awake and he's laughing. He had a good time today. Don't you think he knows when we aren't happy?"

"It has been quite a day."

"It has been quite a day" was repeated in the Kennedy surrey as Andy drove his parents home. Andy was glad of the second drink from Frank's flask, even if Kate was quite content and only making kind remarks. Andy was thinking of the day's events, of the differences in the families, and of what he wanted in the future. He did not want to continue working the family farm; he wanted to have his own farm someday. Frank was his idol; he and Ruth had a good thing going. While Andy didn't want to work in the city, he did want to be independent, and he for sure didn't want to be tied down for a long time. For a while all he wanted was a fast horse and to be looked up to.

His thoughts were interrupted by Meggie's remark, "I had such a good time with the babies today. Even little Willie was fun; he didn't cry all day."

Kate said, "It is quite a comfort to see the young ones coming on. Such a day! When I was Meggie's age I never even dreamed of such a thing as an automobile, and to think we all rode in one today."

"I guess we have made progress," agreed William. "Why, I couldn't even drive a team of horses when we came to Missouri. The Kennedy's are stepping up."

Minnie was happy as she and Eli drove home. "Eli, it was a wonderful day. Did you really mean it when you said you wanted an automobile?"

"Just as soon as the roads improve out our way, we will get one. What did your family say about your fur coat?"

"To tell the truth, they all took on more over little C.A.'s picture than they did my coat."

Eli laughed heartily, "It was a good picture. Claire seems to be holding her own with Kate. I was afraid Claire was so timid that Kate would take over. I never thought Claire could or would hold her own with Kate. Claire will do all right."

Even Will was under the spell of the good day as they drove homeward. Claire chatted happily about how well the four children had gotten along; how the family would all remember the date of their first automobile ride; how they had all been so pleased with C.A's picture. It had been such a good day.

Will was content to let Claire talk; then she said something that really surprised him.

"I have been thinking. I would like to keep the school teacher of Cedar Bluff next year. Estelle said Mr. Henson was looking for a place to board that was near the school. If my garden is good next year, the only cost would be the extra sugar and coffee. Estelle thought he would pay $10 a month. He probably would go home most of the week ends."

Will thought that it would be nice to have someone else to talk to in the evening. "Why, if you want to Claire, it would be all right with me."

The day had been enjoyable for Ruth and Frank too. They were fond of the family but were eager to get back to the city. Ruth laughed, "Frank, they are all dear people but I don't believe your mother likes my being an actress. I hope no one tells her that I sometimes do burlesque!"

"Don't worry, hon', by the time we do marry she will be very happy to have you."

"We do make a good pair."

Stories from the Past

The winter had gone quickly for Claire. Now spring was bursting out all over and she felt the adrenaline flowing. She was looking forward to having the school teacher, Mr. Henson, as a boarder. She just knew an addition to the household would be good for everyone, and besides, it gave her a perfect reason to spruce up the house.

The living room got her attention first. The walls seemed so drab; new wallpaper would fix that and the room would be spring-like. The problem was she couldn't hang wallpaper by herself, and Will was too busy in the field to ask him to help. She thought of Sallie Bryant and her son, Fred. They still worked for other people, even though Sallie was quite elderly. Maybe she could hire them to help with papering.

Claire counted her egg money, looked at the Sears catalogue, and found she had enough money for new paper. She called the Bryants to see if they could help paper the room in a few weeks. They agreed that they could, so Claire ordered the paper.

She looked forward to the new paper making a difference, but she hadn't counted on what the result of the Bryants helping with the work would be.

While Fred hung the paper using a ladder, Sallie measured the next section. Claire and Sallie visited as they worked. "Claire, I was a house-maid for your folks years ago. I was there when your mother died."

"I didn't know that," Claire said. "Papa could never talk about Mama passing."

"I can see why; he was devastated by her death and the babies' too."

Claire was stunned. "Did you say babies?"

"Oh, you didn't know she had twins?"

"No. I was only five at the time. Papa never talked about it, and neither did Aimie. Please tell me what happened."

"Doctor McCaskell had been gone several years by then and the young doctor who came to take his place was out most of the time. He was late getting there when your mother's time came; but I don't think it would have made a difference even if he had been earlier. Those of us who worked in the house were afraid she might have trouble. From the time she knew she was in the family way, she took to her chair and was waited on. Your papa would ask her to go on walks, but she would say,

'No, I'm comfortable here.' She just didn't have the strength she needed when the time came. Such a tragedy. Through the years I have thought a lot about you two little girls left without a mother. I think your father did a fine job with both of you."

Claire was close to tears. "Thank you for telling me about what happened to my mother. I know she was always in my father's thoughts even though he didn't talk about her. Now I know why." As Claire absorbed what Sallie had told her, she began to look at the papering project differently. Now it seemed a tribute to her parents.

Once the living room met with Claire's approval, she moved on to add touches elsewhere in the house. She freshened up Charles' old room for Mr. Henson. She thought it looked quite comfortable by the time she finished. It had a small stove and a table with a good lamp in case Mr. Henson wanted to work in his room. Claire hoped he would spend quite a lot of time in the living room with them after supper. It would mean so much to Will to have another man to converse with; he never seemed to have much to share with her.

More and more, little C.A. filled the lonely place in Claire's heart. She knew she could make a good future for him. Although she loved the farm, Claire wanted C.A. to have an education and decide for himself what he wanted to do. She would preserve the farm for him if he wanted it, but she was not going to be like Kate and try to keep him tied to it!

Besides preparing for Mr. Henson's arrival, dealing with the usual household chores, and caring for little C.A., Claire started the garden. She planted extra to allow for the additional mouth to feed. She had her work list made out, what she would need to can, and the staples she would need to buy.

While she tended to those things, Will had plenty to keep him busy as well. As the spring days grew warmer, he knew it wouldn't be long before the bees would swarm looking for a new home. He got all the things he would need to work with the bees. He enjoyed putting on the protective clothing, heavy gloves, and a broad-brim hat with protective netting over his face. The new hive was ready and he had the pots and pans he would use to get the bees to settle.

Just before noon they heard the swarm of bees coming. Will put on his protective clothing and lit the smoker so he could blow smoke to stun the bees after they settled. Claire got her big heavy spoons to bang on the pans. In short order the bees were settled and the queen was in the new hive. Once that was done, the rest of the bees followed her. The honey they would supply would be a welcome addition to the table.

The highlight of the summer was the gathering of the families at the river for the annual 4th of July picnic. The picnic baskets were something to behold—fried chicken, potato salad, all kinds of pickles, coleslaw, deviled eggs, sliced tomatoes, green beans seasoned with ham, pies, cakes, and fresh blackberry cobbler.

The men played horseshoes on the bank of the river, some fished and others traded stories. The four toddlers were put on a quilt. Their mothers wisely removed their shoes so they would not venture off of the quilt onto the gravel.

Ruth and Frank had brought Meggie a bathing outfit, complete with rubber bathing slippers, stockings and bloomers. She and Ruth enjoyed the water in their matching suits. Meggie's joy knew no bounds.

The mothers and Kate sat around the babies. After lunch and a nap they took the youngsters down to the river for a dip and some splashing in the water. It was a most exhilarating day for them all. Before they left they planned another picnic to celebrate the grain harvest.

Harvest time was hard work, but it was also a community event. Neighbors exchanged work so that each of them would have enough men, wagons, and teams to run the thrasher when it came to his place. While the men folk harvested the grain, the women prepared to feed the thrashing crew.

Will was an expert at stacking the bundles of grain while they waited for the thrashing machine to come. Claire would exchange work with Mrs. Lowes. Estelle was home for a few weeks before the short term at the Teachers College in Springfield, so she would help them too.

Estelle was bubbling with happiness that summer. Her school was her pride and she had met a young man in that community named Aaron Hubbard. As they worked she told Claire and her mother how wonderful he was. It made the work lighter for all of them. "He has a little farm and

74

works in Brandton as a carpenter part time; he is very shy." Mrs. Lowes was as happy as Estelle.

As always, they were excited when the big steam engine pulling the thrashing machine came into hearing. Everyone knew the job they were to do. The women always prepared extra food for those who stopped by to watch. Only those actively involved with the thrashing thought it was work, the onlookers thought it was fascinating.

There was a surprise onlooker in the afternoon. Aaron Hubbard watched the thrashing until the women finished their work in the house. Estelle had said he was shy, but he wasn't too shy to go up to the house and ask Estelle to go with him to look at the Yochum place that was for sale.

As the two of them drove off, Claire told Mrs. Lowes, "I think you are going to have a son-in-law."

"I would really like that, and you can see the Yochum house from my kitchen window. When the leaves are off you can even see the roof top."

Claire's prediction was correct. Aaron planned to sell his small farm and purchase the Yochum place. It was bigger and closer to Brandton for his carpentry work. It didn't take Estelle long to say 'Yes' when he asked her to marry him. The wedding date was set for the week before Estelle's school began. Aaron's cousins in St. Louis had been telling him about the Worlds Fair being in St. Louis the next summer. Aaron and Estelle would take a delayed honeymoon and go to the fair then.

They were married the first Sunday in August in the Lowes's parlor; Will and Claire were their attendants. It was a joyful occasion and they were all surprised when Mrs. Lowes burst into tears. She apologized saying, "I've never been this happy before. I didn't know I would cry." That made them all a little misty-eyed.

The Boarder

Claire had planned well for Mr. Henson to board with them, but even she was pleasantly surprised that it all worked out so nicely. Will enjoyed the talks after supper, often he and Sam would play checkers while Claire cleaned up the kitchen. Claire was glad to have the smell of pipe tobacco in the house again; it reminded her of her papa. Mr. Henson enjoyed the camaraderie with Will and said Claire's meals were the best he'd ever had.

Claire had been concerned their regular breakfast time would be too early for Mr. Henson, but he was going to do the janitor work at the school in addition to teaching, so he wanted to leave early. That gave Claire more time through the day for housework, laundry, cooking, care of the chickens, and most of all, keeping up with C.A. Thinking of the extra money spurred her on.

The evenings when Aaron and Estelle walked over for a visit were the best. They all had enough in common to enjoy each other and conversation was always lively. Mr. Henson became 'Sam' instead of Samuel or Mr. Henson. Little C.A. was passed from one lap to another and usually fell asleep before the evening was over.

On one of these visits Estelle confided to Claire that she was "in the family way."

Claire was excited and happy for her friend. "Our children will have so much fun growing up together. If you have a daughter they might even marry."

"That would be nice," Estelle agreed, then laughed, "Why, Claire, here we are being matchmakers!"

"But what about your school? Will you have to quit?"

"No, as of now I think we can manage. I talked to the wife of the President of the Board and she said since I had been there the school was the best it had ever been. She pleased me very much when she said that I was well liked by both students and parents. With the baby coming in July I can start school by the middle of August. Ma will keep the baby during the day. If you thought Ma was happy when I married you should see her now! She can't do enough for us. She said they would put in extra garden for us this year. I won't go to Teachers College this summer but there is a lot I can do at home."

As they were leaving Estelle said, "I hear Jessie is well on her way to their second heir."

Will overheard Estelle's comment and steeled himself against the familiar feelings of guilt that came whenever he saw or heard something that brought to mind Jessie's wretched life.

On nights when Aaron and Estelle came over they sometimes played Dominoes or Flinch. One evening before the women joined them in the parlor, the men folk held a hushed conversation about the three of them making application to the Masonic Order. They all agreed it would be a worthwhile step. Most of the outstanding citizens of the community belonged.

Aaron said, "Estelle and Claire will enjoy waiting up for us together on meeting nights."

Sam said, "I hope you fellows have been treating your wives all right. Gus Schmidt wanted to put his application in and Joe Randolph told him the way he treated his wife and family he wasn't what they wanted in their membership."

That bit of news brought gloom into Will's spirits. Jessie again! When would he be able to forget her? Even if he hadn't been able to marry her, she didn't have to marry Gus. If it was money she wanted one of the McCaskell boys would have married her in time.

"Neither Will nor I have any skeletons in our closets," Aaron assured Sam. Will struggled to pull his attention back to the conversation, knowing that Aaron's comment wasn't entirely true.

Sam said, "I think this would be a good opportunity to get to know some of the leaders in Brandton, and that could be helpful later. When I get a few more college hours I would eventually like to teach in college."

"Yeah, 'Prof' would fit you well," Aaron said.

Just then, Claire and Estelle joined them to start a game of Flitch. Sam kept score, as usual. Before he had totaled the scores at the end of the game, Claire mentioned that her score and Estelle's were higher than Sam's, Will's, and Aaron's combined.

Sam was amazed that she had added the figures so quickly. "How did you know that, Claire? I haven't even written down the scores yet."

"Why, I've always worked problems in my head. I guess it comes from not having pencil and paper handy."

Estelle said, "You were quick to get the totals. Faster than my students could add one column, you added five."

Aaron agreed, "Not many people could add mentally that quickly."

Will was embarrassed that Claire was getting praise from the others while he couldn't think of a compliment to give her; even more disconcerting was the fact that he had never thought of Claire as being unusually intelligent.

That night Will found sleep slow to come. He wondered if Jessie's brother Joe would vote against him because he had forsaken Jessie. Should he not make application to the Masons or should he take the chance? If he didn't make application it would be difficult to explain to the others why he had changed his mind.

He decided to take the chance, and the luck of the Irish was with him. In due time, all three men were pleased to be accepted for membership. Estelle and Claire were happy too; they planned to take turns visiting each other the nights the men folk went to Lodge. Claire benefited the most, for her it was a chance to visit without having the care of a meal to prepare. When C.A. grew tired of the floor there was always a lap waiting for him.

Estelle enjoyed talking about the upcoming arrival. Hearing about Aaron's comments and the excitement they shared, Claire began to realize that she and Will never had any such exchanges. Wisely she let Estelle hold sway.

Estelle was giving much thought to names. Being a history buff she was thinking of Jackson Aaron Hubbard and use initials if the baby was a boy. For a girl she wanted a Biblical name—Esther, chosen to be Queen of Persia, and Miriam, for Moses and Aaron's sister. Claire thought both names were special.

Estelle said, "Aaron has so many plans for the addition to the family. Most men want a son first; Aaron says he wants a daughter." She surprised Claire by asking, "Which did Will want first?"

Claire replied honestly, "Why, I don't believe he ever said." She was to think about that many times during the coming days. Truly Will never had any plans for anything but the farm. She had to recognize the fact that Will was not a romantic, at least not with her. He said he had never seen Claire at any of the community parties even though she had been there, but she remembered how it had been. Will had been the most hand-some man there and the girls had flocked around him, especially Jessie Randolph. Remembering how he had always seemed to have plenty to say to them seemed to emphasize the distance in their own relationship. She supposed she was thankful she was married and had been able to keep the farm. But she knew something was lacking, even though C.A. was such a pleasure and was filling the void.

It was time to prepare for winter while they still had some mild autumn days. Claire had planted a large garden to be sure she had enough extra for the boarder. In late October, Will dug the potatoes and filled the bins in the cellar. Because of the extra produce, he dug a separate root cellar for the other vegetables and apples. The hole was lined with straw to help insulate it. The produce was placed in the root cellar, more straw was added, and a mound of dirt put over the whole thing. Apples, turnips, and carrots stored this way usually kept good all winter. After the root cellar was finished, Will said, "anything we don't use by the end of winter we will chop up for the pigs."

Claire laughed when Will mentioned the pigs. "Sam has a good appetite; I'll bet we won't have much left over for the pigs by spring."

There was a white Christmas that year! The children enjoyed playing in the huge drifts and were sure that Santa would find them anyway. Most of the usual social gatherings were cancelled, or rescheduled. Each family of the Kennedy clan celebrated the season in their own home instead of gathering together as planned. It was a good Christmas, but they all agreed they missed the big family gathering.

Minnie said to Lucinda, "We should start planning a picnic by the river for the 4th, and hope the weather will be better at Christmas time next year so we can all get together.

A New Namesake

Spring was busy for all of the Kennedy's, but at least they didn't have the added worry of a drought like they often did. The most exciting event was that Eli and Minnie bought a Packard automobile.

When a Winton and a Packard each made separate coast-to-coast trips across the United States, Eli thought the time had come for him to buy an automobile. Minnie was thrilled that they were the first in the family to own one.

She also had family news that should be passed on. One day while visiting with Claire, Minnie had said, "Nat and Lucinda are expecting again. Lucinda is very pleased, because Nat has been so good to her and is such a good father." Without stopping for a breath, she had given a meaningful nod of her head and continued, "Lettie is 'that way' too. Isaac says little Willie needs a playmate. He is finally old enough to entertain himself and the next one, too."

After Minnie's visit, Claire was working in the garden. She hoed at a fast clip, stopping only to pull a stubborn weed now and then. She could do a lot of thinking while she worked and her mind ran back over the conversation with Minnie. It seemed to Claire that her own marriage was different than most other couples' but she didn't know how to change things. If the problems were like weeds she could just chop them out, but it wasn't that simple.

She didn't know what she could do about Will. He always did his share of the work. He was eager to see that things were done on time for the farm and that there was plenty of wood brought in. He kept the fires burning in the stoves and brought the water up from the cistern. It wasn't sharing the work that concerned her. It was the fact that they didn't seem to really share their lives. It puzzled Claire that there was still a feeling of distance between the two of them. If only he would talk to her more.

Before she could ponder on the situation longer, she heard little C.A. awakening. C.A. was her joy! Claire had remarked to Aimie once that she didn't want any more children. She felt she couldn't love another baby as much as she loved C.A. Aimie had laughed at her and replied, "Why Claire, every baby brings its own love. My children are all different but I love them all the same."

"Be that as it may," Claire said out loud now with no one listening, "I want to be sure my children are loved and educated, with the freedom to choose what they want to do for their livelihood. My private nest egg will have to grow."

Her thoughts were interrupted by Will coming in from the field with the team of horses. He called to her, "Claire, I finished in the field. As soon as I take the other horses to the barn, I'll plow the center of the garden and the truck patch for you."

Claire replied, "Thank you, Will. It helps a lot for you to plow between the rows and the big plants in the truck patch. I can hoe around the small things in the garden. The peas are already finished and I pulled the vines."

Will plowed between the rows of corn, beans, Irish and sweet potatoes, okra, and cabbage. When he finished the plowing, Claire carried C.A. close to the horse and let him touch it. He was excited and made happy noises as he patted the big animal. Claire said, "C.A. this is a horse." C.A. tried to say the word himself. "Yes," Claire encouraged him, "Horse."

"When there is not so much to do I will take him horseback riding," Will volunteered.

Claire was encouraged by his offer. "He would like that. He would enjoy that more than a ride in Uncle Eli's Packard car."

"Someday we will have an automobile, too," Will said. "The last drought was a set back but it did give the land a chance to rest. Being fallow for a spell makes the yield greater the next year. Things look pretty good this year. We are building up our beef cattle and should start having some money for extra things."

"We do need to replace several things," Claire commented. "How does that saying go? 'The glory of work and the joy of living.' I think we are ready for the joy of living."

Thinking more of the farm, Will added, "I would like to buy a self-binding harvester. With that I could save what I've been paying others to get my crop done and then do several of the neighbors' fields besides. It would bring in some extra cash."

Claire was disappointed with the direction his thoughts had taken, but made no comment. Will didn't expect her to say anything. She knew they would be buying a self-binding harvester before long. She sighed and hurried to the house to get dinner on the table.

It had been a productive morning. Her garden was looking good, and with Will's plowing there wasn't much more that needed to be done this time. She was pleased it looked so well tended as Aimie's were coming Sunday. Aimie was always pleased when the place looked nice. Claire finished the morning in better spirits than she had expected.

At dinner Claire remarked, "Estelle and Aaron left for the Fair in St. Louis this morning. Mr. Lowes took them to the train at Rolla. Estelle will have a lot to tell when they get back. She said she would bring me something from the Fair. I hope their trip goes well; the weather couldn't be better for it." Will didn't have much of a reply, and the conversation lagged as usual.

Sunday was a brighter day for Claire. As soon as Aimie's arrived, Malinda had C.A. outside enjoying the birds, chickens, and young calves. Her brothers were in charge of Douglas, who was keeping up with them very well for a 3-year-old.

Will and David spent the morning looking over the farm crops, then enjoyed the bountiful dinner Claire and Aimie had prepared. Afterwards they were content to sit on the front porch while the women cleaned up the dishes in record time. C.A. and Dougie were napping so the women joined the men on the porch.

David said, "I took Pa's place in the family when he died. I managed to scrape together enough money for Wesley to go to business school, which has paid off handsomely for him. I got the sisters married, although they still expect me to fill in the gaps for them. It started Aimie and me talking about what we wanted for our children. Malinda is as sharp as a tack. She reads everything she gets her hands on and remembers it. She could easily pass the County Teachers Examination."

Will asked, "Couldn't Wesley help Malinda attend the Academy here?"

David shook his head. "He's too busy with their social life. If they are out on a Sunday afternoon drive they sometimes stop by to see Ma, but they have never even invited any of us to their home. Why, I had to mortgage the place to borrow money for seed to plant this year's crop. Wesley said it was 'just business'. I would have thought my word would have been my bond. I had to sign mortgage papers just as any stranger would have. Aimie and I managed well during the drought, mostly due to Aimie's Scotch heritage. You would never know we had a shortage of anything the way she managed. I really was lucky when I got Aimie. I wouldn't have gotten this far without her. But we'd like something more for our children. When the boys are old enough to work we would like to go to California. It is growing fast and that is where the money is. The oil fields are developing, citrus groves, large vegetable farms, and vineyards. Why, they are even making movies."

Claire said, "Alonzo is handsome enough to be in the movies."

Will said, " He is a fine looking lad."

David continued, "We want to get the farm set up where my sister Lula and her husband Coy could see after it for a few years while we are in California. If we like it there we could sell the farm to them; if we don't like it, we would have a place to come back to. These are long range plans but the drought showed us we need enough money in reserve for long periods when there isn't anything coming in." From that day on, going to California was in the future for all of them.

The emergency ring of the telephone broke up their discussion of prospects of happier days ahead. The community was shocked and saddened by a fire in Brandton. The Deerfield Hotel, owned by Mr. and Mrs. Louis Medlin, burned to the ground with the loss of three lives.

News of the fire spread fast because most families heard the alarm ring on the telephone. Will and Aaron were among the area residents who gathered in response to the alarm. It was a heavy loss to Mr. and Mrs. Medlin, as it represented their united labors for many years. The 22-room, two-story building had not been insured. The pecuniary loss was estimated at $3,500. As Will and Aaron discussed the tragedy, Will remarked, "We know how it is to get nothing for your labor. It surely is too bad."

The fire also impacted the community. The hotel had been an important aspect of life in the Brandton area. Most community members had had dinners there to mark some special occasion, and nearly everyone had enjoyed summer concerts on Saturday afternoons with the band seated on the second story porch of the hotel. The same porch had provided a platform for public speeches during election years.

The Medlin family and two of the guests escaped without injury. Two other guests leaped from second floor windows and received painful cuts and sprained ankles. The fifth guest to escape the fire was in a room away from the heat and smoke on the southwest corner. He grabbed a sock in which he had put his money and watch, and used it to break the window so he could leap to the ground. He sustained burns, cuts, and a strained back.

The blacksmith who lived at the hotel was one of those killed in the blaze. He apparently had not awakened when the fire started; his body was found on the bedsprings. A mother and daughter were the other two casualties of the fire. They had awakened and screamed for help, but by the time a ladder could be brought to their window they were already dead. The entire community mourned the loss of their friends and neighbors. Their section seldom had a disaster but when something catastrophic happened it was felt by all.

With spring work over the Kennedy's turned to summer events. Kate's daughters and daughters-in-law decided to have a basket dinner for the family at William and Kate's instead of going to the river in July. William wouldn't be able to go to the river and they wanted to be with him. Nat and Lucinda were not expected for the day because their baby was due any time.

The first Sunday in July they gathered at the Kennedy farm. The table on the lawn was covered with food. As they were ready to sit down Nat drove up alone. He rushed up saying, "I can only stay a minute; I just wanted you to know that Lucinda and I have a daughter. She was born last night." He went to his mother and put his arms around her. "Ma, we named her Elizabeth Kate Kennedy."

Kate surprised everyone by bursting out crying, "Why, I have never had a namesake. I don't know what to say."

They were all surprised to see Kate's tender side exposed. Some of the in-laws were thinking, "I didn't know the old girl had a heart."

Kate told Nat to wait a minute while she went into the house. She came back with a fifty dollar gold piece. "Tell Elizabeth this is from her Grandma Kate. She is the first granddaughter of the Kennedy name." She didn't know it at the time, but it would be 37 years before another Kennedy daughter would be born, and C.A. would be her father.

Kate's gift of a fifty-dollar gold piece told everyone how much having a namesake meant to her. Kate only had a few gold pieces and it took something really special for her to part with one!

Later Kate told Will, "I have always wanted my name to continue in the family. I was devastated when we lost our first child in New York. I was so happy to have a daughter, I had given her my name. It was so hard to go on when we lost her; but I had to go on for your Pa. We were blessed with six more children; but having a granddaughter to continue my name is a belated blessing.

Will replied, "I am happy for you, Ma. I realize now why having a namesake means so much to you."

The merchants of Brandton had been searching for someone to open an automobile agency in town. Several had purchased cars and had to go to larger towns to find what they needed. They found a group interested in looking the situation over, but the trip was not a success. Owing to delays from breakdowns and bad roads, it took ten hours to travel forty-eight miles. The group told them that Brandton would be a good place for their business but felt that the present roads were not adequate for cars. Brandton folks would have to start a campaign for better roads first.

Will had been watching the price of cars, but he wasn't in a hurry to buy one yet. He had considered the idea of going by car if they went to California. David said he planned to take his family by train. For Will and Claire, California was still a few years ahead, if they even made the trip; Will decided that he would wait to see how things were at the time.

Plans for the Future

Andy was growing restless. With the brothers all gone from home, Kate was always scolding him for something he had done or lecturing him for something he hadn't done. It seemed he never did anything to suit her. Even getting out and going horseback riding wasn't the joy it used to be.

But lately he had begun to notice the little schoolteacher in town, Nancy Harrison. Andy knew she had been courted by one of the Pierce boys but the Pierce family was of a different religion and the Harrison's had forbidden Nancy from keeping company with him. Andy thought they might like a 'nice Irish boy' or at least maybe Nancy would! He set out to woo Miss Nancy. Besides, he reasoned, even if he weren't successful, visits with Nancy would bring him a lot more joy than listening to his mother's scolding.

One Friday afternoon he just happened to be riding by Nancy's school when the students were coming out for recess. The older students headed for the baseball diamond. Andy got off of his horse and walked over to Nancy, "Looks like you have a lot of good baseball material there."

"Yes, and I don't know what to do with it. In three weeks Kent County is going to have a grade school baseball tournament. I know so little about baseball, I feel I have let the boys down."

Andy said, "I play on the district team. I'd enjoy giving them a little help if they would want it."

By that time some of the boys had recognized Andy. One of them said, "He's the best!"

Another one said, "Yeah, I saw him play in the district games last year. Of course, we would like his help."

Andy was encouraged by their enthusiasm. "How about if I come over on Mondays, Wednesdays, and Fridays at the last recess and work with the boys?" Miss Nancy agreed to his plan, and Andy stayed and got the boys to try out for pitcher and other positions. He had never had so much fun. Before he left for the afternoon he told them, "I'll be back Monday afternoon. In the meantime, you boys practice pitching and batting. I want you to run every place you go and read your rule book!" The boys assured him they would do everything he asked.

The boys soon started calling him 'Coach Andy' but he reminded them that Miss Nancy was their Coach and would be on the bench with them at the tournament. He would attend the games but she would have to be the one in charge. The boys knew Miss Nancy was the official coach, but they all looked up to Andy and hung on his every word. More importantly to Andy, Nancy did too!

It fit in well with Andy's plans that Miss Nancy had to learn the rule-book too. He especially liked the part of testing her on what she had learned. Lucky for Andy, Kate didn't catch on to his extra time off. With Nancy and the baseball team as motivation, he got the farm work done in record time so it wouldn't interfere with his coaching duties.

There were so many happy, excited students when the day of the tournament arrived. It was a good day for all, and at the end of the tournament, Miss Nancy's students had won! When the trophy was presented the county superintendent said, "Miss Harrison, your students played like professionals." Andy knew his time had been well spent, both with the students and the teacher!

Andy began stopping by after school and walking Nancy to her boarding place. His horse followed along behind them. Andy was surprised how compatible they were. He felt like whistling when Nancy invited him to her home for Sunday dinner. He could start making plans, but first he had to have an understanding with Ma. He should have a partnership in the farm and at least be treated as an equal. The others had never asked if they could marry and he wouldn't either. He would court Nancy and if she would have him they would live on the Kennedy farm. He knew it would be all right with Pa.

At breakfast the next morning, Andy put forth his plan. "Ma, the place has made the most profit ever. The crops have been good and I did most of the work myself. I want to be a full partner with you. I plan to marry Nancy Harrison. If I stay, she would be your equal in the house and I would be your equal in the field. You know you couldn't hire any-one to work for you for long. If that is not agreeable with you, I will leave like the rest of the boys."

Kate was certainly taken aback by Andy's announcement. She was surprised he had the situation so well thought out, but she had to admit that he was right. This had been the best year for the farm, and Andy hadn't had much outside help.

She didn't look forward to having another woman in the house. But she knew of no one else she could get to run the place. Before she could say anything Andy continued, "I want you to leave us the land with the buildings and the ponds."

William thought Andy's plan was a good one. Kate thought differently, but knew she really didn't have a choice. Of all of her sons, why did it have to be Andy to take over the farm? Grudgingly, she agreed.

Andy was eager for Sunday to come. Now he had something to offer Nancy when the time was right. His horse racing and fighting days were almost over; Andy gave a big sigh but not of regret.

Not long after Andy's ultimatum, their tranquil community was appalled by the discovery of five brutal murders involving three children and their parents. Several pieces of information led the sheriff to believe the killer had also stolen one of the victim's mules. The search began for that mule and the killer. Again the alarm ring on the telephone alerted everyone. In a short time the party line helped to spread the word and the mule was found at the livery stable. The accused murderer was found nearby. Nothing like that had ever happened before in this peaceful section of Missouri. Because the victims were residents of the area, public outrage over the incident was so high the Sheriff moved the suspected murderer to Carthage for safekeeping until his trial. He was tried, found guilty, and was sentenced "to be hung by the neck until dead."

Will told Andy, "Feelings were running high about the horrible thing Jodie Hamilton did. He killed the children, too. Justice was served. What surprised me was that David went to see the hanging and even bought a picture. David is such a gentle person. I wouldn't have thought he would want to be there to see the hanging."

Andy replied, "Yes, it was a horrible crime; justice was served."

The community joined together to provide burial for the family in a nearby cemetery. It was one part of the county's history they wanted to put behind them. The entire incident was so horrible that Claire had nightmares afterwards. It made her appreciate her own family more than ever.

Life was going better for Andy. He had never known chores could be fun before! He was busy making plans for the farm, and thinking about how different it would be when he and Nancy married. His happiness was dimmed by the fact that he could see his father growing weaker day by day. Kate wasn't out in the field very often these days. William was failing and Kate was spending more time with him. After work Andy would visit with William in his room. William was pleased that Andy was maturing so well.

Kate invited Nancy over for dinner one Sunday and she and William had a nice visit. Since then William had been expecting Andy to have an announcement on marriage plans. He was not surprised when Andy told him that he and Nancy planned to marry after the crops were in.

"Well, Son, I rather thought she had captured you. She seems like a fine young lady. Now that just leaves Meggie. Try to look after her when I'm gone."

His remark made Andy sad but he brushed it off by responding, "Meggie is the one taking care of herself."

Due to William's failing health, the family's traditional 4th of July basket dinner was held at the house again. They put a comfortable lounge chair in the yard so William could spend as much time with them as he was able. The family could see he was failing fast but he was interested in what they were doing. He especially enjoyed watching the grandchildren at play.

It did not come as a shock when on the tenth of July word was sent to all the family that William had passed away at sunrise. The funeral would be at the house on the twelfth.

All of the family assembled early, bringing food, their dress clothes, and what garden flowers they had. The house was large enough that the family and the casket could be in the parlor, and friends in the other rooms.

As the day went on and the heat began to rise, it was suggested that they move outside. Nat said, "There is a little breeze and it won't take much to move things to the shade like we did for Sister Lucy." Everyone thought that was a good idea and chairs, casket, and flowers were quickly repositioned under the trees.

Frank asked his mother if she had made arrangements for any songs. Kate said she hadn't thought of it. Frank said, "Ruth has a lovely voice and can sing unaccompanied if you would like her to."

Kate was thankful for the offer and asked if Ruth could include some of Williams' favorite hymns, "Amazing Grace", "Beautiful Isle of Somewhere", and "Sunrise Tomorrow".

The families were arranged for the service by couples with their children. Will put his arm around C.A. and held him close. C.A. looked up at his father and smiled. It was the first time father and son had bonded. Will realized that since his father was gone he was no longer William, Jr.

The service was consoling; Reverend Jordon was at his best, and Ruth sang beautifully. It was a fine tribute to a kind and gentle man. After the service at the cemetery, family and friends returned to the house. Will told Kate she was fortunate that Andy could care for the farm, and that he would help Andy when he was needed. Everyone was pleased that Andy and Nancy would be getting married soon.

Will took Andy aside before he left. "Andy, it is good to see you becoming a farmer and a husband." He gave Andy a hearty slap on the shoulder. "Just wanted you to know I will swap work with you when it gets too much for one. If I can help with any problem, just let me know."

"Thank you, Will. I may need to call on you."

The days following Williams' death were especially difficult for Kate. While William had not been active in working the farm in a long time, she had always looked to him for support and he had been her partner in all her dreams. They had all relied on his judgment and quiet manner.

Kate was the 'ramrod of the family' but William had been the glue that held the family together.

It was all turning out so differently from the way she had planned, and it had been such a lovely plan. She and William would have the main house and her sons would have farm homes around it. Strange how it turned out that the son she thought would leave was the only one staying. Meggie was a comfort now, but she would probably leave too in a few years. Life certainly had a way of changing things around.

Andy missed his father, but he felt better about the future than Kate did. He had his upcoming marriage to Nancy to look forward to. Nancy wanted to be married at home, with just immediate family, two weeks before her school started. Nancy's mother was almost totally blind and her brother, Harold, and his wife had lived with them since her father had died several years ago. Nancy had already been away going to school and teaching, so leaving the family would not be a problem.

It became unusually hot near the end of July. Those lucky enough to have electricity used electric fans; those without opened windows and doors, and sought the shade of trees. Whenever they could, people scheduled their outside work early in the morning and late in the day. It surprised the Russell's maid, Sally, when Mrs. Russell announced she planned to thin a flowerbed in the middle of the day. Sally tried to persuade her not to go out in the heat but Mrs. Russell insisted it would only take a few minutes.

Sally went about her duties and lost track of time. When Mrs. Russell came in she was so hot and flushed that it alarmed Sally. Mrs. Russell sat down while Sally ran for water and to telephone Mr. Russell. By the time Sally came back, Mrs. Russell had fainted. Sally called the doctor but by the time he got there Mrs. Russell was already dead. Mr. Russell arrived and began to notify the family. Lucinda and Nat arrived. They all moved in a daze. A second death so soon after the loss of Nat's father was doubly hard to bear.

Mr. Russell left the funeral arrangements to Lucinda. When Reverend Fields asked what music she wanted she said, "The choir should have the opening and closing hymns but I would like for my dear friend Ruth to sing a solo just after the reading of the obituary. She sang at my father-in-law's funeral, and my mother remarked on her lovely voice and how much she enjoyed the songs."

A morning shower the day of the funeral and the electric fans in the Baptist Church helped to cool the hot summer day. As always, family and friends were there for support. They were all feeling the loss of their loved ones.

The sadness that summer was relieved a little by a happier occasion. On August 5th, 1907, Miss Nancy Harrison became Mrs. Andrew

Kennedy. Reverend Fields preformed the ceremony at Nancy's home with Kate, Meggie, Nancy's mother, her brother Harold, and his wife Bessie, attending. Nat was waiting in the car to take the new couple to the train station. From there they would go to Springfield for a short honeymoon. Frank had wanted them to come to St. Louis but they preferred the more familiar surroundings of Springfield. Later they would go to St. Louis and let Frank and Ruth entertain them.

Andy's friends had planned an old fashioned chivaree after his wedding. Not like the knights of old but with humor. Their plan had included a ride down a bumpy road in a wheelbarrow for Andy. The chivaree was called off due to the recent loss of loved ones.

Kate and Meggie found the house very lonely with Andy away. Kate said she planned to give the young couple an infare dinner in a few weeks. Meggie welcomed the chance to help plan and prepare the traditional homecoming dinner.

Will came over to do Andy's chores while the newlyweds were gone. Sometimes he brought C.A. with him. Meggie enjoyed showing him around. She forgot how protective the old gander was of his territory and his flock until C.A. wandered into the barnyard one day. The gander soon had C.A. by the seat of his pants, beating him with his wings. Meggie saw the situation and came running with her broom to chase the gander back to his flock. Later, C.A. enjoyed telling how exciting it had been and how Aunt Meggie had saved him. The older folk had a lot of fun getting him to tell the story, which got bigger each time. Before long he was saying Aunt Meggie had 'came to his rescue like a whirlwind and hit that old gander so hard with the broom that he walked around the barn-yard in circles'. C.A. had prints from the gander's bill for a number of days but refused to show them.

The traditional infare dinner for the newlyweds was special for all. Everyone brought food, and with what Kate and Meggie had prepared, they had a feast. Minnie and Lucinda brought their maids to serve the meal and clean up afterwards. That gave the women as much visiting time as the men.

Following the meal, the men gathered in the parlor. Nat said, "The country is really moving ahead. To think that in the seven years since the Wright Brothers had the first airplane flight, we now have a fellow in Pasadena, California getting ready to fly to New York! Man, that is progress!"

Will added, "He will probably have to make quite a few stops along the way."

Eli wasn't too concerned about airplanes. "I am more interested in getting more cars in the country. It will help us get better roads."

Frank agreed. "Ford has the Model T at $859 and it will be cheaper when they produce more. They are paying men $2.40 an hour to work in the factory."

The ladies had another interests. Ruth was briefing them on women getting the right to vote. "It will be a few years yet but when it becomes law I want you all to join the 'League of Women Voters.' In the city they are ready to go. It may take a while to get started here, but I hope all of you join as soon as they organize. Women can make a difference. Kate showed she could run a farm as good as any man and Nancy has conducted a school as good as a man. A woman could have done a darn sight better than the men teachers I had in the lower grades!"

After a time, their discussion turned to other matters. Lucinda thought it would be a great idea for them all to get their hair bobbed before the July get-together. Kate was a bit hesitant about the idea. "I'm not sure I should," she said.

Meggie and Nancy responded quickly, "You will have to do it with us."

Lettie also wavered, "I don't know if I should or not."

Meggie joked, "If you come with long hair, we will cut it for you." They all enjoyed a laugh at the idea.

This was a nice welcome into the family for Nancy. Mrs. Harrison, Harold, and Bessie enjoyed the day as well and were impressed with the Kennedy's hospitality. They thought Nancy had done quite well in marrying Andy.

Will and Claire stayed for awhile after the others left for their homes. Will and Andy had work schedules to discuss. Claire and Nancy enjoyed a longer visit and took time to catch up on some mutual friends. Nancy had heard that Sam Henson had just been hired as a teacher at the Teacher's Academy. Claire said she was sorry to lose her good boarder but was glad Sam got the job he wanted.

Will said, "When I see him at Lodge, I'll ask him to come out. We'll have Estelle and Aaron too. You both would enjoy their company." Nancy agreed that it would be nice to visit with them.

Andy's wedding made Kate determined to put a halt to another budding romance. Ben Cox had been stopping by the Kennedy home often lately, causally at first, and then making a point of talking to Meggie. Kate was quick to see what his goal was. She already had one daughter in the Cox family and that had been a lot to bear. Eli was a good provider but he would never be a faithful husband. Ben didn't have Eli's money making ways but he did have the same roving eyes. Kate had thought she might send Meggie to visit the relatives in New York in a year or two, but under the circumstances, she decided to suggest it sooner.

To Kate's satisfaction, Meggie was thrilled at the prospect of a trip and the chance to shop for new clothes. When Ben dropped by one afternoon and asked for a date sometime, Kate was elated to hear Meggie respond, "No, I'm getting ready for a trip."

"At last I've won one," Kate thought to herself.

C.A., Willie, John, and Eli, Jr. were all in school now. As predicted, those cousins would always be especially close. Lettie and Minnie each had three children now, and Nat and Lucinda had two. All of the cousins enjoyed family gatherings. Claire began to think about the possibility of having another child. C.A. was on the go most of his waking time and was not the company he used to be.

Nancy was planning to ride Andy's horse to school. When the weather was bad, Andy would take her in the buggy, and when it was winterish, she could stay where she had boarded before she married. Will laughed, "It will be pretty winterish before Andy can't make it in the buggy."

Malinda was another family member interested in being a teacher. She had been studying Latin, math, and history on her own. She enjoyed school and couldn't imagine why her brothers didn't. If she could pass the County Teacher's Examination, she wanted to teach school the following year. If she could teach a year, she would like to go to the Teachers Academy.

The time came for the test at the County Seat and Malinda was ready. They assembled a few weeks later to hear the County Superintendent announce the results. "This has never happened here before," he stated. "Malinda Jennings has made a perfect score." He assured her that he would recommend her to any school she chose. Malinda wanted Sam Henson's old school so she could board at Aunt Claire's. The school hired her as soon as they received her application. She wanted to help those who wanted to advance; she would be an ideal teacher.

Claire and Will decided that it would be better to send C.A. to school in Brandton than to have him stay at Cedar Bluff. He would have to go there sooner or later, and they thought it would be easier on them both if Malinda didn't have a relative in her class. They knew she wouldn't be partial but there would always be those who would claim 'teacher's pet'. Malinda was sure she could have worked it out but went along with their decision. C.A. could be her pet when they got home from their schools.

Oris Grimes, the County School Superintendent, was in his office when his nephew, James Bradford, dropped by. He told James about the pretty, young woman who had made a perfect score on the Teacher's Examination. James wanted to know how he could meet her.

"Well, find out where she stays, where she goes to church, when they have a school program," his uncle replied. "Man, I can't do it all for you."

Fate was on James' side. Malinda had to go to the County Superintendent's office that day for some forms for her school. When Mr. Grimes introduced them, James was up to the occasion. He said, "Miss Malinda, I haven't had lunch yet; would you be my guest?"

Malinda said, "I have been so busy I haven't had lunch either. I would be happy to go with you."

They found each other's company pleasant and discovered they had many mutual friends. Malinda's father had done business with James's father who bought cattle on a commission for the stockyard in Springfield. He was also an auctioneer, and had been to David's place many times to buy cattle. When James heard that Malinda was boarding with the Kennedy's he said, "I know the place. I've been there many times. This Thursday evening I have a meeting not far from there. Could I stop by for a few minutes on my way to the meeting?"

"Of course; my aunt and uncle always welcome company," Malinda assured him.

That was the beginning of a lasting romance. Claire was happy for Malinda to have company coming. Will told Malinda that the Bradford's were a leading family in the community and one of the first families to settle in the section.

James came by on Thursday evening as planned. Malinda was pleased Aunt Claire had pie and coffee ready. James enjoyed their visit and left reluctantly for his meeting. Malinda invited him to come again.

David and Aimie came early Friday afternoon so they could do some visiting before picking up Malinda for the weekend. They too were pleased to hear about Malinda's friend. David said, "One reason we have waited to go to California was because we wanted Malinda settled in a job or married first. We would like to know the folks and the background of the family she marries into. With the way people are moving into California these days, you would only know what they told you."

Aimie said, "Well, I can help this romance along. We can ask him to go to church with us and have Sunday dinner."

Claire said James could stop by anytime for supper. Will suggested that the matchmakers should allow the two young people to have a say in things.

Malinda arrived at that point and rushed in to greet her parents. "It is so nice to see you. I've met the nicest young man, his name is James Bradford. You already know his family. I hope it is all right that I invited him to church Sunday and to dinner."

Will laughed, "You folks really get quick results from your plans!"

Lucinda wanted Thanksgiving at their home that year; she thought it would be best for her father, who would otherwise be alone; it would also be easier for Kate. The rest of the family agreed.

The gathering was different than in previous years. The men talked more about the war in Europe than they did about cars and roads. They had all voted to re-elect President Wilson who used the slogan 'He kept us out of war.'

Frank said, "I don't see how we can stay out of it. German U-boats are sinking our merchant's ships more often now, and things can only get worse."

Nat agreed, "It doesn't look good. They are buying peach stones to use in making chemical filters for gas masks."

Will expressed everyone's feelings when he said, "I am ready to do what I can to get the war over."

Things were different among the ladies this year too. They didn't talk much about fashion but about the hardships the people in Europe were having. Kate said she had patterns for knitted socks and sweaters. "Those army boots and winter weather are hard on feet and the soldiers are probably always cold. If we help them now maybe our boys won't have to go over there."

All the women agreed they would knit after supper. They would give the finished articles to Ruth to take to the Red Cross in St. Louis. Kate advised them to use brown or dark green yarn. "Never red, because that would make our boys a target."

"They need to send our Missouri General Black Jack Pershing over there," was Mr. Russell's opinion. "He would clean things up."

Before they left, the ladies did ask Ruth to tell them what was new in show business. She told them Broadway was celebrating its tenth anniversary, and the Ziegfeld Follies were paying their girls $75 a week. "The new dance is 'Panama, Pacific Drag'," she said. "If I ate everyday like I did today, I would have to go on Lillian Russell's diet! She enjoys good food and so do I. It would be nice to have a rose named for me like she does." They all agreed that Ruth deserved a rose too.

Minnie and Eli had the family gathering for Christmas. War dominated the news, and the primary question was when, not if, the United States would get involved.

Nat said, "I don't see how we can keep out of it since the Germans sank the Lusitania. There were 128 Americans among the 1,981 lives lost when it went down, and the Germans say they plan to continue such aggression."

Frank said, "What I am hearing in St. Louis is that we should stay out as long as possible and start a drive to build up our military. Those guys have been planning this for a long time and are more prepared than we are."

Will added, "I feel we have already had the best period of our lives."

The women were catching up on what the children were doing. Nancy was sitting by Claire. She leaned over and whispered, "I'll be able to join that conversation next year."

Claire said, "You are—" and gave that knowing nod that announced so many pregnancies.

Nancy said, "Yes."

Claire said, "We are too."

They both began to giggle. Kate said, "Something is going on over there. We all want to know what it is."

Nancy said, "Well, all right. We are both expecting!"

Kate congratulated them both. "For me that is bigger news than the war."

Minnie asked, "Nancy, what about your school?"

"Oh, that is not a problem. They only had enough money to have school until the end of March, and Andy and I have decided I wouldn't teach any more after this term anyway so it all works out just fine."

In the sitting room the men were having a lighter moment by teasing Andy. Nat said, "I have to hand it to Nancy, she has really tamed Andy. I never thought it could be done."

Will added, "Ma should be glad she doesn't have to go to the far side of the field to get him started back anymore."

Andy didn't mind their good-natured ribbing. He got in the last with, "Ah, you're all just jealous because I've had so much fun."

May 28, 1914

In late spring of 1914, the Kennedy's took time out for family matters. Claire had everything ready for the arrival of the new baby. She had extra food prepared, clothes arranged for several days ahead, and of

course, the things for the baby all freshly laundered. On May 28, she called Dr. Holmes and Mrs. Lowes to tell them it was time for the baby. Both Will and Claire had secretly hoped for a girl, but they welcomed James Robert. C.A. was excited about the new baby after twelve years of being an only child.

With the arrival of J.R., Nancy and Andy were even more eager for their baby. On June 2nd Robert Lewis was born. Kate bit her tongue to refrain from telling Nancy that all Kennedy first-born sons should be named William. Kate had learned from past experience that it was pointless to try to tell her in-laws what to name their children.

One Saturday, C.A. walked to town early to buy a copy of the St. Louis Post. It was one way to keep up with what was happening in Europe. The newspapers disappeared almost as quickly as they arrived in Brandton.

He took a little extra money from his piggybank on his errand because there was something he had been wanting to try when he was out alone. The big boys had been talking about a pipe and C.A. had decided he would buy one along with a little sack of tobacco. He planned to wrap the newspaper around his purchases until he was out of town and then try out the pipe on the way home. He could hide it at the end of the lane for the next time the coast was clear.

When he got to the edge of town on the way home, C.A. lit up the pipe. It really wasn't as great as he had expected it to be, but he was sure it would get better with practice. He was so busy trying to keep the pipe going that he didn't see Mrs. Dobbs in her cow pasture.

The next day the Kennedy's went into Brandton for Sunday morning worship. People gathered in small groups to visit after the service. As Will, Claire, and C.A. passed one group, Mrs. Dobbs stopped them with a comment. "I didn't know C.A. had grown up so fast until I saw him go past my place yesterday smoking a pipe." C.A. felt as if the ground had opened up under him and he really wished it had.

Will replied, "Yes, he thinks he is grown up."

C.A. envisioned all kinds of punishment awaiting him when they reached home. After they put up the horse and buggy, Will motioned C.A. into the harness room. Solemnly Will said, "I don't smoke, and your Uncle Nat doesn't. Uncle Frank and Uncle Andy smoke, but they don't try to hide it. The fact that you tried to keep it a secret shows you are not ready to start smoking. If you still want to smoke when you are ready, don't hide it. It wasn't very pleasant hearing about it from Mrs. Dobbs."

C.A. managed a subdued, "Sorry, Pa."

Will didn't tell C.A. the reason he didn't smoke; it even made him sick now to think about it. One day when he was eight he had found a cigar a visitor had left behind. He had hid it until he went to work in the truck patch. It had been a hot July afternoon, and the tall corn had stopped any breeze there might have been. When Will got to the end of the corn row, he had lit up and puffed away. It hadn't been long before he wasn't feeling very well. In fact he felt really terrible. To this day, he couldn't stand the thought of smoking. Too bad C.A.'s experience hadn't made him sick!

Everyone was glad to be together for the traditional 4th of July picnic. Of course the main thing on everyone's mind was the war. Minnie

said, "Let's talk about something pleasant for a change. I brought a picture of Louise and Laura in their Easter outfits." Everyone was polite and said what was expected of them.

On the way home, Lettie said, "Isn't that just like Minnie to bring that picture all that way just to brag about the girls Easter outfits. You know, it is almost funny. Now that I realize that Minnie has had her share of problems, I realize that she is doing what she can to compensate for the things she can't change."

Isaac replied, "You have come a long

way since our talk years ago. I like the new Lettie much better than the old Lettie!"

Lettie laughed, "I told you I was going to try to not be so jealous of Minnie!"

By July 1914 there were a million American troops in Europe, and the American troops were making a difference; the Allies began to make progress in winning the War. Everyone contributed to the war effort. Ruth didn't knit but she sang at a Canteen in St. Louis and delivered the articles the others knitted to the Red Cross.

Like the Kennedy's the nation was one in feeling that the United States should help the Allies win the war. If they should lose, the Central Powers would come after the United States next. The greatest support for the Allies came from communities with German descendants. These groups led the country in purchasing Liberty Bonds too. There were even Liberty Books for children with the slogan 'Lick a stamp and lick the Kaiser.'

The Conscription Law had been passed. As a family man and a farmer Andy could be exempted from the first call for arms. Frank tried to enlist in the Army. He was surprised when they turned him down because of his vision. He was almost blind in his left eye, the result of one of his many fights. He argued that "You only need one eye to sight to shoot" but it didn't make any difference. It hurt his pride to be rejected. One thing was for sure, no one had better ask him "Why is a big strong fellow like you not in the Army?"

The existing Army camps had not been updated for a number of years and were soon overcrowded. An influenza epidemic swept the world killing 20 million worldwide, including 548,000 in the United States. Many of the deaths were in the Army Camps; the close quarters in the camps made it easier for the epidemic to spread.

On January 31, 1917 Germany declared unrestricted submarine warfare. On February 3 the United States cut diplomatic ties with Germany, and on April 6 the United States declared war against Germany.

The Nation rose to the occasion. They had voluntary rationing—wheatless Monday, meatless Tuesday, porkless Thursday and Saturday, and gasless Sunday. Everyone struggled at home and abroad. The only thing Will had a problem with was having cornbread instead of wheat bread. Claire told him to think of it as victory bread.

Will was known for the fine mules he raised, and the Army Quartermaster bought all the mules Will would sell. There was one that Will was glad to see go—Old Jekyll. He was big and strong, a good worker, when he wanted to work, but he had a mind of his own. He lent new meaning to the phrase 'as stubborn as a mule.' A neighbor's son happened to be at the Army camp where Old Jekyll was taken. When the boy was home on furlough he came to see Will. "I saw Old Jekyll the other day," he said.

"Is that right?" Will asked. "How was he doing?"

"Just great. He had a crowd of city dudes around him, and no one could make him move. Sure was a lot of cussin' going on."

Will laughed, "That sounds like Old Jekyll. Well, he got what he always wanted—attention!"

James and Malinda's friendship turned to love and making plans. Aimie called Claire with exciting news that they were to be married in June. They would be going to Ada, Oklahoma, where James would manage a grocery store for his cousin.

Claire shared Aimie's excitement, "I am so happy to hear the good news. We all are fond of James and will welcome him to the family."

Their families were happy with the romance with the exception of C.A. He resented not having as much time with "his Malinda" since she had started seeing James and let his feelings be known at the dinner table one evening when James was a guest. James had just told an amusing story when C.A. remarked, "Malinda, you are sure going to marry a jester like in the Court of St. James."

Claire was shocked and started to scold C.A. but James laughed, "I think that is high praise." His response chastened C.A. more than Claire's scolding would have.

Then at 11:00 a.m. November 11, 1918, bells and sirens sounded to celebrate the signing of the Armistice! Will, C.A., Andy, Aaron and Mr. Lowes joined the celebration in Brandton. Everyone was relieved that the war was finally over!

The next family gathering was at Lettie's. It was a cheerful group; the war was over and the harvest had been good. The baby cousins took naps, older children played games, and the high schoolers talked about school and what they would like to do after graduation.

The big topic in the women's conversation was the Gibson Girl fad that was sweeping the country. Hiked hemlines carried the free look even further.

Lettie said, "I had to do a lot of talking to convince Isaac that bobbing my hair was a good idea. I don't know if he'd go along with me shortening my skirts."

Nancy laughed, "Tell Isaac it is cheaper than buying new skirts."

Ruth said, "Young women are in an interesting time. They are organizing contests in all the states to pick the most beautiful girl. Then probably by next year they will have a Miss United States. It is a relief to hear news about something besides the war."

The men in the parlor were feeling the relief from war days too. Frank said, "Driving down from St. Louis the sky was such a beautiful blue I felt as if I could go on forever."

Will kept his thoughts to himself, but he too had noticed the beautiful blue sky, the color that still reminded him of Jessie.

Nat was thinking about roads and cars, "Our roads are getting better but we have a long way to go before we can call them good. I saw a Duesenberg last time I was in St. Louis. If I had money for one and a good road to put it on, that would be my car! We can thank Henry Ford for making cars everyone can afford."

"Yeah, in 1909 they were $825. Now they are down to $265 for a roadster."

Nat said, "The Duesenberg I saw was a light cream color; she was a beauty."

Mr. Russell remarked, "Henry Ford's slogan is 'We will sell you any color you want, just so it is black.'"

By the end of the day, Kate and George Russell were on a first-name basis. George was surprised how much Kate knew about farming and business. His wife Alice hadn't cared about anything but social events.

As the families were getting ready to go to their homes, Mr. Russell told Kate, "I enjoyed visiting with you. Could I come out some Sunday afternoon?"

Kate was quite pleased, "Why, George, that would be nice. Next Sunday afternoon would be fine."

All who had overheard the conversation had the feeling that this was the beginning of something. Nancy confided to Andy afterwards, "I never thought about them getting together but it would be perfect!"

"Oh, I don't know about that. They are both very opinionated. Ma's had her way most of her life and George has too. It would be nice to have the house to ourselves, but it hasn't happened yet."

Nancy laughed, "Well, I can think about it. What do you think the rest of the family would say?"

"Oh, Lettie would cry; Minnie would ask Eli what to do; Meggie wouldn't care one way or the other. The boys would think it's all right, especially Nat, because Lucinda has been looking after her father and she would have more free time."

"Well, we'll make it easy for them to have time together."

And so it was on June 20, 1920 that Kate Kennedy became Mrs. George Russell. George gave his home to Lucinda and Nat and bought a new bungalow with a few acres at the edge of town. Kate could have a few chickens and a garden there. They told Kate's grandchildren that they could stay with them and go to high school. Two of Lettie's children, William and Rose, did stay there during their school years. Rose stayed during the week and William stayed when the weather was bad. C.A. sometimes stayed with the McCaskell's if the storms were too severe, but he liked the challenge of going home in winter weather.

James and Malinda married later in June. Soon after the newlyweds left for Oklahoma, David and Aimie announced they had decided to move to California when the crops were finished. They planned to go by train. David had a friend who had been giving him information on employment and living conditions and it looked like there wouldn't be a problem with either.

J.R. started to school that fall at Cedar Bluff. Claire kept herself busy during days that seemed too long and too quiet now. C.A. enjoyed helping him with some of his homework and Claire was glad to see the boys becoming closer. The age difference didn't seem to matter since the boys had some common interests. Aimie's verdict was, "J.R and Alonzo take after Papa's side of the family. I think C.A. is more like the Kennedy's with their Irish blue eyes. All our children will be adults before we know it."

Claire knew what she meant. "Where have the years gone? My goodness, C.A. is a senior this year. He especially enjoys teacher training, and is already talking about wanting to teach when he is out of high school."

"Malinda, Nancy, and Estelle will give him a lot of encouragement in that direction. They grow up so fast."

"Yes," Claire agreed. "Will wants to get a car soon so he and C.A. can learn to drive. He wants to drive to California. The Webb's made it in ten days."

"My, it would be such fun if we could both move out there and live closer to each other. Just think," Aimie sighed "electric lights and gas heat."

During the school term Nancy and Estelle tutored C.A. for the Teachers Examination. C.A. said he learned more from them while getting ready for the exam than he learned all year in teacher training class. As soon as he graduated from Brandton High School, C.A. started to the Academy for teacher training.

The Teachers Examination was offered several times during the summer. C.A. took it the first time it was offered and passed! The next step was to find a school needing a teacher.

Aaron heard that Oak Grove School had an opening for that fall. Estelle called to tell C.A. about the opening and advised him to go over on Saturday to see the school board. C.A. was about to embark on his lifelong occupation. Claire was very pleased with his decision. Will would rather C.A. had stayed on the farm but he was proud his son would be a teacher. Teachers were highly regarded in the community.

On Saturday, C.A. put on his suit, got one of the horses saddled up, and rode over to Oak Grove to see the school board. He was fortunate to find all three members at the school checking on the needs for next term. They hired him on the spot! They offered him the janitor's job too but C.A. thought that would take too much time in view of the distance he had to travel. He rode home a very happy young man.

He was surprised to see Will standing by the gate with one of the neighbor's horses. C.A. had talked about that horse for months; it was the best saddle horse around. "Dad, what are you doing with the horse?"

"Well, you will need your own horse now, so I got him for you. His name is Tim. There was a little girl who said they could only sell him if you wouldn't change his name."

"Well, Tim is fine for me too. Thank you, Dad. A mule is OK for transportation, but I'm glad you thought of a horse. He sure is a fine animal."

"I know you will take good care of him."

Thinking how lucky he was to have a horse of his own, C.A. put the horses in the stalls. He thought back to the 4th of July when he'd had to ride one of the mules to the picnic.

The day had gone well until he started home that night. He had bought some Roman candles to shoot off. Looking back, C.A. didn't know what made him do it, but he had decided to shoot off one of the rockets while he was riding along. He had not been prepared for what happened next. The rocket went off between the mule's ears, and the frightened animal hadn't stopped running until he was in their barnyard! Then he'd given a big gasp followed by several loud 'hee-haws'. C.A. had been as frightened as the mule but he was able to stay on for the wild ride. Fortunately for C.A. his parents hadn't heard a thing.

The next weeks were busy ones for C.A. In addition to his classes at the academy, he checked on Missouri requirements, collected study aids, and reviewed a list of students' names, attendance records, and grades from last year. He went to the school several times before opening day and felt he was as well prepared as he could be by the start of the school year.

Beginning a Lifetime Livelihood

At last the long awaited opening day came. C.A. had twenty-two students in eight grades. Some of the seventh and eighth graders were almost as old as he was, and two of them were nearly as big! He was glad that most of the students were anxious to learn; they wanted to get good jobs and hopefully go to St. Louis to work. C.A. soon saw that one of the older boys, Johnny Settles, could become quite a troublemaker. He seemed to go out of his way to disrupt class, and by the end of the day, C.A. had reached the point of exasperation. He told Johnny he would have to stay after school and sent a note of explanation home to Johnny's parents with his sister Blanche.

Drawing on the last of his patience, C.A. began to talk to Johnny after the other students had gone. Maybe by getting to know the boy better he could find a way to reach him. "Have you thought about what you want to do when you grow up?" C.A. asked.

Johnny shrugged, "Awaha, I ain't got no choice 'cept workin' on my folks' farm. Go on an' whoop me 'cause I gotta git home an' do the chores. I ain't got time to waste on book learnin'."

Something in Johnny's tone caught C.A.'s attention. "What makes you think you don't have any choice?"

"Somebody's gotta take care of the farm. My dad's been sickly for as long as I can remember."

C.A. asked, "Who takes care of the chores now?"

"I get up early and take care of things before I come to school, and then do the rest when I come home. It would be easier to get everything done if I didn't have to spend so much time here. I'm gonna quit soon as I can convince Ma it's best."

C.A. nodded thoughtfully. "Johnny, you're filling a man's shoes before you're ready to be a man. That's commendable, but do you really like working on the farm?"

Johnny was puzzled at the question. "Farmin's not as good as buildin' things, but like I told ya', I ain't got no choice. My Dad's too sickly to take care of the farm."

C.A. was thinking fast. "You have four brothers in school," he reminded Johnny. "They're young now but they'll soon be big enough to do some of the work. Do any of them like farm work?"

Johnny thought a minute before answering, "Hiram used to always be in the way trying to do things. I guess he kinda liked farm work."

"Hiram is eleven now, does he still get in the way?"

"Naw, about the time he was worth anything, he stopped hangin' 'round much."

"Well," C.A. replied, "I'd hate to see you drop out of school before you know enough about arithmetic. Being able to measure and cipher is important to carpenters. Have you ever thought about showing Hiram how you do things so he could help with the farm chores? It's just an idea, but it might take part of the load off of you. Well, you better go home now before your folks get worried. We can talk more some other day."

Johnny was surprised; "Aren't you gonna whoop me?"

"No," C.A. replied. "We have an understanding, don't we? You know what is acceptable here and I am sure that from now on, you will do what's right." C.A. began to gather his things together, leaving Johnny to head for home, puzzling over the conversation. C.A. hoped he had given the boy something to think about.

The conversation left C.A. with a desire to come up with something to really help Johnny. If Johnny taught Hiram how to do the tasks he was doing now and later Hiram taught the next brother, it would amount to more productive hours on the family farm. He talked it over with his Dad that night.

Will was proud of the way C.A. had handled the situation. "That is good advice for Johnny." He wished someone had given him that advice when he had been the main laborer on his family's farm and had younger brothers running around looking for a good time. He thought if they had that things might have been different for him and Jessie.

In the coming days, C.A. was pleased to see the plan was working. Besides the Settles getting more work done, now that Johnny realized that learning arithmetic could be useful in building things, he was eager to learn.

C.A. had heard that the father of one of the students was a bootlegger. He didn't know for sure until Christmas when his presents were put on his desk. Among the gifts was a fruit jar wrapped in a paper bag. C.A. peeked inside the bag and immediately guessed what was in the jar! He tried to act as if it was a perfectly normal gift for a teacher to receive from a student. He thanked all of the students, wished them a Merry Christmas, and gave each of them a bag of candy and an orange. Will was amused when C.A. showed him the gift and suggested C.A. save the bottle for Frank. Claire wasn't sure Frank should drink it. They all agreed the student had given C.A. the best gift she had to give.

After the Christmas holiday the children came back with lots of head colds and too few handkerchiefs. By the end of the school day C.A. was tired of seeing sleeves and backs of hands being used as nose wipes! As soon as he returned home he asked, "Mom, do you have anything you can cut up into handkerchiefs?"

"What on earth do you want them for?"

"It seems as if everyone in the whole school has a head cold and not many of them have handkerchiefs," C.A. explained.

"Aren't you afraid you'll make some parents angry?"

"Not likely. Who knows, their mothers may be ill and couldn't get them ready for school. Anyway I have to do something."

"I will help you make soft handkerchiefs. I'll get some cloth, you get the scissors, and we will get started."

The next day C.A. took the stack of crude handkerchiefs to school. He quietly handed them out saying, "This may help you get rid of that cold." There was not one angry parent and their hands and sleeves looked cleaner! Blowing was better than swiping and they were all able to breathe better.

Late one afternoon in early April, C.A. was surprised to see the President of the school board, Mr. Crews, walking up the path. C.A.'s first thought was, "Oh, no, I hope there isn't a problem." Then he noticed Mr. Crews was smiling. That was a good sign.

C.A. went to meet Mr. Crews with his hand outstretched. Mr. Crews took his hand and clasped it firmly. "Mr. Kennedy, I am happy to shake your hand. You've done a mighty fine job with our little school this year. Everyone I've talked to can't say enough good words about you! I will have to admit, when I met you last year and learned you were only eighteen, I thought you were mighty young to take on this big a task. I honestly thought you'd leave before Christmas. But my friend, Deward Cameron said to me, 'Why, you don't need to worry about him!' Deward said he'd known your Pa for a long time and that you were a chip off the old block. He said the Kennedy's were fine folks and that if they said they'd do something they would do it. He said you might be young, but that we could count on you. I've decided Deward was right about you. We all sure hope you'll come back next term! We would like to keep you as long as you will stay with us."

By this time C.A. didn't know what to say. He managed to smile and say, "Why, thank you very much. I really do like to teach, and I would like to stay here a few more years. That way I can go to school in the summers and start working on a degree in Education. I enjoy seeing young people improve their future by learning. I have had a good group to work with here. They are so eager to learn. I hope the girls who helped with the beginners will go on and become teachers."

Mr. Crews replied, "Anyone can tell you really like to teach. That is why you have done such a good job. Another thing I wanted to talk to you about is Johnny Settles."

"I hope his parents aren't angry that he has been coming home late," C.A. said quickly. "I asked his sister, Blanche, to take a note to them so they wouldn't worry."

Mr. Crews continued, "Everybody knows how much trouble Johnny has caused for every teacher we've had since he started to school seven years ago. His folks say he seems to like school now. What did you do?"

"Well," C.A. explained, "I asked him to stay after school the first day because he had really been exasperating. At first I intended it to be a punishment, but then I realized I needed to get to know the boy if I ever hoped to get him to improve. I started talking to Johnny that day, and he told me he liked to build things. I told him that he needed to learn arithmetic so he could measure and cipher how many trees he needed to cut and so forth. Once he saw that school could help him get what he wanted in life, he had a change in attitude. I offered to work with him after school because he was having trouble with the homework. He told me it was all right with his folks, but I suppose I should have talked with them myself. I hope they aren't too upset that he's been staying after."

"Quite the opposite," Mr. Crews assured C.A. His folks can't believe that he actually likes school now. I could see why he might have trouble with homework. He hasn't exactly been a model student in the past."

"Johnny's a good kid," C.A. said. "He just didn't see any point in going to school before. Now he does."

Mr. Crews nodded in agreement. "You've really turned him around. I am glad my three daughters are in this school. You know how to bring out the best in your students."

C.A. smiled with satisfaction as he rode home that evening. Will was in the barn when C.A. went to put the horse away and asked what had him smiling so. C.A. told his Dad what Mr. Crews had said.

Will chuckled about his friend Deward's comment that C.A. was 'a chip off the old block'. "Those are mighty fine words they said about you, C.A. I know you must have done a good job this year to get such high praise."

C.A. taught at Oak Grove three more years. It seemed that the time flew by. He had decided to go to the State Teachers College in Springfield full-time the next year, so May 18th, 1925 was to be his last day to teach at Oak Grove. The last day of school was a tribute to both teacher and students. The students were quite exuberant; they wanted the day to be one everyone would remember. There were games in the morning and a basket dinner at noon. Each family with children in school brought baskets of food and joined in the fun. The table was laden with sliced ham and chicken, potato salad, beets, pickles, all kinds of cookies, pies, and cakes, and fresh things from spring gardens. Nancy kept J.R so Claire could be there too. She brought green beans seasoned with ham and her famous sweet potato pie. C.A. was proud of the skill his students displayed as they presented a ciphering match, spelling bee, and recitations. C.A. had a feeling of a job well done.

Several parents made short speeches praising C.A. The comment that especially pleased C.A. was made by Bertha Settles. "Mr. Kennedy, my husband and I will always be grateful for what you have done for our children, especially Johnny. If you hadn't come to Oak Grove, Johnny would have dropped out of school. He would have been a very unhappy young man. You gave him reason to want to learn. We thank you."

C.A. beamed with pleasure; Claire was so proud!

Mr. Crews said, "Mr. Kennedy, let me add my thanks to what Mrs. Settles has just said. You have made a difference for all of us. We wish you well. I hope you will continue to teach and help others."

Mr. Hanley, President of the school board who first hired C.A., was there too. Mr. Grimes included the endorsement, "This young man possesses a lot of good horse sense." That recommendation was the one C.A. valued most through the years.

Claire told Will all about the exciting day. After going to great detail about the students' part of the program, she told Will about Mrs. Settles' comments. Then she told him about the flattering things Mr. Hanley and Mr. Crews said about C.A. and his teaching. "I wish you could have been there, Will. I think you would understand why C.A. wants to be a teacher."

Will replied, "It does sound like it was a good program."

C.A. would ask Will about Johnny Settles from time to time over the years, and knew that Johnny remained in Brandton and was in demand as a carpenter. He often credited 'Mr. Kennedy' with keeping him in school until he learned enough math to be a good carpenter.

C.A. had a few weeks between closing Oak Grove and starting classes at STC in Springfield. Will said that would be a good time to buy a car so they both could get used to driving before they went to California the following summer.

The New Car!

Will and C.A. had considered the matter of buying a car very carefully. They needed to think about something to negotiate the roads around Brandton and to travel the distance to California. They got a lot of advice from the others, especially Frank and Nat. They decided the Ford touring car was the best on all counts.

There were two auto agencies in Brandton now. The cars came to the Ford dealer unassembled in carload lots. The dealer's profit was fifteen percent. Some of the models were cheaper than the touring car, but they agreed it was worth the extra money. The $376 price would, of course, have to be paid in cash. C.A. had saved $210 from his $16 weekly teacher's pay; Will and Claire could manage the rest. Will had sold the mule to the army for $52, and three calves for $59. Claire had $43 in the egg fund. That meant they only needed to take $12 out of savings.

Both Frank and Nat had given Will and C.A. driving lessons. Nat always started his driving instructions with, "Know where your brake is and how to stop before you ever start the car." C.A. would go over the procedures every night before he went to sleep—the right way to hold the crank in the palm of your hand, how to adjust the spark so the car wouldn't kick like a mean mule, the three pedals on the floorboard and how they were used. The left pedal made the car go; down for low, out for high. The middle one was for reverse; the pedal on the right was the brake. The throttle was on the right side of the steering wheel and the spark advance lever was on the left.

Frank had a suggestion for driving in hilly country. He said the fuel was fed to the carburetor by gravity and if a hill was too steep, the engine might not get enough fuel to make it up. Sometimes you had to back up the hill so the fuel tank would be above the carburetor. Another trick was to run the front end of the car down in a ditch and let the carburetor run full of gas and then go up the hill.

Nat said, "One of our young Brandton swains loosened the exhaust pipe from the manifold to make the car sound louder. He was backing up Johnson Hill when the carburetor caught on fire and burned the car up."

"Have you heard the story making the rounds on Alfred Hemphill?" Frank asked. "He had his Dad's new car out for a drive and was driving faster than he should down Johnson Hill. He struck some loose gravel and landed in the ditch. Alfred couldn't get himself out so he started walking to get a tow truck. He hadn't gone far when he met the tow truck. Alfred stopped them and asked the driver where they were going. He replied, 'Some dumb guy is in the ditch by Johnson Hill.' 'It's OK,' Alfred said. 'I'll ride back with you, I'm the dumb guy!'

C.A. appreciated their advice. "I'm sure we need all of the information we can get!"

Will countered with "I'm getting more instructions than I can remember! I'm glad C.A.'s school term is over now. I am anxious to get the car, but I'm not sure I am eager to drive it. When do you suppose it will be here?"

C.A. thought it would arrive soon. "Mr. Ferguson said he would call when it comes in." Two days later they got the call they had been expecting. Mr. Ferguson said the car was ready and filled with a free tank of gas. It would be parked in front of the garage when they were ready to pick it up.

Will and C.A. went into Brandton the next Saturday to get their new car. Will said he would drive the buggy home while C.A. drove the car. C.A. started to protest but Will cut him off. "Both Nat and Frank said you are a better driver." Finally C.A. agreed. Truth be known, he could hardly wait to get behind the wheel!

They went into the office, paid for the car, and listened to more advice. Finally C.A. got behind the steering wheel. "I'm even more excited than when I rode Tim for the first time!" he exclaimed.

Their first trip was out to see Kate and George. Will said, "Ma, we came to take you and George for a ride. C.A. will be the chauffeur." Will sat in the front seat beside C.A. Claire was already in the back with J.R. in her lap; George and Kate climbed in beside her. C.A. walked to the front of the car, "Everyone ready?"

They all said, "Yes!"

C.A. grasped the crank firmly and followed the instructions he had read so many times. The car started on the first spin of the crank. "Then, hold on!" C.A. called out as he got back in the car.

The main road in front of the house was narrow, bumpy, and rutted. C.A. hoped they didn't meet much traffic. There were very few places wide enough for two vehicles to pass. Meeting another car wasn't likely because there weren't very many in the area, but horses and mules were a different matter. The noisy engine probably wouldn't bother a mule, but C.A. hoped they didn't meet a horse and buggy.

Everyone was in good spirits. George started singing 'Sweet Adeline' and they all chimed in. When that song finished, George took Kate's hand and began another well-known tune. Everyone listened as he sang to Kate.

"K-K-K-Katy, beautiful Katy, you're the only g-g-g-girl that I adore. When the m-moon shines over the cow shed, I'll be waiting by the k-k-k-kitchen door."

When the song ended, Kate squeezed his hand. "That is the first time anyone has ever sung to me. I thank you for the song George, and thank you for being so good to me."

Claire was thinking, "I wish Will would sing to me."

When they came back, George said, "That was a good outing."

"I enjoyed it too!" Kate agreed, "Life has certainly been good to me. When I was a young girl in the old country, planning and dreaming about coming to America, I expected life to be better and easier over here. But I never dreamed it would be this wonderful! Here my oldest son has a wonderful family and a good farm. My other children are doing well too. I have a grandson who is a schoolteacher. George and I are living comfortably. We all have so much to be thankful for."

Will smiled, "Ma, we do indeed have a lot to be thankful for."

They were all quite thrilled with the car. They took many practice drives, usually with C.A. behind the wheel, Will riding in front, and the others in the back. Will occasionally drove, but only when someone suggested he should. The truth was, he had trouble regulating the speed with the gas throttle. When he drove, C.A. had to sit beside him and control the speed for him. When C.A. brought them back home, he always parked the car so Will wouldn't have to reverse; he had trouble with that too.

As the time came closer for C.A. to go to College, Claire became concerned that Will would not be able to drive without help. Claire took C.A. aside, "You will be going to Springfield soon, and your Dad must manage driving on his own. If you keep helping, he will let you. I might be able to help, but your Dad wouldn't like that. Today, when we get started home, don't touch the gas. Regardless of what happens, don't move. Don't you touch the gas."

They got their shopping done and prepared to start home. C.A. said, "Dad, I leave for the State Teachers College next Tuesday. You're soon going to have to manage driving on your own. This is a good time for you to take over the throttle, too."

They started for home at a good speed; all was going well. It was a little bumpy, but Will didn't say anything until they got to their lane. "Cut the speed, C.A." C.A. just sat there. Will yelled in desperation as they drove closer to the gate, "Damn it, C.A., cut the speed!" It was the first time C.A. had heard his Dad use profanity but he still didn't move. Through the gate they went, and around the barn twice. Finally Will turned the key off and the car stopped. Will turned to C.A. and said, "Close the gate."

C.A. wisely refrained from reminding his Dad about Nat's advice to 'know how to stop before you start to drive.' Will never became a really good driver but he did learn to drive adequately to take them back and forth to town and to visit friends and relatives who lived in the area.

Changes for the Future

On June 9th many in the community saw a large balloon pass over Brandton. It was the 'U. S. Navy No. 6', and it caused quite a lot of excitement. The local paper reported it was one of twelve balloons entered in a national race that had begun in Milwaukee, Wisconsin. The balloon landed about 100 miles from Brandton after covering 535 miles and placing third in the race. It was another marvel of how the country was progressing. The Kennedy family would see a lot of changes in the coming months. All of them were affected in some way.

Nat and Lucinda had decided to sell their home and holdings in Brandton and move to St. Louis. They thought their children would have more opportunities in the city. Since George and Kate had married, Lucinda felt free to make a change. Nat was taking a job with the street-car company, and Ruth had assured them Lucinda was so gifted in sewing that she could do well as a seamstress.

C.A. started summer classes at the State Teachers College as planned. Being in Springfield showed C.A. one thing about the future—those with higher education would get the best jobs. Going to California next year would be a wonderful opportunity to go to one of the universities. He would like to attend the University of Southern California; whether he remained in teaching or not, it would be prestigious to have a degree from there. In the meantime, he had plenty to occupy his mind. He liked his classes and his lodgings at the boarding house.

C.A. enjoyed the camaraderie at the boarding house. There were several other boarders from nearby towns and even one from Brandton. Some of the men were in the same classes he was; others had taken them already, or would be taking them later. Besides their serious discussions, he also enjoyed the high jinks and pranks they played. As a country boy new to the city, the friendships he established at the boarding house were important to him.

After two weeks of the summer term at STC, C.A. was eager to go home to tell the family how exciting it all was. He had ridden in a train, a streetcar, and a taxicab! He had also gotten a job as janitor at the College. Claire was worried that it might take too much of his time but he assured her it was really quite easy and interesting. "They have a vacuum sweeper with a long hose and cord. There are hookups for both in each hallway of the buildings; you just plug in the cord, hook up the hose, push the sweeper around, and the dirt is pulled out with the hose. You'll see how easy electricity has made things when you get to California. Maybe there will be electricity for rural folk when you get back to Missouri."

Claire was pleased C.A. had taken another step toward a teaching career by enrolling in the Teacher's College. Will was becoming resigned to the idea that C.A. preferred an occupation other than farming. If that was to be the case, he felt teaching was a good choice. Maybe J.R. would be the one to carry on at the farm.

Claire received many glowing letters from Aimie telling how much she enjoyed living in California. She and David were looking for just the right place to buy; when they found one, they had decided to sell their Missouri farm. David and the older boys all had good jobs. Aimie was eager for Claire and the family to come out. She said Claire's housework would be a breeze there, with running water in the house, electricity, and a bathroom. There would even be time to visit neighbors.

Claire looked forward to a change for a few years, but she would want to come back to the farm. She thought Will liked the plan even more than she did. It gave Will a sense of security to know they would have the farm to come back to. The idea of working a while in California to earn extra money to fix up the farm appealed to him. He had put his heart and soul into the farm; it was something he wouldn't give up. He had always worked hard, first on his parents' farm, and then on his own. The move would be a chance to see another part of the country and to visit relatives and former neighbors who had also made the move to California without giving up what they had here. Aimie and David would probably be buried in California, but Will knew he would not want to spend the rest of his life there.

Claire received a letter from Aimie saying that they had bought a little place just outside of Bakersfield. She described a nice stucco house with a flower garden, vegetable garden, fruit trees, and a Thompson grape arbor. There was a shed and a few acres of alfalfa for a cow, and a pen with a little chicken house. Best of all, Aimie was excited that Malinda, James, and their new baby were coming to California too. James already had an office job with an oil company. Things were working out perfectly.

Quite a few of the Brandton neighbors already had relatives in California. Many more were planning to move there as well because of the good jobs that were available. It was getting easier to make the trip by car, and several families planned to travel together. Most towns used their parks for campgrounds. Firewood was usually available, and for a small fee, there were showers.

Through the winter, they planned their trip. By spring the road maps were well used and they all knew their route. They were going to the oil fields near Bakersfield and Taft. Their biggest concerns were the mountains and Death Valley in the Mojave Desert.

One couple, Ike and Dora Jordan, had made the trip before. Dora told the women, "When you start across the desert, put on as much lipstick as you can to keep your lips from cracking."

Will asked Ike what the men folk did. Ike's quick reply brought a laugh, "Why, you kiss the women!"

Will and C.A. gathered what they would need for the car—a well-stocked tool kit, two spare tires and several smaller items. Will also spent time getting everything in shape on the farm for while they would be gone. Some things would be sold while others would be kept for their return.

C.A. was in a quandary about what to do with Tim. He couldn't take the horse to California, but he didn't want just anyone riding him. Andy, being a lover of horseflesh, offered to buy Tim. If C.A. returned from California and wanted Tim back, Andy would sell him back at a fair price. C.A. was pleased with the arrangement; he knew Uncle Andy would take good care of Tim.

Claire was upset when she saw her organ listed on the sale bill. Will explained, "By the time we come back the mice would have eaten all the cords and everything not wood. It will be cheaper to buy a new one."

"But it was my mother's!" protested Claire, but the organ remained on the sale bill and was sold for $250.

Aimie had written that she had enough extra kitchen things for light housekeeping. She advised them to fold any quilts or blankets they wanted to bring and put them on the back car seat. "You will probably wish you had feather beds to sit on when you come to some of the roads."

Claire was as excited to be going to California as the rest of the group. A problem everyone shared was not being able to take everything they would like. It helped to talk about their problems. Ike kept track of what each family was taking. He took their lists, deleted some things, and suggested others. It was a congenial group who would always be 'one for all and all for one.'

They had decided to start the trip in the middle of May. Some had wanted to go in April but Ike advised again it. "Chances for rain are greater then, and the mud in Oklahoma is quite an obstacle course. We will probably still encounter some rain in May, but it won't be like the spring rains."

Traveling by car involved a lot of unknowns, so they didn't set an arrival date. Fixing flats would probably be a common occurrence; they were prepared with spare tires and tools. They would take each day as it came and see when they got to California. Will was glad C.A. was going too. Will realized he wasn't much of a mechanic, even when he was working on equipment he knew about. This new-fangled car and the way it operated was new to all of them, but C.A. seemed to pick things up quickly. Will was sure C.A. would be able to figure it out.

J.R. was one of four school age children on the trip. There were also two infants they called 'lap babies' because they enjoyed being held. Claire predicted, "They will probably want to continue being held after the trip."

C.A. had enjoyed his part in the planning. He felt every phase had been covered and he was getting eager to put the plan into practice. His personal touch was to put a baseball and gloves in his belongings. They would surely find some time to play catch after a long day on the road, and it would help loosen tired muscles. Others took some small things like dolls, marbles, puzzles, and books to fill the time if need should arise. At last they were all ready! Plans were complete, cars were serviced and loaded, and everyone was looking forward to their future in California.

California, Here We Come!

On Monday, May 15th, 1926, they assembled at the Brandton Fairgrounds. Everyone was there earlier than the time they had agreed upon, so in true "Wagons Ho" style they left at first light. The first day was familiar territory and would be the easiest traveling day. They camped that night on what would later become the downtown public square in Springfield, Missouri. It was a spot they would point out to friends and family many times saying, "This is where we camped on the first night of our trip out west to California."

Grace Jordan kept a detailed journal of the trip that would prove interesting for many years. Anytime one of the travelers wanted to check a date, a place, or mileage, they would contact Grace. Years later, when Grace was in college, she would use the information to write an essay.

It was exciting to see new country every day and the group made good time. They couldn't get used to paying for water for their radiators and air for their tires. Everyone still agreed that this was a wonderful part of the country. They enjoyed the showers at the campgrounds as well as a few tourist cabins available along the way. They only encountered light rain on two occasions.

Their greatest challenge was driving on boards across the desert sand. Ike had told them to watch for boards placed along the sides of the road. "If you see boards along the way that probably means you might get stuck because others have! Place the boards in the tracks. After you cross the first part, move the boards behind you to the front and keep going until you are across to the firm ground. It is courteous to help any car you meet get through the sand. Then put the boards back on the sides of the road."

Ike's advice was good and all five of the vehicles managed to help each other through the loose spots. They would all remember the motorist from New York who welcomed their help and then sped away without even offering to help any of them!

When the mountains came in sight Ike asked how long they thought it would take to get to them. To their amazement no one gave the right time. They were surprised the distance was so deceiving. The travelers were in awe of the mountains and found seeing them well worth the trip.

After nine days on the road, they arrived in California without any of the disasters they had worried about; they were grateful the trip went so well. They would always have a special friendship with their traveling companions.

David and Aimie lived just outside the city limits of Bakersfield. Aimie had sent instructions on how to find their place and the family soon was in the midst of a joyful reunion.

Claire was delighted with the rental house available for them a short distance from Aimie's. The other families were living on their company's lease where all of the men had jobs.

J.R. was proud to have his birthday be their first celebration after arriving in California. C.A. stayed for the festivities and then took the train to Los Angeles the next day. He would look for a job there and start at USC as soon as possible. Claire was sorry to see him leave and told Aimie she would like to see C.A. get married and settle down. Aimie assured her, "There are several nice girls around who have parents from Missouri. Both Alonzo and Ephrim married girls from Missouri families we know. C.A. will find the right one."

"He plans to get his education first; he says all his friends who got married first never did finish." Claire sighed, "I'll have to be content with being Great Aunt while you are Grandma."

C.A. had expected it to take several days to find a job, but he found something right away. He called Will and Claire in Bakersfield with the news that he had been hired at the first place he applied. He would be working for the Los Angeles Gas and Electric Company. "The supervisor said the fact that I'm from Missouri was a plus because their employees from Missouri are their best workers. I found a place to stay that fills my needs very well, and I think I'll be able to start taking some classes at USC that will fit my work schedule."

Claire was glad C.A. had found a job and a place to live. If he thought it was important to get his education before he got married and settled down, she supposed she should be glad he had found something that would allow him to take classes at the University, but she hoped he wouldn't put off finding the right girl too long. Will said if C.A. was going to be a teacher instead of a farmer he ought to get whatever education would help him to be the best teacher he could be.

The next Sunday, the travelers gathered at the Bakersfield City Park. They all had relatives near the park and had planned to meet there for a picnic after they were settled in their new homes. It had only been a short

time, but everyone liked where they were living and the men said they found their jobs easy.

All of the others planned to stay in California, but not Will and Claire. Even before they left Missouri, Will had plans to return to the farm. Will said he liked his job and the wages but he still planned to go back to Missouri after he made enough money. Claire said, "By the time we do go back to the farm, I hope we will have electricity. I like having a fan and my wringer washing machine makes laundry much easier."

"In that case, we may have to stay a little longer," Will said. They all laughed but others knew they wouldn't want to go back to kerosene lamps, wood stoves, or washboards either.

Since they had arrived in California, Will had been pondering the 'what ifs' of his relationship with Jessie. If he had known how easy it was to find work in California at the time he wanted to start life with Jessie, he could have come out and worked until he had enough money for a farm in Missouri. He asked himself if Jessie would have waited that long, but he already knew the answer. It hadn't taken her long to decide on Gus Schmidt; she wouldn't have waited. Eventually he came to the same conclusion as always; he had taken the best of the options open to him. At least he had the farm.

C.A. found everything interesting in Los Angeles. When he wasn't working or sleeping, he was checking out the city. He wrote to tell his folks how much he enjoyed the ocean and the beach on weekends. He was sure J.R. would love it, and so would his mother. He knew his Dad would never drive in the traffic to take them himself, so C.A. promised to take them as soon as he could.

One thing that surprised C.A. was that the people he met were all from somewhere else. He had yet to meet a native Californian. Everyone seemed to like the state. It definitely motivated people and things were progressing faster than in other states. California was the place to be!

Neither Aimie nor Claire could drive, so Malinda was their chauffeur and they were nannies for Malinda's toddler, Wayne. It was a nice arrangement for all of them. Each outing would eventually involve a visit to one of the area parks. Other women and children gathered there as well.

117

Aimie said, "I am glad there are such nice parks here in California. It is cooler in the shade and the grassy area is better than the sand for the children."

Malinda replied, "The valley here is a nice place to live most of the time but you have to water everything you want to be green. You can tell someone waters the park so it stays green."

Claire said, "Well in Missouri you don't have to water to keep everything green most of the year, but some years the summers are so dry that everything burns up. At least here everything is set up so they can water things when they need it."

J.R. liked his school and especially enjoyed the extra curricular activities. Track was his favorite sport; he wasn't interested in football or basketball. Claire was concerned because J.R. got more sunburned with every track meet. She finally took him to the doctor. Doctor Curtis said "Young man your skin is burned just like you have been in a fire. You must stay out of the sun unless you are protected with a hat and clothing." He gave J.R. one ointment to heal his burns and a second one to use before going out in the sun after his burns were healed. He was to put it on his face, neck, hands, and any other part of his body that wasn't covered with clothing. The doctor was concerned that the burns would get infected.

Most Sundays, at least part of the group would gather at the Bakersfield Park for a picnic. Malinda's sons Wyatt and Wayne were younger than J.R. but the cousins enjoyed being together. On one such outing, Claire said, "Malinda, your sons are closer in age than C.A. and J.R. They seem to get along very well together."

"Yes," Malinda said thoughtfully, "they have always gotten along fine. Wyatt is very protective of Wayne."

"Malinda, I know you must love both of them, just as I love both of mine. Aimie, I have thought often of what you said to me many years ago when I said I didn't think I could love another child as much as I loved C.A. Do you remember? You said 'each child brings its own love'."

"Yes, I remember," Aimie said. I'll admit I have watched you through the years and I am sure you have decided you can!"

"You were right," Claire said. "Each child is different and each child is special."

They were all careful with their money. It was fortunate they found their surroundings so interesting that they spent little on entertainment. In the summer there were gatherings at the park. Family and friends would bring food and make a day of it. The children had room to play and there was a horseshoe pit for the men. The women had a place to sit in the shade and exchange information on where to find things, what was new, what they had heard from their families in Missouri.

One day Will had a disturbing letter from Andy. He read it to Claire:

Will,

Ma and George are having trouble. Ma wanted them to go for a visit to New York to see Meggie. She is going to marry a widower with two children and Ma wants to go for the wedding, but George doesn't want to go. Ma said she would go without him and George said if she did, he would divorce her. You know Ma; she is going.

Andy

When Will finished reading the letter, he said, "Yes, and I know George; he will divorce her."

They also received a letter from Meggie telling all about her Edward. She said he was a vegetable farmer and doing quite well. He had two nicely behaved children. She thought Ma was coming for the wedding and planned to stay awhile. Will commented, "She may stay for quite a while."

The next letter from Andy was very brief.

Will and Claire,

Mom left last week for New York. George divorced her like he said he would. Lucinda is quite upset. We don't know what to do.

Andy

When the Kennedy's met at the park the next Sunday, everyone was aghast at the turn of events. They were all anxious for Kate and George to get back together.

More than anyone, Lucinda hoped they would make peace. Since she and Nat lived in St. Louis now she couldn't care for her father. Lucinda had written,

Will and Claire,

Dad certainly wasn't thinking about what people would say when he got a divorce. I am really upset with both of them. I asked Andy when Kate is coming back, and he said she would be back the 7th of September. I know Dad misses her. Just recently he told me how much he enjoyed their long talks in the evenings and what a good cook she is. I am angry with both of them for making themselves the gossip of Brandton. Andy says he agrees that Kate could have handled it differently too.

Andy has come up with an idea. He said when Ma lets him know what time to meet her train, he'll let Nat know and we will let Dad know. Maybe Dad can meet the train and they will mend the break. We have all decided it is worth a try.

Lucinda

Back in Missouri, the groundwork was laid for Kate's homecoming. Andy was early to meet the train but kept out of sight. He was relieved when he saw George arrive with a big bouquet of flowers. Andy still did not come out of hiding. The train was on time. George was waiting when Kate alighted from the train. Andy saw them embrace and shortly afterwards made his presence known.

George turned to him, "Young man, you are just in time to be a witness to the wedding of two very foolish people."

"Nothing would make me happier," Andy said as he gave his mother a big hug. George had hoped for a reconciliation and already had the license and an appointment with a minister. Kate was happy and relieved that the episode was over.

Andy took time to call Lucinda before he joined them at the parsonage. She was delighted! "Nat and I were wondering what would happen if I had to take Dad and he had to take his mother! Thankfully they are both back where they belong." That sentiment was echoed throughout the family.

Back in California, the group had settled into a comfortable routine. Claire was content; she had never had so much free time. She enjoyed the outings during the week and the get togethers on Sunday. It was always nice to hear from the relatives in Missouri. Claire had to admit she wasn't ready to go back. Of course she would be sometime, but not soon! Will, on the other hand, had set March of 1929 as the time they would go back to the farm. He wanted to be back in time to continue the tradition of planting potatoes on St. Patrick's Day.

C.A. had no plans to go back to Missouri right now. He and his folks rarely discussed their plans, feelings, or even their dreams with each other; each of them kept their own council, but he had actually never intended to go back. He found he would soon have enough college hours to teach in a California high school. He decided he would like to teach during the regular term and go to school at USC in the summer. His classes and work still left him time to explore California and he was taking advantage of it.

Claire kept in touch with all of the family. Nancy and Ruth were good correspondents. They were all excited about Ruth and Frank's trip to New York. They saw the musical "Show Boat" that opened in December. The ladies greeted the news with 'Ah's' and 'Oh's'. The men said they would rather have been at Roosevelt Field to see Lindbergh take off for his solo flight to France in the Spirit of St. Louis. Aimie responded, "Just wait; next year a woman will fly across the Atlantic Ocean too. Amelia Earhart from Kansas is thinking about it."

The coming presidential election was a favorite topic. They had never been especially interested in politics before but it seemed everyone in California had an opinion. They had been satisfied with Coolidge so they would stay with the party and vote for Hoover.

The years in California were good ones, but by the end of 1928 jobs were less plentiful. Will and his friends were grateful the jobs they had found were steady and paid well.

Aimie's came for dinner one Sunday in February. David commented that the companies were not expanding like they had in the past. "They are not updating their plants now. I think you're going to see things stationary for awhile."

Claire commented, "Well, Will, at least we're not in Missouri this winter. You didn't have to chop the ice off the pond and shovel snow."

"Yes, I know, but we really do need to get back to the farm in time to plant."

Claire was in no hurry to return to Missouri. Although she loved the farm, the time in California had been a welcome change. The letters from Nancy telling of doing the washing, weeding the garden, and milking the cows twice a day made her tired just thinking about all the chores. It would be good to be at family gatherings with them but she was going to enjoy every moment of being in California. She hadn't known there were so many things you could do with leisure time.

Will continued his plans to go back to the farm the first of March. "I've made enough to have life a little easier in Missouri. Claire and Aimie will really miss each other, but you have vacations that you can come and see us. And David, you have your brother and sisters to visit."

David said, "I'm grateful for my job here. I never would have gotten ahead in Missouri. My family just expected me to do too much for them. They all seem to be doing better solving their problems now that I've been gone. Wesley has never helped the family in any way, nor has he ever said thank you for the financial help I gave him."

Will said, "I bet you sleep better at night than he does." They enjoyed a hearty laugh together.

C.A. was finding the employment situation very good. The oil industry had slowed, but the Los Angeles area was still growing quickly. What had been just a little settlement a short time ago was becoming a thriving city. Large companies were building stores; citizens were organizing city governments. Several new schools had been built, and there was a shortage of teachers to staff them. The beginning teacher's salary was the highest in the nation.

C.A. told his folks he had looked at several places and liked them all. He said it was a new experience to be able to pick and choose among several good options. He chose a position where he could teach high school mathematics and be assistant coach for the track team. Claire told him it was good that he wouldn't be teaching younger students because she wouldn't be there to make handkerchiefs for him if they went back to Missouri.

Will had been talking to J.R. about what they would do when they got back to the farm. J.R. said he liked it in California and asked why they couldn't stay. "Sooner or later we need to go back," Will said. "We'll sell the old car and ride the train back. Then we can get another car when we're back in Missouri. I was thinking of buying you a full-size bicycle when we get back too." The idea of a train ride and a bicycle perked J.R. up a little.

The Sunday before they left for Missouri there was a big reunion of those who had traveled to California together and their friends and families. Many felt they would never have made the move if Will hadn't made the plan; they were sorry to see them leave.

C.A. came up for the weekend. He promised his mother he would come to Missouri when be got ready to pick a wife. That cheered Claire up, especially when he said, "These California girls wouldn't be a help-mate to me like you have been to Dad." Claire thought it might be tough to live up to that compliment when she got back to being a farmer's wife.

Back to the Farm

The train trip was long but interesting; they all enjoyed the scenery along the way. Will visited up and down the aisles. He enjoyed finding out where people were from and what organizations they belonged to; he was especially pleased when he ran across a fellow Mason. He wrote down names and addresses of the people he met; he didn't plan to write himself, but he expected Claire to keep in touch with them.

Andy and Nancy were at the station to meet them when they arrived. J.R. and R.L. quickly renewed their friendship and soon started to scuffle good-naturedly. They hadn't realized how much they had missed each other. The same could be said for their parents.

Nancy said, "Come home with us for supper and spend the night. We'll all go over to the farm in the morning after breakfast and open up the house. Andy can take Will into town for what supplies you need. It certainly is good to have you home."

Claire surprised herself by meaning it when she said, "It is good to be home." And it was good to be back where she knew she belonged. After one of Nancy's Missouri suppers they talked into the night. J.R. and R.L. talked themselves to sleep.

In the morning they went over to the farm. Everything seemed to be in good shape. Claire made a list of their needs and the men went to town. The women aired the house and set about cleaning out the dust and cobwebs. It wasn't long before it was livable again.

Each time she walked through the parlor Claire couldn't help noticing the empty place where her mother's organ used to be. She moved a few pieces of furniture around, putting a chair in its place. Yes, that did look a little bit better. Will had said they could get another organ. Claire sighed; maybe so, but it just wouldn't be the same.

As the women worked, they continued catching up on the happenings on both sides of the Rocky Mountains. True to his promise, Will bought J.R. a bicycle. He and R.L. wasted no time in trying it out. They had some spills but soon mastered the bike. It made the homecoming special for J.R. and this was a big day in the boys' lives.

That evening Will said, "It sure is good to be back home. I'm glad we went to California, but it never did feel like it was home."

Claire agreed, "Yes, I know what you mean. But I did like having electricity. When do you think they will get the power on here?"

"They were talking about that when I was in town. Most seem to think they will turn the power on before too many years."

Claire said, "I sure do hope so. I have places picked out for the fan, toaster, coffeepot, and reading lamp we brought back from California. I wish they would hurry and turn on the switch!" Claire sighed, "I miss C.A; I wish he had come back, too."

Will said, "The boy has a good head on his shoulders, and he's getting a good education in California. He'll come back to Missouri sometime. He promised he would come to see us."

Claire looked at the baby picture of C.A. she had given Will for Christmas long ago. "It doesn't seem like twenty-seven years since that picture was taken."

Will replied, "No, it doesn't."

"He still has the dimple in his chin."

The next day the car salesmen started arriving. Will wanted something heavier than a Ford. Claire wouldn't say what she thought they should buy; she knew Will would make his own decision. The larger car Will wanted had a stick shift, which would mean another learning experience. He didn't look forward to that, but he knew he would be better satisfied later. When the Winton salesman came by and offered to take them for a ride, they drove around and eventually went by to show the Winton to Kate and George. When the salesman heard that Will was the son of Mrs. George Russell, he offered them a ten percent discount. "George is one of our oldest merchants." Will had wanted a Winton ever since Eli had bought his Packard. Will knew he couldn't get a better deal than the discount. He told Claire, "As you often say, 'The glory of work is the joy of living'. We need to step up with a better car."

"Why, Will, that is fine with me," Claire replied. Needless to say, they bought the car that afternoon.

Will practiced driving up and down the driveway until he was sure he could handle the new car. He told Claire the Winton drove easier than the Ford. Their first outing was back to see Kate and George; they weren't surprised to see Will, Claire, and J.R. drive up in the Winton. Kate extended their hospitality and everyone enjoyed refreshments while they visited. Kate was pleased that Will had done so well out West. Grudgingly she admitted to herself, 'I guess Will could have done worse than marry Claire. Maybe she's not a milk sop after all.'

It wasn't long until Will and Claire were back in the old routine. They had returned just in time for planting—Will in the fields and Claire in the garden. They replaced the chickens and cattle they had sold and Will gathered together the livestock he had contracted out while they were gone. He was pleased with the care the animals had received, especially his mules. They seemed eager to get in the field. Both Will and Claire were surprised at how wonderful their Missouri life felt again. Their life went on in the way it had before the trip to California—keeping the farm going, visiting family and enjoying the gatherings.

The big news at one of the gatherings was the arrest of a man in a nearby community who was believed to be a notorious bandit wanted in several bank and post office robberies. He was living under a different name and building a modern ten-room house.

Another event that captured everyone's attention and saddened the nation was the kidnapping of Charles Lindbergh, Jr. on March 12, 1931. The toddler was found dead on May 12. Things like that didn't happen in the United States and certainly not to the son of one of their heroes. They felt shame it had happened. The tribute Will Rogers published in the paper expressed their feelings eloquently.

The outcome of the presidential election was not a surprise. None of them had been pleased with President Hoover. Everyone thought Roosevelt couldn't do worse than Hoover. They weren't sure that was still the case when President Roosevelt ordered all banks closed. The local bank was closed under a six-day moratorium. Wesley Jennings announced that he believed the bank's assets would be more than sufficient to pay all depositors in full. Because of the drought and low prices, several of the farmers couldn't pay their mortgages. The prices of farm products were low; farmers were even asking grocers to stop selling Oleomargarine, claiming that it was keeping the price of butter down. Will said they were still in good shape and he was confident the bank would reopen before long. "We need something to get our financial system stable."

With letters and phone calls, Claire and Will kept in touch with C.A., Aimie's, and Malinda's.

Claire was excited to get a letter from C.A. that he had a new job and would tell them about it when he called Sunday.

When she heard C.A.'s voice on the phone, she asked about his new job. "Yes," C.A. said, "I have a new job at the Midvale, Arizona High School. I am going to teach mathematics; they said I was just the man for the job. Once again they were happy I'm from Missouri!"

"That's wonderful. Good luck on your new job, son!"

"Thank you. I'm looking forward to a change."

"Wait a minute, did you say Midvale, Arizona?"

"That's what I said."

"Why Arizona?"

C.A. laughed. "That's where the job is. One of my classmates is from Arizona and told me about the opening. The climate is still great in Arizona with no snow to shovel. You know, I've been thinking, I'd like to teach in every state."

"We can't come to see you in every state!"

"Well, that would be one way for all of us to see the country."

"I don't think your dad would travel that much. I wish you would just settle down and come back to Missouri!"

C.A. replied, "Well, at least I can come back to Missouri to visit from wherever I am. I am really enjoying seeing the country."

"We miss you. Take good care and come see us when you can."

"I love you both. You take good care of each other. If I don't write I'll call soon."

News came from Washington, D.C. that the Rural Electrification Administration had been created. That was good news to those living in rural areas, especially the housewives. It meant that electricity would be coming soon. Houses, and even some barns, began to be wired for electricity.

Will and Claire's house was among the first to be wired, along with their barn. They knew the electricians would be so busy once the electric company was in operation that there would be a long waiting list. Claire didn't want to miss a day once electricity became available!

Minnie had been busy with an addition on their house and hadn't been out to any community activities. She told Eli, "I haven't been out of the house in ages. I don't know when I've seen any of the family. Now that we have the screened porch and sunroom finished, I'd like to have the family for Sunday dinner a week from this Sunday."

"Sounds good to me; I always enjoy the group."

Minnie started making phone calls. Lettie's were first, then Will's, Andy's, and George and Kate. She would have to write to Nat's and Frank and Ruth and hope that they would be able to come down. Lettie said she felt so old she wasn't sure she could make it. The others nearby all said they thought it was a great idea to get the family together and they would plan to be there.

Everyone came, even Lettie. The day was spent more in reminiscing about the past than talking about the present or the future. The most exciting news from St. Louis this time was Frank's new car. He had bought a Model A Ford and was so proud of it. The men took turns sitting in the driver's seat and agreed that it was a very good car.

The phone rang for Will and Claire about 2:00 p.m. the following Sunday. As Claire started for the phone, she said to Will, "It's C.A.'s usual Sunday call." She answered with, "Hello from Missouri!"

C.A. laughed, "Hello from Arizona! I wish you could be here to see the desert in the spring. We have always looked forward to the coming of spring but in Arizona the sounds, the smells, and the sights of spring are overwhelming. There are hummingbirds and bees in the blooming cactus. I have never seen so many hummingbirds. You would like the flowering cactus; flowers of all colors. You would especially like all of the reds! I have never been so taken with any place I have lived before. I have changed my mind; I don't need to teach in every state. I think I'll stay here for awhile longer."

Claire replied, "The geese have started flying north. I heard the frogs last night, and the serviceberry is blooming already. It won't be long before the redbud and the dogwood will make our Missouri spring mighty pretty too! I was thinking you were probably calling to tell us you were coming back to Missouri soon."

C.A. laughed, "Not yet. I will probably come back at least to visit before too long, but I have already signed up to coach baseball here at Midvale this summer. Uncle Andy would like my job here. As good as he was in baseball he would have been a great coach."

"Yes, he would," Claire agreed.

After visiting a few minutes C.A. said, "You and Dad take good care of each other; I'll call again next week."

"Be careful, son. We love you!"

Kate followed a regular morning schedule; she would feed and milk the cow and feed the chickens, and then would go in to cook breakfast. This particular morning she had finished the chores and decided to sit on the porch steps to rest a bit before fixing breakfast. Her granddaughter Rose came out a few minutes later to speak with Grandma and soon realized that something wasn't right; she called for George. He came quickly and confirmed Rose's fears that Kate had passed away.

He called Will, "This is George. My heart is broken; my Kate is gone. She seemed fine this morning when she went out to do the chores. Rose found her sitting on the front steps. I can't believe she is gone. I don't know what I will do without her."

Will replied, "I know how you feel, George, this is quite a shock to us too. All of us appreciate all that you have done for Ma these past few years. They were good years for her. We will all miss her. I am glad she didn't have to suffer. Would you like for me to call the rest of the family and take care of her service?"

"Yes, that would be such a help."

Will just sat there holding the phone. "She worked until the very last as she would have wanted. We will all miss her. "

Claire took the phone and said, "Yes, we will. I am so sorry. I will call the others for you."

"That would help me so much, Claire. Thank you." The party line helped to spread the sad news.

Claire called C.A. "The family would understand if you didn't come."

"Mom, I want to be there. Some of my best childhood memories are of being with Grandma. When she was fishing in the pond, I had to be very quiet or she would send me to the house. I still enjoyed being with her. In all ways she was a tower of strength. I will be there for her service. I want to be there to be with Dad."

They decided to have the service at the Baptist Church. Kate had been going there with George since they married. It was a consoling service and a sad reunion for the family.

The weather in Missouri in May is usually pleasant but one Sunday the air seemed heavy. Although Will and Claire had only done the regular chores that day, everything seemed to be an effort, as if they were not getting enough air. Clouds were rolling in and it looked like it could rain at anytime.

After supper Will said, "I'll keep my eye on the clouds. We might have to go to the cellar. Keep your shoes by the bed and maybe a shawl." He had just finished speaking when the wind struck with extreme force. Things were flying all around, objects hit the house, and there was a loud roaring sound.

Will yelled, "It's a cyclone! Come on; we have to go to the cellar now." By the time they got to the door, the wind was blowing it open. Will shouted, "It's too late; help me close the door." It took both of them to close it part way and hold it.

They watched the damaging winds take their toll. They saw the barn go, heard their big parlor window shatter, and saw some big trees come down. They were never sure how long it lasted, but they were completely exhausted by the time it was over.

When the winds stopped, it took some time for them to recover from the shock of the storm. Will said, "It's too dangerous to go outside before daylight."

Claire went to the parlor to see how badly it was damaged. "What are those lights in the lane?" she asked. Gradually the lights drew closer and they could make out figures carrying lanterns. "Will, it's the neighbors coming to see about us." Throughout the storm, Claire had been very brave and kept her emotions in check, but the idea of neighbors hurrying over to check on them so quickly was too much to subdue. She began to weep uncontrollably.

Will had never seen her like this. He had seen her cry when she was very happy and when she was sad or angry; but not like this! He put his arm around her and awkwardly drew her close. "Claire, it will be all right. We will get through this. We still have the land. We can fix the rest."

She smiled at him and said, "You're right. We still have the land. We have always made it through."

With the light from the lanterns, they could see enough to check on the damage. Even though they had seen some of it as it happened, they were hardly prepared for the extent of the destruction caused by the storm. The barn, the equipment shed, and the outhouse were completely gone. The damage to the house seemed repairable and the garage seemed all right. Will hadn't even thought about the new car. One of the neighbors speculated that when the parlor window broke out in the beginning it may have helped equalize the air pressure and kept the house from exploding. For whatever reason, they were thankful that they weren't injured, the house was still intact, and nothing had been destroyed that couldn't be replaced.

It was good fortune too that J.R. had spent the night with R.L. Someone called Andy and he came over without the boys. Someone brought a bucket of coffee and another brought a cake left over from Sunday dinner. Someone found cups for the coffee and plates for the cake and served the gathering. They made plans when to come back to help.

Will was fortunate to have insurance. His agent was with the group, "Will, you will have to agree we're here when you need us. Go in and order your material in the morning. Get whatever you need. We don't know how much damage the storm has done over the country and they may run short on things before all of the storm damage is repaired."

Andy and Aaron came early the next morning to go with Will to the lumberyard. Aaron had been doing some building for others and had several blueprints of barns. Now Will could build a new barn that would be even better than the old one!

Claire suggested they build the new barn on the southeast side of the house because the slope there would provide good drainage. Will thought that the new location would be much better too. He also agreed with Claire's other recommendation—that they rebuild the outhouse first.

Claire was amazed how fast and far the news of the storm traveled. They had calls from Aimie, Malinda, and the other friends who had gone to California with them. But the call that surprised and pleased her most came from C.A. "Mom, are you and Dad all right?"

Claire assured him they were fine. "We weren't hurt, just scared to death."

C.A. replied, "I'm glad my school is almost finished. I'm coming home to help out. I will leave Saturday and will be there in few days."

With the help of family and friends, Will and Claire started cleaning up. The men got to work cutting up the fallen trees. J.R. and R.L. carried brush and stacked wood. Everyone found some way to be helpful. None of the other family members lived in the path of the storm. Lettie, Isaac, Andy, Nancy, Estelle, Minnie, and Eli came to help. Nat, Lucinda, Frank and Ruth came down for the weekend. George came on Saturday afternoon. This was the first time since Kate's funeral the family had been together. They all deeply felt the void and realized just how much Kate had meant to each of them. Even Claire admitted to herself that Kate had mellowed through the years and she would be missed. Kate had held the family together. They were glad they still had each other.

The outhouse was the first project on the agenda. Once that project was underway, everything in the parlor had to be taken out and dried. The rug was hung over the clothesline. Claire decided to move the parlor rug to the bedroom and get a new one for the parlor.

Johnny and Hiram Settles were now employees with the lumber company and came with the truck bringing some of the materials. Their first job was to install the glass in the parlor window. Then they repaired the door that had come off its hinges. Claire told them what happened to the hinges. Johnny said, "As hard as the wind blew, I don't know how you and Mr. Kennedy could hold it in place. No wonder it broke the hinges."

Claire said, "I don't know how we managed either. How is your mother? I haven't seen her since the end of school picnic all those years ago."

"She is doing well. I will have to tell you that she can't say enough good things about Mr. Kennedy."

"Thank her for her kind words"

It wasn't long before the house was functioning again. Will and Aaron planned the barn Will had always wanted. Aaron drew up the blueprints. The new barn would take the place of both the barn and the equipment shed that had been destroyed. It was to have a hay fork in the loft, a driveway large enough for all the farm equipment, horse stalls on one side, cow stanchions on the other side, a crib with a concrete floor, a holding pen for the calves, and benches in front of the horse stalls. Will liked the idea of having the equipment in the barn instead of in a separate building.

The help and concern of the neighbors overwhelmed Claire. She couldn't imagine what they would have done without every one of them.

Reminders of their thoughtfulness appeared everywhere. Aimie sent a beautiful set of parlor curtains, Malinda sent a Seth Thomas clock, and there were other gifts from family and friends. Each item reminded Claire of good people.

Life returned to normal for Will and Claire. "Will, we have so much to be grateful for. I have always believed the Lord has a master plan and everything happens for a reason. I believe the cyclone happened so we would not forget what good friends and family we have and to count our blessings every day."

Will replied, "I think you are right, Claire. Things do happen for a reason. C.A. told me the day he came back that he had a three-year contract to teach at Midvale in his pocket when he heard the news about the cyclone here. The cyclone helped him decide to come home to help us instead of signing it."

Claire replied, "Thank you, God!"

Will smiled and said, "Yes, thank you, God."

Their troubles seemed insignificant when they heard that their favorite comedian/philosopher, Will Rogers, had been killed in Alaska along with the aviator, Wiley Post. They all felt the loss and grieved with the rest of the world. Will said, "Will Rogers was like a good neighbor. He gave us something to lift our spirits. There will never be another man like him. If he had lived, I believe he could have been President."

They all agreed.

Missouri Girl

While they waited for more building materials to be delivered, C.A. looked for a teaching position. It wasn't long before he found exactly what he was looking for, and he signed a contract as Principal, science teacher, and boys' basketball coach at Bradfield High School. He hurried home to tell the family that he would be staying in Missouri. Claire was quite pleased with the news and couldn't resist saying, "It's time to look for that Missouri girl." C.A. just smiled and made no reply.

The building materials soon arrived, and construction began on the new barn. With help from family and friends, it was finished by the 4th of July. Before they moved anything in, they decided to invite the family and workers to gather to celebrate their comeback from the storm. As Will said, "It is a monument to man's will to recover from disaster."

The men put boards on the sawhorses to make a long table and added extra benches for seating. Everyone brought in food to share for the celebration. It was a happy occasion. All of the storm damage had been either replaced or mended. There was so much talking and laughter that someone remarked, "This is really a barn raising."

Will was talking to Johnny and Hiram Settles. "We sure do appreciate all the help you boys have been."

Johnny replied, "I am happy I was able to help. That is my way of saying 'Thank you' for the help your son gave me when I was his student at Oak Grove. I am glad he didn't just whip me and send me home that first day. I would probably be home working on my folks farm now."

Hiram laughed, "And still trying to get me to help with the chores! Everyone in the family is happy that our brother Elmer enjoys farming and is taking care of the place so we don't have to!"

Johnny said, "I have been looking for Mr. Kennedy. I can't call him C.A., he is still Mr. Kennedy to me."

Will said "Both of the boys are in the barn up in the hay loft."

C.A. and J.R. were in the loft looking out the big door that afforded a fine view of the farm. C.A. commented, "This is sure a fine new barn. You know, I like the farm but I never want to be a farmer."

J.R. agreed, "I want to see the place kept up, after all, it was Mom's parents' place, but I don't want to farm either. It always seemed kind of odd to me, but I think Dad likes this farm even more than Mom does.

Guess it's the Irish in him. Now, take Cousin William, he has that Irish love of the land too. He's a better farmer than Uncle Isaac. He gets it from Aunt Lettie, I suppose. It has sure been good to have you home, C.A., even besides all the help you have been getting the place back in shape."

"It is good to be back. If it hadn't been for the cyclone, I would probably have stayed in Arizona awhile longer. I had a three year contract in my pocket when I heard about the cyclone."

Johnny and Hiram joined them in the loft. C.A. was glad to see them. "I haven't seen you boys since the last day of school all those years ago. Dad tells me both of you work for the lumberyard now. Did you get your farm chores done before you came today?"

Hiram said, "Thanks to you, Elmer is home taking care of the farm now and we don't have to!"

"Neither C.A. nor I want to work our family farm either. That is what keeps me going to school so I can do something else when I finish!"

Johnny said, "I see your brother has helped you to see the value of an education too. To C.A. he said, "Mr. Kennedy, I am glad you didn't just whip me and send me home that first day! I would still be taking care of the farm."

"And making me help," said Hiram.

They all laughed and expressed appreciation for the help each had given and the Settles boys went back to join the others.

It felt good to C.A. to think about the time when he first started teaching. He had to admit he was glad to be back in Missouri. J.R. was so grown up now. Time had slipped by during the years he had been out west.

"Tomorrow I am going to look for a place to stay over in Bradfield where I'll be teaching," C.A. told J.R. "Would you like to ride along?"

"Sure, it would be fun."

The brothers enjoyed the time together the next day. It gave them the opportunity for some serious talk about the future. C.A. and J.R. went to the school first and met the superintendent, a few teachers, and the school secretary—a young woman named Maria. A few students were playing basketball in the gym; C.A. introduced himself and J.R. to them. They were impressed that their coach had reported early and C.A. was pleased the boys were enthused about basketball.

C.A. asked around about apartments near the school and got several prospects. One happened to belong to the aunt of the school secretary, although he didn't know it until he had rented it. He was just leaving when Maria came up the walk. "Are you going to be staying at my Aunt's?"

"Is this your aunt's place? I just signed up." C.A. replied. "Where do you live?"

133

"Just at the edge of town. I come by Aunt Lula's often, and sometimes have a meal with her. I hope you will like Bradfield."

"My brother and I like what we've seen so far. I will move over next week."

Aunt Lula came to the door with the announcement, "It is customary for those who dwell under my roof to have Sunday dinner with me."

Maria laughed, "That means you will also enjoy church. Dinner comes after church."

C.A. laughed. "I can do that."

On the way home J.R. said, "If I were a little older I would go over to Bradfield and do some sparking."

"Oh, which one, Aunt Lula or Maria?"

J.R. laughed, "Ah, you know which one. I bet you already have plans for Maria."

C.A. laughed with him but didn't respond to J.R.'s teasing.

Claire was happy that both of her boys were in Missouri now. C.A. kept in touch by visits, letters, and phone calls. The storm damage had been repaired, Will seemed happy with the new barn, they had enough rain, the garden was weed-free...Claire was sure she had never been happier; but something else topped every one of those things. C.A. was courting a Missouri girl! They didn't know her yet but J.R. gave a glowing report about C.A.'s new girl.

It was a busy school year for C.A. Between physical education and science classes, he tended his duties as principal. Thankfully, there were few problems needing his attention. He had a good science class; they were eager to learn. During basketball season, his physical education classes mainly played basketball but C.A. tried to work all the students into the game. The boys' basketball team practiced after school and on Saturday mornings.

Then there was Maria. C.A. saw her in the office every day and on Sundays. When the basketball team had an away game, C.A. went on one bus with the boys' basketball team; Maria went on another bus as chaperon for the girls' cheering squad.

Claire was especially pleased every time C.A. mentioned something that involved Maria. She was even more pleased when she suspected Maria's Aunt Lula shared her hopes for a match between the two.

During the past several months, Aunt Lula had been playing match-

134

maker, inviting a carefully selected string of eligible bachelors to join her for Sunday dinner and, of course, including Maria. Now that C.A. was there for Sunday dinner that didn't seem necessary anymore; after all, he was an eligible bachelor! Lula thought C.A. and Maria were a good match; Maria thought so too. From the beginning, C.A. knew he had found his special Missouri Girl!

Early in December, C.A. invited Maria to go to Springfield to see a Laurel and Hardy movie. When they had dinner, amazingly they both ordered sirloin steak cooked medium, baked potato with butter, a garden salad, and green beans; and for dessert—hot tea with lemon, and apple pie. "We do seem to like the same things," C.A. remarked.

Christmas shopping was next on the agenda. C.A. needed gifts for Claire, Will, and J.R., and of course, Aunt Lula. Maria suggested they go to Heers. "They have a wide selection; maybe we can find something nice for all of them there."

C.A. said, "I never know what to get Mom. She always acts like she likes what I give her, but this year I would like for it to be really special. This has been an especially difficult year. I was thinking maybe a nice bottle of perfume in a pretty glass bottle, maybe 'Evening in Paris.' What do you think she would like?"

Maria said thoughtfully, "Perfume would be nice, or does she have a vanity set with a nice mirror, comb, brush, and manicure set?"

"I don't think she has a vanity set. I don't remember seeing anything like that at the farm. She uses an old mirror that is very cloudy. One day she mentioned that her mirror was so cloudy she couldn't be sure if her rouge was on right. I think she would like that."

"Let's try to find a set with celluloid handles, maybe with a neat silver trim. What is her favorite color?" Maria asked.

C.A. thought about it and decided, "She likes bright colors like red, pink, yellow, and green."

"Most of the ones I've seen are soft, pastel colors. Aunt Lula has a pretty blue one. Does your Mom like blue?"

"No, I don't think so. I don't remember ever seeing her wear blue." They selected a set with soft pink handles and silver trim. They decided on a tan wool muffler for Will and a new safety razor with an adjustable handle for J.R. A crystal fruit bowl for Aunt Lula completed the list. C.A. had already chosen Maria's present—a handsome perfume bottle with an intricate, cut-glass stopper.

Claire had invited Andy, Nancy, and R.L. for dinner the Sunday before Christmas. J.R. would be there too. In early December Claire had written to C.A. hoping he would be able to come home for the holidays and join the family. C.A. had written back that the school would be on Christmas holiday starting the 19th and be off until after New Years. He had also asked if he could bring a friend along.

"Oh," Claire exclaimed when she read his letter, "I just know he is bringing his Missouri girl!"

"Yes," confirmed C.A. during their next phone call. "I would like for you to meet Maria. We will come early Sunday morning and I will take her home on Monday. I thought she could have the room you used when you had the boarder."

"Yes," Claire said excitedly, "that will work out fine. I am so pleased you will be coming! I am anxious to meet Maria. Will you be coming back home for Christmas Day? Andy and Nancy have invited the whole family to come for Christmas dinner. This will be the first Christmas since Kate passed away."

"Mom, I don't think I will be able to come back for Christmas day this time. Maria has invited me to join her family for Christmas dinner. Her Aunt Lula will be there, of course, and her sister Lois and her family are coming from Alabama. I have never met them. Don't you think I should go to Maria's?"

"Yes," Claire said laughingly, "I think you should go to Maria's."

Early Sunday morning, C.A. loaded the carefully wrapped gifts and a large box of oranges he had purchased on Friday. Then he went to get Maria. She was waiting and ran out when he drove up. C.A. had never seen her look lovelier. "I like your red dress and so will Mom."

"Oh, I hope so. I hope your family will like me."

"Of course they will," he replied.

The day went very well, even better than C.A. had hoped. Claire was happy to meet Maria and welcomed her warmly. Claire had the table laden with food. C.A. was sure she must have been cooking and baking for days. After dinner Will told Maria some of his best stories. Andy, Nancy, J.R., and R.L. kept the conversation lively; everyone was glad to meet C.A.'s new friend! C.A. was sure Maria would be welcomed into the family; he hoped she would say "yes" to the question he planned to ask her.

After Andy's left, C.A said he had brought some Christmas gifts. When she opened her gift, Claire was overcome; she took a deep breath, spread out her arms and said happily, "I couldn't be more pleased. How did you know what I wanted? My old mirror is getting so cloudy it is hard to see my face!"

C.A. smiled at Claire and then at Maria, "I had help selecting my gifts this time."

Claire smiled happily at both of them. "Oh, that makes it even more special."

Will liked his muffler, too. "My old one is soiled and not very warm. Thanks, C.A."

When he opened the safety razor J.R. said, "This is just in time. I nicked my neck with my old straight edge yesterday morning."

As C.A. and Maria drove back to Bradfield on Monday morning, Maria was in good spirits, "I liked your family so much! I hope they liked me."

C.A. assured her with a smile, "Of course they liked you! Mom was elated. I haven't seen her that happy in years."

"I hope you like my family as well as I like yours."

C.A. told her, "I already know I like your parents and Aunt Lula. You have read me letters from your sister Lois. She sounds pleasant. If she is anything like you, I know I shall like her."

Christmas Day made a picture post card with fresh, white snow. Many sleds, horse drawn sleighs, groups of carolers, and children playing in the snow making snow angels added to the season. The day could not have been better! This was to portent many, many glorious Christmases C.A., Maria, and their families would spend together!

When it was time to say goodnight, C.A. and Maria stood for a few minutes on the porch looking at the full moon. C.A. put his arm around her, of course to keep her warm. The neighborhood children had spent all afternoon building a snowman with a carrot nose, sticks for arms, and coal for eyes. C.A. pulled her closer; "Even if that snowman is watching..." His kiss was returned. It had been a glorious day!

When C.A. was at the farm a few weeks later, J.R. casually asked, "How are you getting along with Maria?"

"Oh, we are quite compatible," C.A. replied.

"That sounds as good as an engagement announcement, to me." laughed J.R.

"Perhaps it is," responded C.A. but he was thinking, 'it actually is!' He was serious enough to ask Maria to marry him. Of course she said 'Yes!' The next Saturday they went to Springfield and selected her engagement ring; they chose a wedding date in August. That would give them enough time to find a house and get settled.

On August 20th, 1936, Miss Maria Stewart became Mrs. Charles Arthur Kennedy. The ceremony took place at the Methodist parsonage with J.R. and Maria's sister Lois as their attendants. After the ceremony they left on a short honeymoon to Springfield, then on to Branson, and back to their new home. Claire was thrilled that C.A. had found his Missouri Girl!

The Boys Head West

C.A. enjoyed another year teaching and coaching at Bradfield. In the spring he was offered a contract for another year, but he hesitated to sign it. Although they were doing well, he thought they should be doing even better. He remembered how it had been profitable for his parents go to California to build a larger nest egg. When they had returned to Missouri, they had enough money to make them more comfortable on the farm. Teachers' salaries in California were higher than in Missouri, and salaries in the oil fields were even better. C.A. thought California might be the answer for them, too. He shared his thoughts with Maria and they discussed the options available and decided to make the move. C.A. especially looked forward to introducing Maria to the family in California and showing her around the places he had enjoyed. He didn't look forward to telling his Mom they would be leaving Missouri!

As expected, Claire was dismayed at the news. "But I hoped you would stay in Missouri! It's been so nice having you close."

"It has been nice being here," C.A. said, "but I think it's a good move for our future. You and Dad taught me to always plan ahead." Claire couldn't argue with his logic, but she was still disappointed they were moving so far away. Will didn't say much on the subject either way, but he did remind Claire that at least C.A. had found his Missouri girl before moving back west.

C.A. and Maria decided to make the trip at a leisurely pace and really see the scenery on the way. They were both excited about the challenges ahead. It would be the trip they would call 'the perfect trip' in later years.

When they arrived in California, they stopped at Aimie's in Bakersfield first to spend a few days. Aimie hugged Maria, "I feel like I know you already. Claire has told me so much about you! C.A., we have missed you. We have a lot of catching up to do." Aimie insisted they call Claire and Will and let them know they had arrived safely, then they all had a great time getting the Missouri news and bringing C.A. up to date on happenings of old friends. It was a most enjoyable reunion.

Then they went on to James' and Malinda's home in Taft where they were greeted enthusiastically. Malinda said, "We're so glad you came. I have wanted to meet Maria. My, we have so much to talk about. How did you leave Aunt Claire and Uncle Will?"

C.A. answered, "Mom is doing great; Dad is working hard from sun up to sun down. He has the farm in better shape now than before they came out here."

James said, "It sure is good to see you two. Let's go to the shade. Later I will show you around what we laughingly call 'Our Ranch'. We picked this spot because we like to grow things and have some living things around."

Malinda added, "Wayne should be home from school soon; he is a freshman this year. Wyatt works at a gas station on the Ridge and will be here in time for supper."

"Where is the Ridge?" Maria wanted to know.

James laughed. We are in the San Joaquin Valley. When you head west from here you will know when you go over the Ridge. All of the sudden, you come over the ridge and it is several degrees cooler and the breeze feels wonderful. I guess 'the Ridge' is really a lot of mountain ridges that run mostly north and south all along the coast and for several miles inland. As you head farther east from the coast the ridges get lower and the last one before you get to our valley we locals call 'the ridge'. The ridge is a good place for a filling station. Everyone wants a full tank of gas and plenty of water before they head into the valley."

When Wayne arrived, C.A shook his hand warmly and introduced him to Maria. Wayne said, "I'm glad to meet you, it is nice to have a new cousin. I hope you like living here; we all do."

James had the barbecue set up to cook their steaks for supper. They visited while the meal cooked.

Wyatt came in later in the afternoon. C.A. was glad to see him again, "Wyatt, I haven't seen you in a few years and you are all grown up now."

Wyatt laughed and said to Maria, "Aunt Claire talks about C.A.'s Maria in every letter so I feel like I already know you. Aunt Claire sure does think you're great!"

C.A. said, "So do I!" They all laughed.

It was a joyous reunion with them as well. The conversation never lagged. After dinner Malinda said, "While James cleans up I want to show Maria the house. I love the porches and windows. There is usually a breeze through the house, so we seldom run the air conditioner." They started in the living room. "I just got the divan," Malinda told Maria. "I like it, but it makes the piano look old. I never play it anymore; guess I should get rid of it."

Maria said, "I love piano music. Please play something for me."

"Oh, all right, but you asked for it," Malinda said with a laugh.

After Malinda finished playing Maria said, "I love that piece, 'Christian Endeavor' is one of my favorites. My friend, Winona, plays it because it is special for her. When her grandfather was very ill, he liked

139

for his daughter, Winona's mother, to play for him to pass the time. He asked her to play 'Christian Endeavor' for him one day. She did, and when she finished they found Grandpa had passed away while she was playing."

"That's a beautiful story," said Malinda. "Aunt Claire taught me to play that piece. You are the first person I have played it for who knew the title."

Maria said, "It is even more special to me since C.A.'s mother taught you to play it."

Malinda continued, "Aunt Claire taught C.A. to play, too."

Maria was surprised, "I didn't know C.A. could play the piano."

"Oh yes," Malinda replied, "at least Aunt Claire taught him to play his Grandmother Lafever's organ. The fingering would be the same."

Maria replied, "C.A.'s mother mentioned that her mother used to have an organ, but I have never seen one at the farm."

"No," Malinda replied, "it was sold before they came out here a few years ago."

James laughed, "I bet C.A. can still play 'Drop My Dolly in the Dirt'."

C.A. shook his head. "I doubt I could even do that, although I still remember singing the tune; I might be able to figure it out."

Maria added to the merriment when she said, "I didn't know I had married a musician'!"

James and Malinda invited C.A. and Maria to spend a few days with them at their cabin on the coast near Cayucos. It allowed them to spend a few more days together. Maria thought the scenery was beautiful and enjoyed being on the Pacific. Fishing was good and they all enjoyed eating what they caught.

After the much deserved vacation time, C.A. started looking for employment. He decided to take a job with Texaco Oil Company in Taft rather than continue teaching. It would pay a lot more and would start immediately. The location was ideal, being near both sets of relatives. They were especially fortunate in that an engineer for Texaco had been assigned elsewhere, making a house on the lease available for them. That meant they wouldn't have to find housing, and a house on the lease included utilities.

C.A. told Maria she could select the furnishings for the house. They would have some things shipped from Bradfield and the rest would be sold. Maria was happy Malinda could accompany her on the shopping trip for furnishings. C.A. approved of their choices and it wasn't long until the house was ready for them to move in.

Malinda and James were their first dinner guests. C.A. barbecued steaks and Maria did the rest. C.A. couldn't top James' jokes, but they had a good time.

They kept in touch with Claire and Will by phone and letter. They were pleased that C.A. had found a job and a place to live so quickly. They could remember the places C.A. and Maria told about from their own time in California.

On Christmas Day Aimie had all of her family as well as C.A. and Maria for a traditional Christmas feast. Her table was laden with good things, among which was a sugar-cured ham Claire had sent as a Christmas gift. Malinda said, "Let's call Aunt Claire and tell her how much we enjoyed the ham."

When Claire answered the phone Malinda said, "Merry Christmas to you both. C.A. and Maria are here with my family. I wish you were here too; we all have enjoyed the ham you sent."

C.A. came over to Malinda and said, "May I wish the folks a Merry Christmas, too?"

"Of course," Malinda replied as she handed him the phone.

"Hello, Mom, Merry Christmas to you and Dad. We're enjoying a very special Christmas here with Malinda and James and the family. I wanted to tell you our good news. We are going to have a child in June."

"Oh, I am going to be a grandmother!" exclaimed Claire. "I can't wait to tell your Dad the news. He's out feeding the cows now. That's the best Christmas gift you could have given me. Oh, I'll go out and tell your Dad right now; it will take too long for him to come in. I can hardly wait to call Nancy. Does Aimie know?"

C.A. laughed at her excitement. "She does now. She and David are sitting here at the dinner table."

"Could I talk to Maria?" Claire asked. C.A. handed the phone to Maria with a warm smile. "Maria, I couldn't be more pleased. I feel like I have the daughter I always wanted and now you are giving me a grandchild. Thank you for the most wonderful gift. I will always remember this very special Christmas!"

"I'm happy about it too." Maria said, squeezing C.A's hand. C.A. hugged her as they passed the phone around for everyone to share holiday greetings. It was a very special day!

J.R. had tried college for a time in Springfield. Claire very much wanted him to go, and had let him have her egg money for expenses, but they both finally realized that more education wasn't in his plan. At last she suggested he try working in the oil fields for a while instead. She hated the idea of both her boys being so far away, but was comforted by the thought that they would be close to each other and to Aimie's and Malinda's.

J.R. was really sorry he had disappointed Mom by not staying in college. Maybe he would get back to it some day, but for now, he just didn't find it interesting. A job in the oil fields and a regular paycheck sounded great to him! With a full-time job, he could have a car of his own in no time.

J.R. took her advice and went to California. He stayed with Aimie for a few days before taking a room at the bunkhouse on the lease. He really didn't mind the work in the oil fields; he had worked harder on the farm. And besides, he was usually thinking of a great evening while he worked. But he missed his friends and family back in Missouri. He had Sundays off and enjoyed the family get-togethers at C.A's, Aimie's or Malinda's. Aimie's meals were so much like Mom's that they made him miss home even more. It was harder moving away from home than he had thought it would be. It was harder saving money than he had thought it would be, too. He had managed to save some from every check, not much, but it was a start. He really wanted a car—just one to run around in for now, later he would get something fancier. He didn't like to ask to borrow C.A's car too often, but if he borrowed a friend's car he almost had to take the friend along. That meant more money. Maybe he'd be better off back in Missouri after all.

Missouri had been especially severe winter that year. In early March, Claire said to Will, "This is the seventh snow this winter! I wish we were out in California with the boys!"

"I miss it sometimes too, but even when I have to cut the ice off the ponds for the animals I still would rather be here. After a time you would have grown tired of being in California. I am glad we went and have the extra money, but our life is better here on the farm than it would be there. I know you miss the boys and Aimie's and Malinda's, but the rest of the Kennedys are here in Missouri. I guess James and David will want to stay in California, but I hope the boys will come back home someday."

"I hope the boys will come back to Missouri, too."

C.A. and Maria kept busy for the rest of the winter. They agreed it was wonderful not to worry about things freezing or shoveling snow. C.A. was gone all day during the week and Maria occupied her time knitting blue baby blankets, and a blue sweater and bootie set. It seemed safer to make blue things. No Kennedy son could wear pink; but a Kennedy daughter could wear blue. C.A. had said he would like to have at least two sons. Maria had told him she didn't care how many sons she had but she hoped for at least one daughter.

April 16, 1938

One nice spring morning in mid April, Maria was getting ready for the day. She looked at her maternity wardrobe to decide which dress to wear. She decided to save the sky blue dress for Easter the next day and wear the navy one that day. She wanted to get the grocery shopping done early so she could get back home before the heat of the day. C.A. had gone to work with a friend so she could keep the car. As Maria hurried down the walk, she tripped and fell over something. She was stunned for a few moments and was alarmed when she couldn't get up. She didn't think any bones were broken but she seemed to hurt all over.

She quickly began to feel uncomfortably warm in the bright sun. A grape arbor beside the walk between the house and the garage blocked the view from the street, and C.A. wouldn't be home for hours. She knew she would have to get herself back to the house. By extreme will power she managed to get the thirty feet back to the house, up the three steps, and through the house to the bedroom.

It was hard to say where she hurt the most. It seemed her right hand and her knees had taken the main force of the impact. "I think I protected the baby," she said over and over to herself. By now her head was throbbing too. Maria decided the best thing she could do would be to try to stay calm, keep cool with the fan, and drink plenty of liquids.

C.A. was alarmed when he came home and found Maria in bed. "I'm going to call the doctor just in case. At least he can give you something for the pain."

Dr. Dycus was there quickly. He said, "She must go to the hospital right now." Then he added, "I think you will be a father before morning!"

C.A. was happy about being a father but he was worried that the baby would be too small. He was also concerned about Maria's scratches and bruises.

Dr. Dycus had Maria checked in and then gave orders to send her directly to the delivery room. After what seemed a very long time to C.A., the nurse came to say the doctor wanted to see him. "You have a fine son and there is another child coming soon!"

C.A. had mixed feelings. He was pleased he had a son, but he was worried about the other baby. Soon Dr. Dycus said, "Congratulations, you have a healthy pair of sons! These little fellows will need extra care because they're premature but they will grow up strong. I have twin sons that are in high school now. They have been my pride and joy. You will have many happy times ahead with your family. I would like for the mother and babies to stay in the hospital for at least ten days. I don't expect problems, but they need the extra care for a few days."

When C.A. got to talk to Maria she said, "You have your two sons."

"And I couldn't be happier. They are going to be all right and you are doing fine." He told her what the doctor had said about staying in the hospital for ten days. "The extra time here will give me time to double up what we had ready for one. Malinda will help me."

Maria asked if he had called the folks back in Missouri to tell them the news. "Not yet," said C.A. "I was so worried about you and the baby that I didn't think about calling earlier. Now I think we should decide what we're going to name the babies before we call."

"What about names?" Maria asked. "We hadn't even decided on one yet, and now we need two."

"Any you want," replied C.A. "You have ten days to decide."

Maria set about choosing names. She wanted both babies' names to reflect their father, but how could one name do for both? Then she had the idea to divide C.A.'s name between the twins and have each of them keep the same initials as their father. Number one son became Charles Ansel and number two son became Caroll Arthur.

C.A. said, "You did a good job selecting those names. Mom will be pleased. I was named for her father and now my sons will carry on the name. I'll be glad when you can all come home."

Maria said, "I'm glad I made so many blue baby things."

C.A. laughed. "That may be the secret of having a boy. Whatever it was, I am delighted to have two sons."

Claire answered the phone when C.A. called to tell them the news. "Hello, Grandma." he said.

"Grandma! Aren't you a little early with calling me Grandma?"

"I think two grandsons qualify you to be called Grandma," C.A. replied.

It took a second for the news to sink in. "Two grandsons! Oh, a double blessing. Are they alright?"

"Yes, we have twins. And yes, mother and babies are doing just fine." C.A. assured her. "Mom, we have decided to name them Charles Ansel and Caroll Arthur; Maria picked the names." As he had predicted, Claire was delighted with the choice of names. They talked for a few more minutes before ending the call. C.A. said he would write with more details. Claire told him to send pictures with his letter. She couldn't wait for Will to come in from the field, so she found him to tell him the good news! Of course he was pleased.

"Twins are really special, Frank and Minnie are twins and they were always especially close, even closer than the rest of us. It will be especially nice since they are both boys." When Claire told him the names, he replied, "Those are nice names." To himself he said, 'Humph, C.A. didn't hold with the Kennedy tradition for the name William either.'

Next Claire called Nancy, then Estelle and Lucinda; the party lines were busy the rest of the morning.

Easter morning came and Maria smiled when she thought that just yesterday she had been wondering what she would wear today. It had been decided for her.

Malinda and Aimie came to the hospital to visit and bring gifts. Aimie's eyes filled with tears when she heard the babies' names. "Oh, you used Papa's name. I didn't use it for any of my sons and thinking back afterwards I was sorry that I hadn't."

When the ten days were up, Maria was glad to be going home. C.A. had the nurse who lived on the lease, Mrs. Griffin, to stay for two weeks. They all were sure each baby had a different sounding cry. Mrs. Griffin referred to Arthur as 'the dark-haired one' and Ansel 'the light-haired one'. Maria felt they should get used to calling the boys by their correct names from the start. They got along splendidly and everyone soon adjusted to a workable schedule.

C.A. was good to help, especially with the laundry. He laughed about hanging up all of the diapers. By the time he finished hanging the last ones, the first ones were dry!

C.A. and Maria had been so busy with the new babies that C.A. decided to give the folks a call to let them know how well the babies were doing instead of writing.

Claire was happy to hear from them and she had big news too! "They turned our electricity on at the farm on April 28th. I can finally use the things I brought back from California!" Everyone was happy to have so much good news.

Claire was pleased to have grandchildren at last. Her only regret was that they were so far away. She wished they were close enough for her to see them on a regular basis. C.A. assured her they would come for a visit when the twins were old enough to travel.

Letters were an important means of keeping in touch. Claire had an expression, "Only those who writes letters gets letters". Weather, crops, who visited, who died, and who married were all topics covered in Claire's letters. As she went about her daily chores, she kept a mental note of anything that would be of interest in her correspondence. But her favorite subject was 'when are you coming to visit'? Will sometimes added a note thanking Maria and C.A. for pictures they had sent or commenting on the growth of the children. The news from Europe and the possibility of war worried the Kennedy's in both states and was a topic included in their letters as well. It looked even more likely that the United States would have to become involved. Each household looked forward to the letters that kept their relationships strong.

Sometimes when they received a letter from C.A. and Maria, Claire would say, "They're answering my letter." Then she would spend a long time reading and re-reading it. After a time Will would grow impatient and ask, "How are they getting along?" Then she would let him read the letter.

C.A. and Maria had always planned to take the twins to Missouri for a visit to see and be seen by relatives. They made notes of any tips they found for traveling with young children. They made a checklist of things they would need to take with them and took short trips to see what they had left off the list. They acquired two car baby beds and a small trailer to accommodate everything they would need for an extended trip. C.A. wrote to his mother, 'I bought a trailer today for when we bring the twins to Missouri.'

He got a letter by return mail. 'C.A., don't you put those babies in a trailer.'

C.A. promptly called his mother to explain that the trailer was not for the children but for all of the things they would need. The trailer proved to be very serviceable. They found they could arrange things so they were easily found when needed. C.A. fixed a holder for bottles and baby food on the manifold and a cover in front of the radiator to hold in the heat. They could open the engine hood and put a bottle of water or milk on the manifold. Food in metal containers could be warmed in about 5 minutes at 40 miles an hour. They would stop at tourist courts with a kitchenette so they could cook dinner and breakfast. A big pan with a lid was part of the necessary equipment so they could sterilize the bottles every evening.

The babies loved to ride and slept well in the car beds, and could be carried into the house without even waking up! The boys soon learned when they were getting ready to go somewhere.

Plans were perfected, the car and the trailer were loaded, and they left early on Monday, August 17th, planning to be away two or three weeks.

It worked out better to stop and rest at regular intervals anyway so they planned to stop at something interesting at feeding times. The schedule worked perfectly and the twins were on time for every feeding. They usually attracted some onlookers when they stopped. C.A.'s clever apparatus to heat the food on the manifold was applauded regularly.

When they arrived in Missouri, Claire and Will were so happy to have them and to finally see the twins they had heard so much about. Claire remarked, "I am glad they aren't at the stage where they are afraid of all strangers."

C.A. was surprised at the statement, but had to admit that even the grandparents were strangers to the boys. The uncles, aunts, and cousins were interested in the twins too. Those who could came to visit.

Lettie made the remark, "It is good to get together for a happy occasion and not a funeral. The twins are darling; I wish you lived closer so we could see them more often."

C.A. laughed, "You sound just like Mom!"

Minnie came up about that time, "C.A., I am glad that you have twins. Frank and I had our ups and downs but there was always a special bond between us. Your boys will enjoy growing up together."

"We have already noticed that as young as they are they do entertain each other."

It was time to re-load the car and trailer for the trip to Bradfield. Aunt Lula and the Stewart grandparents were looking forward to meeting the twins as well! It was fun for C.A. and Maria to visit Bradfield and visit with the Stewart relatives. At school, several teachers were getting ready for school to begin soon; it brought back happy memories. Maria could not resist saying, "Mr. Kennedy, I am so glad you came to Bradfield as our Principal. It has been a real pleasure to meet you!"

C.A. laughed, "It has been a real pleasure to meet you too!"

Their visiting time was over all too quickly, and they had to pack the car and trailer for the return trip to California. Both families were amazed that the children had traveled so well. C.A. said, "It was all in the planning." In later years they would talk about "another perfect trip."

In early October Maria suggested to C.A. that they make arrangements to have the twins Christened on October 16th in honor of the grand-parent's anniversary. Maria asked, "Do you think they would come to California for the occasion?"

C.A. laughed and said, "I don't think we could get Dad to come and Mom probably wouldn't come without him!"

Maria made arrangements at the Methodist Church in Taft and called Aimee and Malinda to be sure they would be there.

October 16th was a beautiful day and the twins were happy to be going on an outing. They looked so sweet in their white outfits with the soft blue trim. Maria had wrapped them in the blue blankets Aimie had given them. C.A. took their picture so they could share the occasion with the grandparents. Aimie's, Malinda's, and several families who had traveled from Brandton to California with Will's group were in the congregation. This was the first time the twins had gone to church; there were so many new things to see. The twins were quite calm during the service, it was their parents who were nervous but they had no cause for concern.

After the service C.A. and Maria invited Aimie's to have lunch with them. After lunch C.A. said, "I am going to call the folks since it is their anniversary. Hearing about the twins christening would make it even more special." Before he could pick up the telephone it started to ring. He answered it, and to his surprise it was Claire.

She was so excited she began talking as soon as C.A. answered the phone. "We just heard that the twins were christened this morning. Rebecca Pierce was at church there too. She called her Aunt Nellie here is Brandton."

C.A. began to laugh, "I had just started to call you folks to tell you about the Christening and that we remembered your anniversary. I am glad it was good news that traveled fast. Do we have a party line even at this long distance?"

The following December C.A. asked Maria what she wanted for her birthday. Her request was for a family picture taken at a studio. "Oh, how about one of just the boys?" asked C.A.

"They could have some separate ones as well, but I want one of both of us with the boys. If the picture is good we can have copies made to give everyone for Christmas," Maria replied.

"Oh, all right. I am sure it would please Mom," C.A. agreed. "That picture in the front bedroom at home was a Christmas present for the family when I was a baby. Mom had it made to surprise Dad. She had saved her egg money and also gave the photographer two extra chickens to pay for it. Dad had to admit he was pleased. I know how much Mom treasures it. Go ahead and make the appointment with the photographer."

The usual Christmas dinner that year was at Aimie and David's. There was quite a gathering of all the family. Claire and Will had sent the traditional sugar cured ham. Maria brought a cherry pie with Oregon cherries, Malinda brought potato casserole; the table was laden with food. After dinner C.A. presented each family a copy of the picture. It was received with many compliments.

Aimie exclaimed, "This is a wonderful photograph. You surely had one made for Claire and Will, too."

C.A. assured her they had. "Maria mailed it to them last week. I hope they got it before today."

148

"Let's call them and find out," David suggested.

When Claire answered the phone, David said "Merry Christmas to you both! Again this year we have all enjoyed your ham. I hope you never lose your special recipe!"

Claire said, "I'm glad you like Will's ham; you'll have to come back to the farm to try his new hot sausage because we can't send it to you. Is C.A. there, too?"

"Yes, I'll hand him the phone."

"C.A., your picture came in the mail yesterday. I am so pleased! I hung it in the front bedroom next to your baby picture. It doesn't seem like thirty-six years since you were the Christmas baby."

C.A. laughed, "It doesn't seem like that long to me either!"

Will walked up and held out his hand for the phone. "That's a mighty fine bunch of Kennedys in that picture." They talked a few minutes before Will gave the phone back to Claire.

Claire said, "It looks like Arthur's dimple in his chin is getting deeper, but it's not as deep as yours. I wish we could all be together today, but at least we can talk to you on the phone."

Everyone at the table had a turn exchanging Christmas greetings. Aimie said goodbye last and suggested that Will and Claire come to see them. She even offered to pay their way on the train if they would come.

Claire laughed and said, "That's a good offer. I'll talk to Will about it. I would love to come see all of you."

A short time later, Aimie was downtown shopping when she passed the photographer's studio. To her surprise the display in the window included an enlargement of the family photo.

The 1939 World's Fair was in San Francisco. Everyone was saying it was the best one in years. C.A. and Maria thought it would be a shame to miss it since it was so close. Maria shared the news about their visit:

> *Dear Mom,*
>
> *Malinda offered to keep Ansel and Arthur while we went to the World's Fair. She said she would rather stay home with them than bump elbows with the Fair crowd. We really appreciated her offer, and I know the boys did better with Aunt Malinda than they would have at the Fair.*
>
> *We had a wonderful time looking at all the exhibits and demonstrations. One of the most fascinating was a demonstration of how TV studios produce the picture to your TV set. The demonstrator even interviewed us for the program. We saw ourselves on tv! We also enjoyed the livestock exhibits. Dad would have been impressed*

at the size of the hogs and the weight of the cattle. You would have especially enjoyed the home management department.

When we got back to pick up the boys, James tried to impress us with a trick he had taught the boys. They were both playing with blocks when we arrived. James said, "Wink for your folks, Ansel and Arthur." Arthur laughed and winked again and again. But Ansel watched him for a minute and then continued working on his building. I guess he didn't feel like winking!

All our love,

C.A., Maria, and family

In one of her letters Maria mentioned that both of the boys said 'Mama' first. C.A. and Maria had a laugh when they got Will's short reply:

Dear Children,

Good to hear from you folks. Nice the twins are talking. C.A., you must spend more time talking to them and saying 'I am Daddy.' In no time they will be saying 'DaDa'.

Hope you can come visit again before long.

Love Grandpa

Maria said. "It would be nice to take the boys back to the farm to visit this summer. You know your folks would love it."
"Yes. Let's plan on that."

Back to Missouri Again

J.R. was beginning to think about going back to Missouri too. He had moved back and forth between Missouri and California twice already, and found that each place had something to offer. He really liked it in California, but Missouri was home and he missed it when he was gone. The California relatives always included him, but it wasn't the same. He needed to feel he really belonged to someone; he wouldn't admit it to anyone else, but he was homesick.

Suddenly he realized he could do whatever he wanted! He had saved enough money to buy a car and that had been the goal when he came to California this time. Tomorrow he would tell C.A.'s he was going home, then he would take the train and go. He knew Mom would be pleased. She would fix special food and fuss over him. And of course there was always the old gang to run around with and something going on. He felt better just from making the decision to go back home.

C.A. was not surprised when J.R. came by to tell them he was going home. "Don't tell Mom I'm coming, I want to surprise them."

"We will miss you but I know the folks will be glad to have you home. Tell them we send our love. We will probably settle down in Missouri ourselves someday. We can't get away from our roots," laughed C.A.

C.A. had been thinking about possibly moving back too. The twins would soon be two years old, and he didn't like the idea of the boys growing up looking at pictures of family they didn't really know.

C.A. said to Maria, "You know, I've been doing some thinking lately. We're doing fine here, and the salary is good with the Oil Company, but there is something missing when the only exciting thing about a job is payday. There is no excitement with this job, no challenge involved. I've realized lately that I really miss teaching. I spent all that time getting my master's degree so I feel like I should be using it. I would like the responsibility of being Superintendent. The weather is certainly a plus here, but I also think that if I am going back to teaching, I would rather teach in Missouri. What would you think?"

Maria was not surprised by his question. "I think it would be good for you to get back into teaching, and I know several people who would be happy to have us closer. We have tried to keep in close contact through letters and phone calls but that's just not as good as living close enough to be together often. You can't build very strong family bonds when you aren't together."

"It's decided then; we'll go back to Missouri. Since April is the time schools will be serious about finding replacements for next year, we ought to go as soon as we can make arrangements. I'll call and tell the folks the news."

He placed the call and exchanged greetings with his Mom before telling her their decision. "Mom, we're coming home!"

"Oh, good!" exclaimed Claire. "How long can you stay this time? I hope it is longer than the last time."

"We plan to find a place and stay this time. We're moving back to Missouri!"

"That's wonderful! When will you be here?"

"Maria and I just decided today, so it will be a few days before we can get everything taken care of here. Would it be all right for us to stay at the farm for a while until I can find a school?"

"Why, of course! Just let us know when you will be here. Will, they are moving back to Missouri!"

Will came over to the phone, "That is good news! Be careful driving back."

"We will! See you all before long. Bye for now."

After calling home, C.A. called to let Malinda and James know their plans.

Malinda said, "I'm glad to hear you are going back to teaching. We hate to see you leave California, but I have to admit you are right about being close to family. My children have always been very close to my parents because they were here in California, too. They hardly know the Missouri relatives even though we have visited when we could and tried to keep in touch with calls and letters. When will you be leaving?"

"We just decided today that we would be moving. It will take a few days to get everything arranged, but we need to make the move right away for the best chance at a position."

"We will miss all of you. It has been great being close and seeing the boys while they are small. We will keep in touch with you and your family, and we'd love to have you come back and visit."

"We will do our best. All of you will have to come visit us too."

Next C.A. called Aimie and David, "Aunt Aimie, Maria and I have decided to move back to Missouri. We decided we want the boys to grow up knowing their grandparents."

"I know a grandma who will be happy to hear that! I have been blessed through the years that my grandchildren live close. Give Claire and Will our love and do come to visit us when you can. You are always welcome here."

"We have enjoyed our years in California and especially have enjoyed being close to you and your family."

"Have a safe trip, C.A., and do plan to keep in touch!

C.A. and Maria began making plans for their move right away. C.A. gave his notice at the Oil Company; since he hadn't signed a contract, it was not a problem for him to leave immediately. A week later everything was packed and they were ready to head to Missouri. C.A. called Claire with the news. "Mom, we're leaving early in the morning and should get to the farm in four or five days. We have had practice by now and the boys are seasoned travelers!"

"Be careful."

"Of course we will."

The trip was long but uneventful; the boys entertained each other on the long drive. Springfield was on the way to the farm so C.A. planned to stop at the Southwest Missouri State Teachers College Placement Office on the way through. On the way to the Placement Office C.A. met a friend from his college days at the boarding house, Milton Walker. Milton had just placed an ad at the Placement Office about a Superintendent of Schools opening. He had held the position for eight years but now had an opportunity to go into a State Department position. He had two years left on a three-year contract as superintendent but his school board said they would release him from the contract if he could find a good replacement. He offered to recommend C.A. for the position and the two of them made arrangements for C.A. to meet with the school board for an interview. The school was only about thirty miles from Will and Claire's farm.

When they arrived at the farm, Will and Claire were happy to see them. The interview on Tuesday was an added bonus and seemed to forecast good things to come.

When Tuesday came, the interview went even better than C.A. had hoped. With no hesitation the board agreed to offer C.A. a contract, which he was pleased to accept. He was to start immediately to allow Milton to move on to his new job.

After the board meeting, C.A. thanked his friend and said, "I hope everything goes well for you in Jeff City. It will be nice to have a friend in the State Department. Now that I have a job, we will need to find a house."

Milton said, "I can help you with that too." He had a comfortable house that he was willing to rent or sell. C.A. decided to rent with an option to buy. He was anxious to get back to the farm with his good news. Everyone was excited; even the twins knew something good was happening!

In two weeks the family was settled in their new home, and C.A. was the new Superintendent at Grovesboro Schools. Maria said, "C.A. let's invite your parents over for Sunday dinner, and have Aunt Nancy and Uncle Andy too." C.A. though it was a good suggestion and offered to call with the invitations.

For dinner Maria prepared a large roast with carrots and potatoes, buttered peas, coleslaw, pickled okra, and her special angel food pie. Everyone enjoyed the meal. Claire said, "This roast is as good as Will's mother used to fix. You have prepared such a nice meal, Maria. It must have cost at least $5."

Maria just smiled and made no comment. After the family left, C.A. said, "I'll bet the roast by itself cost more than $5." Maria admitted it had. C.A. said, "Mom and Dad would both be unhappy if they had to buy their groceries at the store. They have always grown what they needed. I hope that will always be the case."

One extra job C.A. took on besides being Superintendent was the result of a group of students being interested in football. They came to C.A. and asked if the school could hire a football coach. When he told them that the budget wouldn't allow the expense of an additional coach they asked if he would coach if they got enough players for a team.

C.A. told the boys that he'd never coached football, but they persisted until he agreed to give it a try. It would be a learning experience for everyone.

C.A. got a book on football and rules. It had some good advice on equipment, drills, and other aspects of the game. C.A. was able to obtain uniforms from a neighboring school that had purchased new ones for their own team. The enthusiasm of the players impressed C.A. The boys seemed to know a great deal about the game and what positions they wanted to play. They had a good time learning more about the game. The boys were a quick study. When a problem came up C.A. would say, "Read your book."

Some of the boys were friends with the boys from Rollings, the school that gave them their old uniforms. They talked football when they got together. One thing led to another until a Rollings student suggested the two teams play a game for fun. C.A. cautioned his players. "You know that motto, 'It's not whether you win or lose but how you play the game'. Do you think you could take it like a good sport if you lose?"

They all said they could, but that they didn't intend to lose!

C.A. said, "That's the spirit! But read the book!"

The day of the big game came. The Grovesboro boys did everything by the book and to the surprise of everyone but the Grovesboro boys, they won the game with a score of 13 to 6. They were ecstatic over their win. When C.A. told Will and Claire about the unexpected results Will said, "Those boys must have really read that book and you must have read the book too!"

One evening as they watched the twins play at the city park Maria said to C.A., "Grovesboro is a pleasant little town with a lot of nice people, isn't it?"

"Yes, I think this has been a good move for all of us."

"You seem happy about things at school."

"I am. Milton said everything was going well when he left and I don't see any reason to make any changes; at least not now. The board has been supportive and the faculty members are all enthusiastic. I look forward to going to work now."

"I'm glad. I hope it will be just enough of a challenge to be better than the oil company job."

"So far it has been. Grovesboro is a good place for the boys also. It is nice to watch them play. I know what Mom means when she says she forgets about the problems of the world when she watches the children playing."

The War Years

The war clouds grew heavier when France and Britain officially declared war on Germany. The Selective Service in the county registered 2,028 men. The War Department established the Seventh Corps Area Training Center in the Mark Twain National Forest and named it Fort Leonard Wood. J.R. decided to make a little money by helping to build it. In May of 1941, the local newspaper reported that the fort was 92% complete and had 4,500 troops there.

Will and Claire remembered the way to 'make do' from their World War I days and got ready to do their part in the war effort. The Civilian Defense Volunteer opened in January. The Chamber of Commerce took the lead in establishing a Red Cross War Relief Fund. Auto tires were rationed to everyone; only eight tires were allotted for Kent County for the month of February. Will was thankful he wouldn't be needing any right away. He contributed all the metal he could find to the scrap iron supply.

Claire knitted scarves and sweaters again for the Red Cross. When the young housewives complained about War Ration Books for sugar, coffee, butter, and meat, she taught them how to manage with substitutes and gave them recipes she had used during World War I. Her favorite was the cake recipe made with honey instead of sugar; with her advice they learned to compensate quite well. They knew they were more fortunate than those overseas.

"If this war goes on I will eventually have to serve," J.R. told C.A. "If I volunteer before I'm drafted I can choose my job."

"And what would that be?" asked C.A.

"A cook."

"Well, why not?" replied C.A. "You always were better in the kitchen than the field."

In September, J.R. volunteered and was assigned to the kitchen at Fort Leonard Wood. He still had training to do but was relieved to know he got the job he wanted.

J.R. was home from Fort Leonard Wood fairly regularly, usually bringing a buddy along. They enjoyed the home cooking and it was a pleasure for Claire to fix meals that brought J.R. home often. One weekend in early October, J.R. surprised Claire by coming home alone.

"Where is your friend, J.R.?" she asked.

"He didn't come this time. Can I borrow the car tonight?

"Do you have plans?"

"I have a date."

"A date! Who with?"

"Leann Davis."

"Leann Davis! Isn't she a little young to go on a date?"

"Mom, she is seventeen now and quite grown up. Haven't you seen her lately?"

"I guess it has been awhile. Yes, you can borrow the car. I am sure that will be all right with your Dad."

After that, Claire noticed that J.R.'s visits seemed to get more frequent. He would visit a few minutes with her and Will, have a quick supper, and then ask to borrow their car. Then he would be gone all evening. She knew he was seeing Leann Davis as often as he could.

The family did what they could to ease military life for J.R. On his birthday C.A and Maria decided to make a surprise visit to the Fort. Claire offered to keep the twins for the day.

J.R. was sitting in the barracks when they arrived. 'What a way to spend a birthday,' he thought. 'Rain pouring down, and I didn't even get a lousy birthday card.' Just then C.A. stepped in the barracks and asked, "Is there a Private J.R. Kennedy here?"

J.R. was happy to see them. "I didn't think anyone remembered my birthday!"

"Well they did. Maria and I want to take you to the movies and Mom sent you a cake. We passed the theatre trying to find this place. The movie showing is prefect for the occassion; it is "Sergeant York", starring Gary Cooper."

J.R. said, "That movie was great. We need someone like Sergeant York to help us with this war. This has turned out to be a better birthday than I thought it would be. C.A., do you remember my last birthday in California? I do apologize to you and Maria for my behavior."

"Oh, it makes a good story," C.A. laughed. "Why, just last week I told someone about the time my brother wanted to borrow my car and asked me to have a drink with him for his birthday. I had to refuse you on both requests. Maria and I were going to a movie and I didn't want a drink beforehand. It sure would have been easier if I had accepted the drink then! You were back at the door again at midnight. Then, when I said I would have a drink with you for your birthday, you said, 'Oh, it's all gone'."

They all laughed at the memory. Maria said, "J.R., there was a girl back in California who wanted to change your merry ways."

"I know," said J.R. "She had plans for our future, but I just didn't feel that way about her! But there is a girl I've been dating that I would give up my wild and wicked ways for, and I don't want to wait too long. I think she is planning to go to St. Louis to work this summer and she might find someone else."

"Do I know her?" C.A. asked.

"You know the family. It's Leann Davis, Roscoe Davis' daughter."

"Oh yes, her brother was a star basketball player. Does Mom know about you and Leann? I know the folks would be pleased to have you married. Mom would be especially pleased that you are dating a local girl that she knows the family!"

"Mom knows I have been borrowing the car to go see Leann. I haven't asked Leann to marry me yet, but I may before long. The rumor going around has it that my group is going to be sent to a base in Columbia, South Carolina."

"Well, good luck with Leann. Let's hope that next year will bring peace to all countries. Until it does, you take care."

"Thanks for making my birthday special and tell Mom thanks for the cake. Say, C.A., do you still plan to teach for the Army Air Corps?"

"Yes, there is a program for instructors for the Army that I've been looking into. I applied last summer. If I am accepted, I will be teaching pilots and mechanics how to test engines and determine what kind of problems they might have. I think I will know soon. I don't think I'll be drafted since I am married and near the top of the age bracket, but I want to do something for the war effort. Who knows, we might be close enough to do some visiting. Well, we had better go; Mom probably won't close an eye even if the twins are sleeping away."

"She's had a good day. She and Dad are so happy to see the family going on. Having your boys close by has been great for the folks; they forget their aches and pains when the grandchildren are there."

"Yes, and Mom looks for reasons to keep them longer."

"You are right! I'm glad you and Maria came. Thank you for making my birthday special."

Most Americans had expected Japan to create an incident to bring the United States into the war but no one expected anything of the magnitude of the surprise attack on Pearl Harbor. It was unbelievable that such a thing could occur. The loss was incredible—19 ships sunk and 2,300 seamen lost. The country's determination to win was even more resolved than ever, if that could be possible. Everyone settled in to doing what they could—even World War I veterans tried to enlist again. One big difference between this war and the last for Will and Claire was the fact that this time they had sons and nephews who could be involved.

Claire wrote to Aimie and suggested that they come back to Missouri because Bakersfield was too close to the war now. Claire told her the farm could provide vegetables, eggs, meat, chicken, fruit, and plenty of honey; and it would be nice to have the company. Aimie elected to stay in California but said that if the war got too close they would all accept Claire's offer.

Christmas that year was more subdued than other years. The main topic, of course, was the war and how it affected all of their lives. Lucinda and Nat's son, John Russell, had chosen the Army as a career. Now news of war seemed even more real. It wasn't just going on 'over there'; one of their own was involved. The children played, opened gifts, and sang carols. They all agreed that it was good to be together.

That winter J.R. went to Brandton whenever he had a day off. After a visit and one of Claire's special meals, he would always borrow the car and visit Leann.

One weekend in April when J.R. was packing to go back to the Fort, Claire said, "Son, I have invited your Uncle Andy and Aunt Nancy for dinner next Sunday. Will you be home then?"

J.R. said, "Yes, I have the weekend off."

"Good, I would also like to invite Leann Davis."

J.R. gave Claire a big hug and kissed her on the cheek. "Is this your official 'welcome to the family' dinner? Do we have your approval?"

"You sure do have my approval, Son."

J.R. smiled, "Well I haven't officially asked Leann to be my wife, but I plan to soon. I'll call her right now to be sure she can come next Sunday."

Of course Leann was pleased with Claire's invitation to Sunday dinner. J.R. said, "Yes, she will be here for dinner Sunday. I heard several clicks; the party line is already spreading the news!"

After J.R. left, Claire called Nancy, "I hope you and Andy will come to dinner next Sunday."

Nancy replied, "You sound excited, who else is coming?"

"J.R. and Leann Davis!"

"Ooooh! Of course we will come."

Claire couldn't wait for Will to come in from doing the chores; she went to the barn to find him. "Will, J.R. is bringing Leann Davis to dinner next Sunday!"

Will replied, "That's nice."

Claire smiled and said, "You aren't fooling me, you are as happy as I am about it."

Will just smiled and made no comment.

Claire spent the week planning, cooking, and baking. By Saturday she had made apple and cherry pies, had the chicken ready to roast, and the dressing ingredients prepared; she was almost ready for the special Sunday dinner.

In the afternoon, J.R. came in from the Fort and remarked on the obvious preparations. "You have been busy this week, Mom. Is there anything you need me to do to help you get ready?"

"You can bring eight or ten potatoes, two jars of green beans, and a jar of sauerkraut, pickles, and beets from the cellar."

J.R. came back with the requested items, put them on the cabinet, and asked if there was anything else he could help with.

"Not anything more today. I'll wait till tomorrow to gather the things I want from the garden," Claire said. "Thank you for bringing the things from the cellar."

"I'll help you gather the things from the garden in the morning. There are some pretty flowers out front. Would it be all right if I picked some of them in the morning too?"

Claire told him that would be fine and thanked him again for his help before he asked to borrow the car and left for the evening.

After J.R. left, Claire called Nancy. "I can't believe the change in J.R! He actually asked what he could do to help me today. I don't think he's ever noticed my jonquils before, and now he wants to pick some for dinner tomorrow!"

Nancy laughed, "He must be serious about Leann!"

"I think so, too," agreed Claire. "It's about time!"

Sunday morning J.R. came in early for breakfast in very good spirits. "Mom, I'll go pick the things from the garden. Would you like for me to wash them too?"

"I can do that later, Son. Just bring in about two dozen radishes, a dozen onions, and three large bunches of lettuce." To herself she thought 'he's so excited about Leann coming today that he'd waste a lot of water!'

In addition to the vegetables, J.R. also brought in a large handful of jonquils. "Would it be all right to put these in Grandma Lefever's vase?"

"Yes, that would be nice."

Sunday dinner was everything Claire had hoped for. J.R. and Leann were sweet together and Claire was sure wedding bells would be ringing soon. Leann did seem much more grown up than her seventeen years. Claire reminded herself that she was only eighteen when she and Will married.

Being in the military made J.R. appreciate letters, especially letters from Leann!

Dear J.R.,

Hope you got back to Camp with time to spare. I enjoyed Sunday dinner at your home. You have a nice family. I hope they liked me!

I am going to St. Louis soon to look for a job. As you know, there aren't any jobs here in Brandton. I think we pretty well discussed our plans for the future last weekend! I know you plan to save some of your pay. Now I want to save a little extra money, too.

How did you do in the Mess Hall today? You probably are a better cook than I am. You can teach me. We will have fun cooking together.

Yours truly,
Leann

Over the next few months J.R came to Brandton whenever he had time off at the fort. Claire's instincts were correct. J.R. told the family he and Leann were planning to be married. They hadn't set the date because he wanted to see where his unit would be stationed and Leann wanted to work awhile first. Claire made sure the party line spread the news!

Dear J.R.,

When I got to St. Louis everyone I talked to told me I had to come back to Brandton to get the School Superintendent to sign a form saying I graduated. Since I am just 17 he has to verify that I will be eligible to work. Uncle Joe said I could stay with them. I am going back up tomorrow.

You take good care. I love you.

Yours truly,
Leann

Dear J.R.,

> *I got a job in a Pencil Factory. The salary is not too great but the work is easy. The job I wanted would have paid more money but my uncle wanted me to turn it down. He said the place was in an area that wasn't safe for me and the workers were ruffians. He probably knows best. I miss you!*

> *Yours truly!*
> *Leann*

In early November 1942, J.R.'s unit was transferred to Fort Jackson Army Base in Columbia, South Carolina. Claire was just getting used to J.R. leaving Missouri when C.A. received word he had been accepted to the instructors' position for the Army and would be reporting to Champaign, Illinois for training in late November. Maria and the boys would be staying in their home in Grovesboro during his training and in the spring they would all go to Seymour Johnson Army Base near Goldsboro, North Carolina. Claire was very proud that both of her sons were doing their part for the war, but she was not looking forward to the families being so far apart.

C.A. and Maria had been discussing what plans they could make for Christmas. It was difficult, especially when all services were being delayed. The mail, trains, and buses all had problems. For C.A. and Maria the mail service was the biggest annoyance. Although they wrote frequently it was almost impossible to put events in the right time frame. That led to a mix-up at Christmas.

C.A. originally thought he would have plenty of time off to come home for Christmas, then the Administration decided they needed to escalate the program and shortened the time off for all personnel. He wrote Maria about the change and said she and the boys should come to Illinois.

About the same time C.A. wrote to her, she wrote to him to 'come home for Christmas, even if you have just a few days'.

The letters crossed in the mail, and they both made plans too hastily. They were probably in Rolla at the train station within an hour of each other.

When Maria and the boys arrived in Champaign, a man came up to her and asked if she was Mrs. Kennedy. He told her he was in the same program as C.A. and that he recognized them from their pictures. Then he told her that C.A. had left for Missouri earlier that day.

They decided that it wouldn't take C.A. long to figure out what had happened when there was no one there to meet him, and that the best thing for Maria and the boys to do was to stay in Champaign until C.A. contacted them. C.A.'s friend took them to C.A.'s house to wait.

When C.A. arrived at the station and there was no one to meet him, he called Claude Howell. Claude told C.A. that he had taken Maria and the boys to the train that morning to go to Champaign. C.A. quickly called his home in Champaign to be sure Maria was there and told them he was on his way back. He was exhausted when he finally arrived back in Champaign.

Ansel and Arthur enjoyed playing in the snowdrifts which remained from the last snow. They weren't ready to leave their Dad when it came time to go. Maria reminded them about their Christmas presents waiting for them in Missouri.

It was a Christmas C.A. and Maria would always remember, but they both vowed to be more careful in making plans in the future.

In January, Maria took the boys to visit Will and Claire for a few days. Snow was predicted and Maria thought it would be fun for all of them to be snowed in together.

When she called to be sure it would be all right with the folks for them to visit, Claire said, "Of course. Will never likes being snowed in. He will enjoy having the boys here to entertain. Do hurry on over before the storm comes."

Maria laughed, "We'll head your way soon and be there in about an hour." Everyone enjoyed the companionship, and the twins had a great time. They loved going out with Grandma and Grandpa to 'help' with the chores. They enjoyed playing in the snow, knowing Grandma would have big sugar cookies and hot chocolate waiting for them inside. In the evenings Grandpa made popcorn and shared stories about times when he was a boy.

Ansel and Arthur spent hours looking at the Sears catalogue. They especially liked some play soldier suits that were pictured and talked about how much fun they would be. Claire told the boys she would get the suits for them if her hens laid well.

When it was time for Maria and the boys to leave Claire said, "I'm so glad you came. Can you all come over every time it snows?"

Maria laughed, "Maybe the ones this winter; it will be hard to do once we go to North Carolina."

"I know," said Claire; "that's why we want to spend as much time with the boys as possible before you leave."

In February, all the families had a surprise announcement in the mail. Will brought the mail in and called to Claire, "We have a letter from Frank."

Claire told him, "Go ahead and open it; I'm busy."

Will opened the letter and gave a big 'whoop'. "Come in here. You aren't too busy for this!"

Claire came in a hurry and Will handed her the letter. Claire read it and began laughing. "After all these years they marry on Valentine's Day and are coming back home."

She had barely finished speaking when the telephone began to ring. It was Lettie. "Did you know that Frank and Ruth married and are retiring to the Stimson's place?"

"Yes," Claire told her, "we know. I guess they sent announcements to all of us."

"Why get married after being together all of these years?" Lettie said. "She is 60 if she's a day! What would Ma have said?"

"I think your mother would be pleased; Ruth is a fine person." They always said they would know when the time was right," Claire replied.

"She's a little too modern for me," Lettie retorted, "and too modern for Ma too."

Claire added, "I think it will be nice to have them at our gatherings; just like old times!"

Will laughed when the call was over. "Well, I'm glad they are coming home. I always knew it would turn out all right."

Claire replied, "I'm glad, too! Ruth always added something interesting to our gatherings."

Claire was even more excited about another marriage in the family! J.R. and Leann had set a wedding date. J.R. planned to take the train from Columbia, South Carolina to St. Louis. Leann knew he would arrive on March 8th but she didn't know which train he would be able to catch. A big snowstorm made travel difficult on the day J.R. was to arrive. Leann dressed in her blue wedding suit with the lace collar and made the trek to the station in time for the first train in spite of the storm. No, J.R. this time! Three trips later J.R arrived looking handsome in his uniform. They were married at the court house by a Justice of the Peace; then they collected Leann's belongings, and traveled by train back to Columbia.

J.R. had arranged for a tiny apartment on the base and Leann made it as homey as she could. In March, C.A.'s training in Champaign, Illinois was finished. He came back home to Grovesboro to get ready for the move to North Carolina.

C.A. and Maria made one last trip to visit Will and Claire before they left for North Carolina. They would store some things at the farm during the few years they would be gone. They told Claire she should use the refrigerator instead of just storing it.

C.A. said "I know you'll like the convenience, Mom, but Dad may not like the bigger electric bills."

"I am thrilled to have a refrigerator! If your dad is unhappy about the electric bill, I will use my egg money."

C.A. laughed. "Your egg money always comes in handy."

Claire said, "When you get to North Carolina, the visits will be few and far between. We will miss you. I am glad you have been closer for awhile."

Maria said, "It has been a special time for all of us to be back in Missouri."

"We will keep in touch," C.A. promised."

It was especially hard for her to see C.A.'s moving away because they were expecting their third child in May. Claire would have loved to have the next grandchild close by, but she knew C.A. was looking forward to his new job and seeing a new part of the country.

After they arrived in Goldsboro, C.A. and Maria had a few days to look for a place to live. Claire was glad to get a letter soon after they were settled and shared the news with Will. "Maria writes that they found a very nice apartment in a wonderful old Colonial house a short distance from Goldsboro. It has lots of windows and a wrap-around porch. Upstairs has another porch and a balcony. She says they would have loved to have the whole house, but there are three other apartments. They are downstairs, which is better for the boys. C.A. says his instructor's job is going well and that it is quite different than teaching high school. He says the warm sunny days are quite a change from Missouri snow."

Letters told about C.A. and Maria's friends whose husbands would soon be sent overseas. Maria told about Ansel and Arthur standing at the end of the walk waving to the soldiers passing through on the trains. Claire smiled to picture the boys' waves being returned by the soldiers. Claire liked stories about the boys even though reading the stories made her miss them even more. Claire was happy about the maid named Clissia that their landlady had found to help C.A. with the boys. The $5 a day they would have to pay Clissia seemed like too much money!

Claire wished she could go to North Carolina to help. She could just picture C.A. and Maria sitting on the porch of the big Colonial house watching the twins play. She would have loved being a part of the preparations for the new baby. But she was thankful that neither of her boys had been sent overseas.

Often when Maria would write to Will and Claire, Ansel and Arthur would want her to ask how Grandma's chickens were doing. It puzzled Maria until one day a package arrived addressed to Ansel and Arthur. It contained two play soldier suits from Claire. Finally Maria understood why the twins had been interested in Grandma's chickens! Maria took pictures of the twins in the suits and sent them to Grandma along with thank-you notes she helped the twins write.

C.A. wrote that he liked having time to play with the boys when he came home from work in the evening, and that he and Maria enjoyed sitting on the porch after the boys were bathed and in bed. Will nodded his satisfaction when C.A. wrote that it reminded him of the porch at the farm but that it wasn't as peaceful there. It reminded Will again of how glad he was to have the farm and own his own land, in spite of what he'd given up to get it.

Will enjoyed the letters from C.A. and Maria, but he didn't get as excited over them as Claire did. She was usually still reading when he headed back to work. Or else she was calling Nancy or someone else in the family to pass along the latest news.

It was Claire who kept C.A., Maria, J.R. and Leann up to date with what was happening in Missouri. She told them about the weather and the farm. She told them the news from family and friends; she told them about weddings, births, and funerals.

Claire was also the one who shared the news she received with the rest of the family. Claire was especially excited when she shared the news with everyone that Maria had written that she was keeping her things ready to go to the hospital because the doctor said it wouldn't be long before there was a new Kennedy baby!

May 18, 1943

Early on the morning of May 18, Maria awakened C.A. and told him they needed to go to the hospital. They told their landlady they were leaving, kissed the sleeping boys, and were on their way. They didn't have to wait too long for the arrival of William Ryan Kennedy. C.A. went back to check on the twins and tell them they had a new brother; then he called his folks to tell them that they had a healthy new grandson and that mother and baby were doing fine. Claire's pleasure was evident in her voice when C.A. told her the new baby's name. "Your Dad will be so pleased."

The next day C.A. dressed the twins and brought them to the hospital. They came tiptoeing into Maria's room and looked around. Ansel asked, "Where are the babies?"

Maria explained, "We only got one this time."

"Why?" they wanted to know. "We thought we would get two!"

Maria said, "I am just thankful you are all so healthy. You boys look so handsome! C.A., I'm so glad you brought Ansel and Arthur today. You have them scrubbed and brushed and polished. Children usually aren't allowed in the patient's rooms. How in the world did you manage to get them in?"

C.A. laughed, "I didn't realize they wouldn't get to come in, so I got them ready to come to see you. The receptionist said we could come on in anyway because the boys looked so clean and neat!"

"You did a good job. This is a wonderful surprise! I am so happy. I love all of you. I will be so glad to come home!"

Within a few days they had a letter from Claire.

Dear Family,

I told your Dad "At last you have your William". I told him he should do something special for his namesake. It is too bad they called in all of the gold a few years ago and we don't have $50 gold piece to give William Ryan like your Grandma Kennedy gave her namesake, Elizabeth Kate. Your Dad is sending William Ryan $5.00. He said tradition dies hard for the Kennedy's.

I am so proud that C.A. is a good father. He must have really done a good job getting the boys ready to visit you in the hospital if they made an exception and let them come in anyway.

We have had a lot of rain this spring. I hope it isn't as dry this summer as it was last. We have the garden planted now and we are enjoying the lettuce, radishes, onions and peas. There are already little tomatoes on the plants your Dad started in the parlor window. I hope you can come back this summer to help us eat all we have planted.

Love,
Grandma

Dear Grandpa,

Thank you for William's $5.00. We have started a savings account in his name with it. We will bring William and the boys to see Grandpa and Grandma as soon as C.A. can get some time off. The twins were surprised we got only one baby this time. They thought we would get two!

I hope you're still having enough rain and that your garden is still doing well. Think of us when you're enjoying all the fresh, home-grown vegetables.

Grandma, the boys certainly enjoy their soldier suits. Thank you again for sending them.

Take good care of each other. We miss you.

Love,
Maria and family

At last the War Housing Project near the Base was ready for C.A.'s. The whole family was happy to have the larger place with a spacious, safer play area. Playmates were always available for the twins. C.A. was now closer to his work and he could join the family for lunch. It was close to the stores, near the Community Center, and just a short distance from the Field.

One of the residents had a teen-age daughter who wanted to be a teacher. She volunteered to do a story hour twice a week at the

Community Center. The twins adored Miss Margaret and looked forward to each session. Everyone in the complex was connected with the Base and the wives had a lot in common and formed lasting friendships. The boys liked the new place because they could see the planes better; adults and children alike would stop what they doing to watch the planes. When the B-17s started pulling gliders there was a lot of speculation regarding what part they would play. Rumors were going around that something big was being planned and gliders would be used to take troops and supplies behind enemy lines.

> *Dear Grandma and Grandpa,*
>
> *We are all doing fine and hope you are too. The children keep us busy and we rarely have any leisure time. There is always something to do. All of us are enjoying the new apartment. It is larger and more convenient. The boys like it because Daddy can come home for lunch.*
> *The boys are fascinated with the planes. C.A. knows all about the different planes and is teaching the boys; they enjoy telling me what kind of plane we are watching. Lately we are seeing the B-17s towing gliders. It makes me sad to think about those boys training to go to war. I know you are glad that J.R. isn't flying, and so are we. We pray that God will watch over John Russell and keep him safe.*
> *Take care of each other. We miss you.*
>
> *Love,*
> *Maria and family*

Will and Claire continued to do what they could for the cause. Everyone kept abreast of the news. Already their community had suffered losses. A neighbor boy, who had been listed as a POW in the Philippines, was reported dead. Two other prisoners were from their County as well. The community was thankful for a short wave radio message saying that one, a U.S. Army Nurse, had been released. They knew it was just the beginning of more war casualties. The news that a concentration camp had been built at Fort Leonard Wood for enemy aliens seemed to bring the war even closer to home.

When the grandparents heard that William was scheduled to be christened at the Methodist Church in Goldsboro in early July, Will decided they would go by bus to be there for the occasion. Both C.A. and

Maria were surprised but very pleased. They knew what a trial the bus ride would be for Will and Claire, but it showed them how important the children were to the grandparents. Will was quite moved to see his namesake christened. It was a good visit for all of them. William liked all the extra attention he received and he was outstanding in a knitted suit the shade of his Irish blue eyes.

Some things went on as usual. "Oklahoma" opened on Broadway; Frank and Ruth went but had to go by train because of the rationing of gasoline for cars.

When C.A. got his orders to report to Keesler Air Force Base near Biloxi, Mississippi, he and Maria both knew the routine and were soon ready for the move. With wisteria, magnolias, and dogwood in bloom, spring was a beautiful time to see the south for the first time.

After staying for a few days in a small tourist court, they were glad to move to the new house C.A. had been promised in the government housing area.

On June 6, 1944, Allied forces invaded Normandy with the greatest amphibious landing in history. They felt that war was at last nearing an end. Everyone was shocked and saddened by President Roosevelt's death a few months later. The whole country lamented the fact that he hadn't lived to see the end of the war.

V-E Day on May 8, 1945 ended the war with Europe.

Missourians were confident Vice President Truman could step up and be a good President. They were right. President Truman warned Japan the atomic bomb would be dropped unless they surrendered. Japan did not surrender; the Enola Gay was ordered to drop the atomic bomb on Hiroshima, Japan, on August 6, 1945 and a few days later, on August 9, another bomb on Nagasaki. This action saved countless lives for all countries involved and hastened the end of the terrible war. Japan had not warned us that they were going to bomb Pearl Harbor; the Kennedy's and rest of the country agreed that President Truman had done the right thing and was a good President. On V-J Day, September 2, 1945 the war was officially over! With jubilation and relief the country started to return to what they liked to think of as normal.

J.R. had decided not to reenlist when his time was up and had gotten out of the military. He and Leann decided to visit C.A. and Maria on their way back to Missouri; it was a good, getting acquainted visit. Maria and Leann were friends immediately, a friendship that was to last the rest of their lives.

In November, Leann wrote that J.R. had a job with the State Department in Jefferson City and she had found a job as a secretary that she was happy about.

They were all glad the war was over. It was a great feeling to make decisions without worrying about what would happen with the war. C.A. and Maria had long talks about their next step. They liked the Gulf Coast very much, and the weather was great the year around. Best of all there were plenty of teaching jobs, both for the government and in the public schools. They decided to stay in Mississippi for a few years. C.A. said, "Let's see about having the wringer washing machine shipped down here now. I know Mom has never even used it."

Maria said, "Oh, yes, that would be such a help. It will be so much easier than using the washboard."

J.R. and Leann wrote that they had bought a new car. C.A. invited them to visit and to bring Will and Claire along. It was a great visit; the men fished while the women and the children enjoyed the beach. Claire especially enjoyed a trip to New Orleans. Will enjoyed the time with the boys. Claire noticed that Will seemed to take a special interest in William, and decided that was because William was his namesake.

Time went at a leisurely pace, the twins were in school, little William turned two, and Maria was expecting another baby in November. Claire offered to come back down and take care of the boys when the baby came. It would be a change for her too. She had missed being with them and welcomed an opportunity to be 'Grandma'.

November 28, 1945

C.A. sent his mother a train ticket to come down the last week in November. Claire left Will with her cousin, Effie, to cook for him while she was gone. Will knew from the start that he wasn't going to be happy with the arrangements. Sure enough, he was right! Cousin Effie made carrot cakes instead of pies, scones instead of pancakes, and he wasn't sure what she did to the meat. But Claire was having a great time with the family. She liked the beach and sitting on the seawall but she didn't like the water.

It was a foggy night when C.A. and Maria awakened Claire and told her they were on the way to the hospital. Claire was getting breakfast when C.A. returned. "I have great news for everyone," he said. "We have a baby girl! Her name is Elizabeth Susan."

The room became a hubbub of excitement. Claire said, "I wouldn't take anything for my boys but I always wanted a girl too. It is nice to add a girl to the family. Which name will you call her?"

C.A. answered, "Maria thought 'Susan' since it is shorter and easier for the boys to say."

"Maria will be good at making bows and curls and frills and ruffles. I know I never would have been able to do them."

C.A. said, "Well, I can't count the times you had to tie my necktie."

Claire laughed, "I was glad when you learned to tie your own tie!"

When they called Will to tell him that Susan had arrived, he said, "That is good news; it's time the family had a girl of the Kennedy name after 37 years. Now when is Claire coming home? I have about had it with Cousin Effie's cookin!"

C.A. told his Dad that Mom would be coming home at the end of the week and that they would let him know her arrival time.

Will replied, "It can't be too soon for me!"

Claire reveled in taking care of her grandchildren. She enjoyed the neighbors dropping by to check on the family. She baked big sugar cookies for the children and their classmates who stopped by on their way home from school. She told C.A. "This has been a vacation for me. But it seems as if your Dad is not enjoying Cousin Effie's cooking. She cooks things the way she likes instead of what he wants. I guess I had better get home before he tells Cousin Effie what he thinks of her cooking!"

They had a special dinner for Claire the evening before she left. The children gave her a bag of shells they had gathered for her on the beach. The shells pleased her even more than the hard-to-get nylon stockings they gave her. They all began to tell her how much they had enjoyed her visit.

Claire said, "I hope you come back to Missouri and find a place near us so we can see the family often."

C.A. replied, "In a few years we will probably come back to Missouri, but we are all enjoying the coast. We like the temperature being so mild the year around; it is good for the children, too. They would enjoy being in a big Missouri snow, but I can't say I would. In fact, I planted a magnolia tree in our yard. It will take a few years, but we like it so much here in Mississippi that we might live here long enough to see it bloom."

Claire replied, "We have dogwood and red bud trees that are mighty pretty in the spring."

"So you've reminded me before," C.A. laughed. "All right, we'll visit in the spring to see them."

They all went with Claire to the depot. She held Susan all the way. It was very exciting for the children to be at the station. Claire was just as excited and so moved by their hugs and kisses of farewell.

Will and Cousin Effie met Claire at the depot at Rolla. It was a joyous reunion. Even the news that Cousin Effie had baked a carrot cake just for the homecoming didn't dim their spirits.

They were all eager to get back to their everyday routines. Will enjoyed Claire's roasted chicken, biscuits, and cherry pie and told Claire he was glad she was home!

C.A. and Maria enjoyed living close to the Gulf and thought that everyone would enjoy having a boat for family outings. C.A. had built a boat several years earlier and had it stored at the farm in Missouri. The estimated $25 to $50 cost to ship the eighteen-foot wooden boat was much less than it would cost to buy another one.

C.A. wrote and told Will and Claire that he had arranged to have a freight company pick up the boat and deliver it to Biloxi.

Two weeks later the boat was delivered to their door. The delivery-man said the shipping costs were $30. Maria found exactly that amount in her purse. It was a good thing she had the full amount when the boat arrived, because she wasn't sure they would have left the boat without receiving the money. C.A. and the twins went out frequently and brought fresh seafood back to the others. They dug for oysters, netted shrimp, and caught various kinds of fish; sheepshead and flounder were their favorites.

The boys had looked forward to having a new playmate but they guessed they would have to wait awhile before Susan could play with them. In the meantime they took turns holding her and bringing Maria the things Susan needed and sometimes things she didn't need!

When Susan arrived, Aunt Lula had sent her grandniece a lovely christening dress. The twins were anxious for the occasion to see how the dress would look.

C.A. made the arrangements and they all got ready. When they got to the church they were ushered down to the front pew. The minister asked all of the family to come up for the ceremony. Afterwards the church secretary asked the twins to sign the certificate for Susan's christening. They were so pleased and proud they could sign.

It was a special occasion and the brothers liked the christening dress so much they didn't understand why Susan couldn't wear it often. Pictures were taken for Claire and Will and, of course, for Aunt Lula too.

Back in Missouri, a problem developed. Will was seldom ill; he hardly ever even had a cold. But for some reason he wasn't feeling well and he couldn't understand why. He thought the feeling would pass in a few days. He was sure he would wear it out before it got worse, but he didn't. He was doubling over with pain when Claire decided to call Dr. Holmes.

In a few minutes Will said, "Call Doc back, I've gotten easy."

"No, I want to know what caused you so much pain."

In a short time the doctor was there. As soon they told Dr. Holmes Will's symptoms he said, "Will, this is serious. You have appendicitis and your appendix has ruptured; that is why you got easy. You are going to have to go to the hospital in St. Louis. You can't go in a car; you will have to go by ambulance. Claire can go with you. Claire, pack a bag. Call Nat to meet you at the hospital and call Andy to look after the place. Now hurry, we have to move!"

Andy assured them everything would be taken care of while they were gone. Claire was ready before the ambulance arrived and they were soon on their way. The Doctor rode with the driver and told him to make all the speed he could, because it was critical to get Will to the hospital as fast as possible. After the appendix has ruptured, chances of survival were not at all good. Dr. Holmes hadn't wanted to alarm Claire by telling her how serious the situation was, he had called ahead so everything would be ready at the hospital when the ambulance arrived.

Dr. Holmes had given Will a shot before they left home and he slept all the way. Claire was bewildered by the rushed arrangements and wondered how she would manage when they got to the hospital; she hardly noticed how fast they were going.

When they pulled up to the hospital entrance, a medical team met them and rushed Will to the operating room. A nurse and an aide showed Claire to Will's room but told her the operation would take awhile and that she might want to walk around instead of waiting in the room. By that time Nat and Lucinda had arrived, and Claire was relieved to have someone to keep her company.

Lucinda invited Claire to stay with them while Will was in the hospital. "Nat has to go to work but we will be back tonight to take you home with us." It would be a much better arrangement than trying to sleep in a chair at the hospital.

Claire didn't know how long she had been waiting, but she was standing at the window crying when the nurse came in. "It won't be too much longer until they will be bringing your husband back. We can't have you crying when he gets here."

Claire said, "I'll be all right by then."

Dr. Holmes came in to see Claire. "I am pleased to be able to tell you Will is going to make it! A few years ago a ruptured appendix was almost always fatal, but we have a new drug called Penicillin that has just lately come into use and it has worked wonders. Will is lucky that his clean living and hard work gave him a strong body and that we got him here in time."

Claire was feeling more cheerful by the time they brought Will to the room. They told her he wouldn't be aware of much for a while, but she could sit by him. They would be in often to check on him, but he was doing unusually well considering the circumstances.

Claire was sitting by the bed when Will began to mumble. She moved closer and couldn't believe what she heard. "Jessie, I am so sorry I couldn't marry you but I didn't have anything. Claire had a farm. Oh, I feel so terrible; I just want to sleep."

Claire had never been so hurt and angry. She cried again, but this time they were tears of anger. The letter had been true! Jessie had been right to think Will was going to marry her, and the blue dress at the dressmakers was to have been Jessie's wedding dress. She knew now that Will had married her instead of Jessie because of the farm.

After more angry tears, reason returned. Claire asked herself where she would be now if it hadn't been for Will. He had worked tirelessly on the farm, and to face the facts, there had been no one else who wanted to marry her. She couldn't have hired anyone to work the place. By now she could have been a lonely old maid, barely getting by. She might have lost the farm and had to go live with some of the relations. Instead she had a hard-working husband, two outstanding sons, and one of the best farms in the community. She might not like Will's reason for marrying her, but her life was better because he had.

J.R. and Leann came later that evening and were relieved that Will's surgery had gone better than the doctors had expected. C.A. took the train to St. Louis and a taxi to the hospital. They all stayed at the hospital until the doctors assured them Will would be fine.

C.A. called Maria, "Dad is going to be all right! I will be home tomorrow."

Maria replied, "I am so relieved; our prayers have been answered!"

When Will was on the road to recovery he asked, "Did I say anything foolish when I was coming to from the ether?"

Claire couldn't tell him what he'd really said. "You said 'Claire, cut me another piece of that cherry pie.' You must have been hungry."

Back to Missouri to Stay

Claire and Maria, with an occasional note tucked in from Will or C.A., kept each family abreast of family happenings. Each letter from Claire would include, "When are you coming home?" or "My how the children have grown. I wish I could see them more often."

Each letter to Missouri contained a picture or two of the children and the promise they would be coming to visit before too long.

Each time they received a letter from a family member telling about the 4th of July picnic, the church ice cream social, someone's birthday, someone's wedding, or someone's funeral, either C.A or Maria would say or think, 'we missed that too.' They both began to realize just how much they had enjoyed a close family as they were growing up. Each family had found time to get together and share the happy times and the sad times.

"Should we stay here in Biloxi?" was a frequently asked question. C.A. said, "We both enjoy the beach, fishing in the Gulf, the weather is mild most of the year, and no snow to shovel. I do enjoy teaching adults but I must admit I miss the young people. Before the war, I enjoyed the responsibility and challenge as Superintendent at Grovesboro. I keep thinking that we really should be closer to the folks. They are getting on in years now, and I can't expect the cousins to see what their needs are."

"You're right," Maria agreed. "Our children should know them better. We have tried to stay in touch with letters and phone calls but it just isn't the same! Have you noticed when we are there your folks both seem to perk up when the children are telling what they are doing?"

Yes, they both wanted to go home to Missouri!

"I must say you have always been great in making all the moves my livelihood has caused," C.A. commented.

"It has been enjoyable. We have many good friends we wouldn't have known and the children have learned about different parts of the country. Now it is time for them to know their relatives."

"And for the relatives to know them," C.A. laughed.

"We need to make a trip home anyway so we may as well combine business and pleasure," C.A. said.

When C.A. called home to share the news that they would be coming to Missouri, Claire was excited, "How long will you be staying? I hope you stay longer than the last time?"

C.A. laughed, "Can we stay at the farm again until I find a job at a school?"

"You mean you're moving back to Missouri! Of course you can stay here as long as you like!"

"We should be there in about a week."

"It seems like we've had this conversation before," laughed Claire. "Be careful, son."

Claire made sure the party line spread the good news!

The children always liked traveling, especially when it included a visit to Grandma and Grandpa's farm.

In just a few weeks C.A. found a position as Superintendent at Elmwood, about a 30-minute drive from the farm.

It didn't take them long to get settled and for Elmwood to feel like home. They liked the community, the school, and the church. So many of the ones in town had relatives in Brandton, it was like having an extended family. Through the years, each of them would consider Elmwood to be home. Elmwood was the only place where the entire family lived at the same time.

They all enjoyed living in Missouri. Most weekends, especially in the summer time, meant going to the farm. The children looked forward to

Grandpa's story time in the evenings and Grandma's roasted chicken, sauerkraut, chiffon cake, and especially her cherry pie! Susan liked the freedom to run in the big lawn and chase Pal, the little family dog. The boys liked to roam the farm and even enjoyed helping out with the chores.

They enjoyed the traditional 4th of July picnic each year, church ice cream socials, special birthdays, weddings, and Christmas celebrations. Shared family times made happy memories for all.

After renting a place in Elmwood for a few years, C.A and Maria bought a large, shady area at the edge of town and built their dream home. It was the first home they had ever owned. Claire took it as a sign that they really intended to stay in Missouri for good!

They had left their refrigerator for Claire to use while they were in North Carolina. Places they had lived since then had always had a refrigerator furnished. Maria told C.A. "We can't just take the refrigerator back. Let her have it and we will get another. They are hard to find and we may have to wait awhile. It will be easier for us to get another one than for her."

C.A. agreed and borrowed the old icebox from his folks to use until he and Maria could get another refrigerator. "I remember you have to empty the water from the icebox as the ice melts. I know what I'll do with the water. I'll use it on the two elm trees I set out. Johnny Appleseed set out apple trees; I like to set out shade trees."

Maria replied, "You have planted trees everywhere we have lived. It will be special to be able to watch these trees grow."

From time to time through the years when they enjoyed the shade from those trees, C.A. would comment, "That ice box water must have been good for those trees I set out. They are beautiful now."

The first time J.R. and Leann brought the folks to visit, Will said, "You have a fine place here, but I still like the farm." C.A. understood what his dad meant.

C.A. shared an incident with his folks that brought him satisfaction. Elmwood needed a coach, and C.A. had posted the vacancy in the placement office at SMS and started spreading the word about the opening. Good news travels fast, and he soon had a call from John Tolbert, one of the players on his first football team at Grovesboro. John had just finished his degree in physical education at SMS and was looking for a teaching position. C.A. made arrangements for John to interview with the school board. The board accepted C.A.'s recommendation and hired John as the new coach.

After the interview, John shook C.A.'s hand firmly and said, "Thank you Mr. Kennedy! Since those high school days, it has been my goal to be a coach like you. You probably didn't realize at the time what an influence you had in my life. Before you came to Grovesboro my biggest thrill was having a good time on Saturday nights. After you came, I knew I wanted to amount to something. Your advice to 'read the book', 'play by the rules', and 'make us proud of you' was probably the best anyone has ever given me. You really made a difference in my life."

C.A. was pleased to know that John gave him credit for changing the direction of his live and told his dad about his former student. After he finished the story, C.A. said, "Dad, that is one of the biggest thrills for a teacher; when years later a student tells you that you changed his life!"

"That means you did a good job."

Claire was excited when she learned that Maria and C.A. were expecting another baby; since they lived close now, she would see this one grow up!

Early in December 1954 Maria started pondering what to do to make Christmas special for the family this year. They planned to attend the church Candlelight Service on Christmas Eve and the Sunday School Christmas program. J.R. and Leann were coming and bringing Will and Claire, as one of them put it, "for an old fashion' Christmas". Everyone hoped the new baby would arrive during the holidays.

The children gathered pine cones from a nearby tract of timber and Maria used them to add fragrance to the Christmas boxes for the family. Christmas cards were sent out early with enclosed letters and pictures in many of them.

A large tree was set up in the living room and decorated with bubble lights. There was lots of popcorn on hand for munching when they gathered around the tree and shared Christmas stories.

Gifts for each of the children, C.A., J.R., Leann, and the grandparents were wrapped in colorful Christmas paper. There was enough food and eggnog on hand for all who might come by.

The day of the Christmas visit was a happy atmosphere. Food, gifts, and laughter were shared by all. They made contact with other relatives and wished them happy holidays. Maria's eggnog may have helped make a very congenial group. They were all sitting around the fireplace enjoying the fire and the Christmas decorations, when Maria said, "Isn't it great to be together as a family? I'm glad to be able to share my life with you C.A. and I'm happy to have your family here today."

Leann said, "Every time we are in a group there is always some girl that will tell me they were sorry J.R. got married, that they had their eye on him!"

Maria laughed, "That is the way it was with C.A. Every girl in the Pep Club had a crush on 'Mr. Kennedy' and thought they would be the one he would choose."

Claire stunned the group with, "I beat the time of the prettiest girl in the community to get Will," and then she gave a little laugh.

Her comment was not much different than Leann's or Maria's but it somehow seemed that way. Especially because of the effect it had on Will. Even though he'd heard it many times over the years, he still reacted the same way. Every time Claire said it, he thought again that it wasn't Claire that beat Jessie's time, it was her farm. No matter how much time had passed, he still felt things would never be as they should have been, and he couldn't accept the way they had turned out.

Maria broke the silence that followed Claire's comment. "Anyway, I am glad we are who we are. I think we are a great family and I am happy to be a part of it!"

J.R. said, "I second the statement! I wouldn't change a thing. We come from a good line and I think we do them proud!"

"Hear! Hear!" they all cheered.

J.R. added to the expression of their feelings. "I made so many trips back and forth to California, I've almost forgotten how many. But here and now I wish to say I am in Missouri to stay for a long, long time, unless Leann should change my mind."

Leann laughed, "I am all for staying in Missouri."

"Good, now that's settled," Will remarked.

"How about another eggnog, Maria?"

"Coming up," Maria replied.

C.A. followed Maria into the kitchen, "Did you see Dad's face when Mom made her statement about beating the prettiest girl's time for Dad? He didn't like that one bit."

Maria whispered back, "I have heard her say that before. She always gives that same little laugh."

The rest of the day was spent happily, sharing gifts, watching the children, listening to carolers, and singing along with them.

At the end of the day, J.R. and Leann took Will and Claire back to the farm, exchanged another round of Christmas wishes, and promised to come back to visit soon.

On the drive to their own home, J.R. asked, "Did you see the funny look on Dad's face when Mom made her comment about beating the prettiest girl's time to get him?"

"Yes, I did! I've heard her make the statement before, but never when your Dad was there."

January 16, 1955

The expected baby did not arrive during the holidays as they had hoped. Days passed and they were becoming worried. Finally the doctor told them on Saturday that Maria should go to the hospital on Sunday. C.A. took the children to the grandparents' for the weekend, and early Sunday morning he and Maria were on their way to the hospital. Before long they had added Steven Malcom to the family.

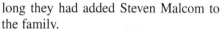

C.A. went to the farm to tell the family the news. "We have added Steven Malcom to our family! Dad, Maria chose the name Malcom in honor of your Grandfather and Steven for her Grandfather who came from Kentucky."

"Maria is more like a Kennedy than some in the family who were born a Kennedy! Both are good names. I am pleased to have a grandson named Malcom. You have added to the family tree, twins in California, a son in North Carolina, a daughter in Mississippi, and now a son in Missouri. I am glad you are back in Missouri now!"

"I think Missouri is just the place to finish raising our family."

C.A. took the children back home for school the next day. The rest of the family looked forward to meeting Steven. Although Susan had been hoping for a sister, she thought Steven was adorable.

When the Stark Nursery catalogue arrived that winter, C.A. ordered a dozen fruit trees. He told Maria, "Fruit trees are 'cheaper by the dozen' and apple and peach trees will be a welcome addition to our yard. What we don't use here I'll plant at the farm."

That spring C.A. planted some of the fruit trees in their yard in Elmwood. The next weekend, the boys helped plant the rest at the farm. Will said, "That is a good idea, C.A. I hope we are all still around when these trees bear fruit."

"I hope so too; if not, others in the family can enjoy the fruit."

Will continued, "C.A. I used to think you didn't have the Irish love of the land like the Kennedys. I have decided you do have that love of the land after all. You plant trees and vegetables instead of farming. You can water what you plant and it will grow even if the rains don't come."

C.A. laughed, "I do love to work in the garden; I like to watch things grow. You are right about being able to water. I have watched you and the uncles and cousins when the rains don't come. I have seen how disappointing it is when everything you worked so hard to plant withers and dies."

Will said, "You are right, but farming is all I know."

C.A. answered, "All in all, farming has been a good life for you and Mom."

"Yes, it has."

When the time came to have Steven christened, Susan suggested that he wear her christening dress and she would wear the Easter dress Maria had made for her. C.A. and Maria wanted the grandparents to be there. Since C.A.'s time was already taken up with school responsibilities, he asked the twins to make the trip to pick up their grandparents. The arrangement suited all of them, especially the twins. So it was that a happy group of Kennedys gathered for Steven's christening at the Elmwood Methodist Church. Will was grateful they could be there for the occasion. He liked to see the family growing and family names from the past continuing. Claire always liked to be with the family. It was meaningful for all of them. After church, the grandparents came for Sunday dinner. It was a special day for all.

C.A. invited his parents along with Uncle Andy and Aunt Nancy for Sunday dinner a few days before Christmas. C.A. considered Andy his favorite uncle, and Maria enjoyed Nancy's company as well. They all looked forward to spending the day together. Claire was looking forward to showing Nancy their new home.

Arthur and Ansel were put in charge of selecting a Christmas tree. C.A. had purchased a section of land near the family farm which had stands of pine and cedar. The boys stopped in to check on their grandparents, and then selected a tree from the property to cut and brought it home to decorate.

Maria could hardly believe her eyes when she saw the size of the tree! It was so large she wondered how it would ever fit through the doorway, but the boys were so proud of their selection that she just had to congratulate them on doing a fine job choosing the tree.

The day of the dinner, Ansel and Arthur informed everyone that they had chosen the tree themselves. It filled the entire picture window, and with ornaments weighting down the top branches it fit perfectly from floor to ceiling.

The boys proudly described how they had secured the tree on top of the car by tying it to the bumper and through both sets of windows. "It stuck out on both ends of the car, and we had to leave the windows down part way because of the rope," Ansel said. "We were pretty cold by the time we got home, but it was worth it."

"I'd say so," agreed Will. "That was quite an engineering feat."

"We had to get more decorations because we didn't have enough," added Susan. "But after it was decorated, our tree won a prize."

"A prize!" exclaimed Claire. "What kind of prize?"

"The Elmwood Chamber of Commerce sponsored a Christmas decoration contest," Maria explained. "Our tree was chosen as the 'Best Decorated Home Christmas Tree'. I think Steven is partly responsible for the award. I was in the kitchen one evening when I noticed colored lights moving in the living room. I found Steven swinging the tree branches, trying to reach the ornaments. I noticed a car driving slowly past the house; at the time I didn't think much about it. Later, when it was announced our tree had won first place, I realized the judging had taken place the same night. I'd say it was a combination of Steven's 'moving lights' and the specially selected tree the boys brought in that won the contest."

"That's the spirit," said Claire. "Everyone working together!" They all enjoyed a laugh at that.

"I remember when R.L. was Steven's age; a two year old can get into mischief quicker than you can turn around," added Nancy.

"That's the truth," agreed C.A. "A few weeks ago he was playing in the kitchen cabinets. Before we realized what he was up to he had taken the labels off all the cans. Maria has had to be creative with meals since that incident. You get some strange combinations when you can't tell for sure what you're going to open. Cranberry sauce and pumpkin sound the same when you shake the can."

Andy laughed, "Here I was looking forward to a wonderful dinner. Now you're saying it's a new kind of 'pot luck'. You invited us to use up the mystery cans quicker."

"No," Maria assured him, joining in the laughter. "Today's menu was planned in advance, and every ingredient was recognizable. But you can be sure Steven has lost his cabinet privileges."

The laugher and good spirits continued throughout the day. On the way home that evening, Andy said, "This has been an especially good visit. I am happy to see C.A. doing so well. He and Maria have a nice family and a nice home."

"Yes," Will replied. "I used to be disappointed that neither of my sons wanted to be farmers, but they both are doing what they enjoy and I can be happy about that."

The Family is Changing

J.R. and Leann continued to live in Jefferson City for several years. As a special gift one year, J.R. decided to give Will and Claire airline tickets to fly to California to see Aimie and David. "Mom and Dad have seen a lot in their lifetimes," J.R. said, "but they have never flown. And it will be a way of paying Mom back for money I borrowed from her during my running around days. She would never take the money when I tried to pay her back."

Claire was excited about the opportunity to visit Aimie in California. Will agreed to make the trip only after C.A. convinced him that the farm would be looked after during his absence.

J.R took the folks to catch the plane in Kansas City and took pictures to share with the others. The one they all liked the best showed Dad helping Mom into the plane.

Malinda and James met Will and Claire at the Los Angeles terminal. Claire could hardly wait to tell them how wonderful the trip had been. "Why, it was as smooth and level as if you were walking across your living room floor."

James and Malinda had contacted several of the Missouri folk who had made the trip to California with Will and Claire years before. They had so many old friends stopping by to see them that Malinda said it was like 'Old Home Week'. It made for a great reunion and a time to celebrate. Several of them told Will and Claire, "We probably wouldn't be here today if it hadn't been for you two and C.A."

James and Malinda took them to Aimie and David's where they saw more old friends. "Flying is the way to travel," Claire told them. "My goodness, how many days did it take for our first trip? Things have improved since then." It was all very enjoyable.

Claire and Aimie spent hours enjoying one another's company and sharing stories about their families, but it wasn't long before Will began to miss the farm. He didn't say anything but Claire guessed that he was getting restless and told Malinda it was time they went back to Missouri. When James and Malinda took them to the airport Will said, "At first I didn't want to make this trip but now I wouldn't have missed it for the world, but it's time we got back home."

Claire said, "We are looking to see you all in Missouri next summer."

"We will plan on it!" James said. "Aunt Claire, I want to put my name in the pot for your chicken and dumplings."

As it turned out, the entire family was at the airport to meet them. It was quite an important occasion that the grandparents had taken such a trip, and the grandchildren were excited about the being at the airport. There was a lot of talking until finally Will said, "This has been a wonderful trip, but I am ready to get on home and just think about it." They all could understand his feelings.

Will and Claire enjoyed having the grandchildren near enough to visit often. Ansel and Arthur helped out on the farm regularly. They enjoyed the work, and trips to their grandparents' had the added bonus of an opportunity to drive. One project they enjoyed was getting rocks to build up the floor of the front porch. It took several loads of rocks, gathered by driving all over the fields, before the concrete was poured. Any task that involved driving was great!

William helped out on the farm, too. Will especially liked to tell about the time the twins asked William to clear the garden of rock, thinking it would keep him busy for hours. "It didn't take him nearly as long as they expected," Will would say when telling the story. "He hung a bucket on each handlebar of his bicycle and filled them with rocks. Then he pushed the bike over to the rock pile, dumped them out, and was back for more in no time. William will do well," he would say proudly. "That boy is a problem solver!"

Claire enjoyed having Susan in the house with her. Having a grand-daughter was even more special because Claire had never had a daughter of her own. The two of them spent a lot of time in the kitchen, in the garden, and just being together. One year Claire used her egg money to have a pleated, red wool skirt made for Susan for Christmas. The new skirt was finished just in time for the annual Brandton Masons' Christmas Oyster Supper. Will beamed with pride as Susan twirled around the room at the dinner. "That's my granddaughter," he couldn't resist saying to everyone around, "She is the first daughter of the Kennedy name in thirty-seven years."

Both Grandma and Grandpa enjoyed watching Steven grow up. Steven enjoyed watching the farm animals and going with Claire to gather the eggs. He was especially interested when they had calves, ponies, or baby chickens. Steven named each of the animals on the farm; Grandma and Grandpa might not remember which one was Sugar or Sally, but Steven did.

Grandma and Grandpa shared special occasions with their grandchildren. They were there when Ansel, Arthur, and later William, received their Eagle Scout Award. They watched proudly when the twins were the first in the District to receive the God and Country Award. "You know," Will told Claire later, "that shows the boys have good character and honors the rest of the family too. I am proud of them."

They even got out at night to watch Ansel and Arthur play basketball. Ansel and Arthur were on the basketball team for Elmwood and Leann's brother, Harry, was on Brandton's team. When Leann heard of an upcoming game between Elmwood and Brandton, she suggested that she and J.R. take both sets of parents to Brandton to see the game. The night of the game, the gymnasium was packed. It was an exciting game with Elmwood winning 86 to 80. Later Claire told Maria, "I got so annoyed with Leann and her mother. Every time Harry did something cute they had to jump up and cheer."

Maria laughed, "Claire, you should have sat in the Elmwood section. We were up quite a few times to cheer for Ansel and Arthur."

Maria told C.A. the next day, "Your mother said Leann and her mother cheered 'every time Harry did something cute'. I don't think she realized it was because he had made a good play."

C.A.'s were glad they were near enough to see the grandparents often. One day when they decided to run over and check on them they were surprised to see Claire out by the gate and to their alarm she was crying.

C.A. hurried to her; "Mom, what is wrong?"

Claire replied with sobs, "I am an orphan now. Aimie died."

Maria said, "We are so sorry; how can we help you? Will you go for the service?"

"James called me; he wants to pay my way. I will leave from Rolla tomorrow morning at 8:00. I am so glad we went to California to visit Aimie. Oh, dear me, I don't know what to do now. I guess I should pack my bag. What should I take?"

"Let's go inside," Maria said, "I will help you get your things together."

Maria helped Claire to pack what she would need for the trip. C.A. said he would take her to the train station the next morning. Before C.A. left, Will said, "Now I can take care of myself while your mother is gone this time. Don't you go and call Cousin Effie!"

C.A. promised he wouldn't call Cousin Effie.

At the train station the next morning C.A. told his mother she should stay as long as Malinda needed her. "We will come every weekend to see that Dad is doing all right. Maria will cook some extra food before we leave today, and she will get things ready for him each weekend when we come. Andy and Nancy said they would help him too."

When Claire returned she was pleased to find that Will had cleaned the garden of the dried summer plants and had it ready for the winter. Tears came to her eyes and she said, "Will, thank you so much for tending to the garden while I was gone. On the way home I was thinking that I would have to hurry to get the old stalks and vines out before the ground froze. Thank you for doing my work."

Will replied, "It needed to be done and I needed to keep busy. I am glad you are home."

When it was time for Ansel and Arthur to start to college, C.A. and Maria decided to sell their land near the farm that they had bought years before. C.A said, "All that tract of land has done for us in the past is furnish Christmas trees."

Maria replied, "Yes, that money will give the boys a good start toward their education. I know once they start something they always finish it; they will get a good education.

C.A. told his dad about their decision, Will said, "Yes, when you started out, you could teach and go to college at the same time. The boys can't do that now. I am glad the land can help the boys get a good start."

C.A. said, "It took me a long time to finish my degree but it was a learning experience too. I appreciated it more when I worked for it! Maria and I want to help the boys, but we won't make it too easy for them!"

Meggie wrote to Minnie that she planned to come for a visit in July to be there over the 4th and hoped they could have all of the family together like they used to; maybe even at the river!

Minnie called Lettie, Frank, Will, Nat, and Andy to give them the good news that Meggie was coming in July and they would all gather at the river on July 4th. Everyone was excited and agreed to be sure their children and grandchildren knew about the picnic.

Lettie said, "Oh, good, I'm glad she is coming! Is she bringing her family?"

"I don't think her husband and the grown children are coming, but she is bringing her younger children."

"I hope they will stay with me!" Lettie responded.

Minnie said, "In her letter Meggie said she would make my place their headquarters."

Lettie said, "I'll write and tell her they are welcome at our place."

Then Minnie called her daughters, Louise, Laura and Edith, to ask for their help in planning and seeing that everything went well. Minnie said to each of them, "I am really looking forward to seeing everyone but arranging things would be difficult for me now."

Louise said, "I was just wishing the other day that we would have an old fashion' gathering at the river. I am glad Aunt Meggie is coming!

Minnie's daughters came early to set up everything for the picnic. Laura said "Look, our picnic area by the river now has even more shade and picnic tables!"

The table was laden as always; grandchildren played, and the oldsters reminised. Lettie and Minnie were filling Meggie in on what friends and acquaintances were doing since Meggie left for New York. Meggie asked, "And what did the prissy Miss Jessie do?"

Minnie answered, "Oh, she married Gus Schmidt, probably had her eye on the Schmidt's money! From the looks of things she didn't get to spend any of it. Jessie broke her arm and couldn't work so she and Gus had to move out to their own place. Schmidt's loaned him the money but he had to pay them back. That is probably why they moved to Texas."

Will overheard their conversation and regret set in. 'Why did Jessie think she would have plenty of money when she married Gus? All of the Schmidt's were known for holding on to their money. I am sorry I heard what Minnie said. Well, at least I don't need to worry every time I go to town that I will run into Jessie.'

Will said to the group, "We should do this more often, the last time we were together was at a funeral." They all agreed 'a good time was had by all' and they wouldn't wait so long to have another get together."

Lettie called Claire after Meggie and the boys left, "We had such a good time at the river, didn't we? Meggie's sons were so grown up. I was very disappointed they didn't stay with me at least part of the time they were here. I even bought a new bed for her."

Claire said, "Maybe next time she'll stay with you and in the mean-time you can enjoy the new bed yourself."

Claire called Nancy. "Lettie is still Lettie! She had to tell someone she was unhappy that Meggie didn't stay with her."

Nancy replied, "Some things never change and I'm glad the good things about the family haven't changed either!"

J.R. and Leann took the Grandparents to Ansel's wedding. Arthur was the best man, William was groomsman, Susan was a bridesmaid, and Steven was the ring bearer. A short time later it was Arthur's wedding and Ansel was the best man. A few years later, William married his high school sweetheart.

Will said "It is good to see these young folk starting life so well prepared. I wish them a long and satisfying life. We have had our ups and downs but we were always there for each other."

Claire smile, patted Will's hand, and replied, "They will do fine, just look at the Kennedy record. Besides, they all married Missouri Girls!"

Will and Claire were pleased to hear that Arthur and Anna and Ansel and Lois were all teachers in the Kansas City area. Will said proudly, "I am glad they are teachers; that was a good profession for C.A. too. We can really retire now; the Kennedy family is in good hands. This generation is going to do all right."

Claire replied, "Will, how can we retire?"

Will continued, "Oh, I don't mean quit, just take it a little easier. I think I'll talk to young William to see if they want to pasture some of their cows on our land and maybe keep the fences and gates in good shape. I don't want any horses or bulls over here."

C.A. and Maria agreed that returning to Missouri had been a good move for all concerned. It was good for the family to be able to do things they enjoyed. It was a good place for the children to grow up. It was a good time for Will and Claire too. It wasn't so much the help the family gave, although they appreciated that; it was the company. Having the grandchildren nearby gave them something else to think about as they grew older.

Sad Days Ahead

Claire loved having family over to visit through the years. Will said she was spinning like a top all day taking care of the household and getting ready for their visits. It came as a shock one morning when Claire didn't get out of bed promptly as she usually did. When Will helped her up, she seemed puzzled as to what to do next, and then she turned around and got back in bed. Will called Dr. Holmes, who came quickly. He wasn't long in making his diagnosis. "Will, Claire has had a massive stroke. She should go to a hospital. Since J.R. is in Jefferson City, I would suggest going to one close to him. I will call an ambulance."

Will said, "Do what you need to do. What should I do now?"

Dr. Holmes replied, "Call J.R. to meet us at the hospital. Then call C.A."

Will called J.R. "Your Mom has had a stroke. Dr. Holmes said she must go to the hospital in Jeff. They will take her in an ambulance. Will you call C.A.?"

J.R. was stunned. "I will call C.A. We will meet you at the hospital."

Dr. Holmes said, "You will want to stay at J.R.'s so you can be close to Claire. You should pack some things you will need. Hurry; the ambulance will be here soon. You will want to ride with Claire."

Will went into the bedroom, took out the suitcase and opened the top drawer of the chest. "I don't know what to take. J.R. will have to come get my things later."

The ambulance came and Will rode in the front seat by the driver. When Claire arrived at the hospital, the nurses made her as comfortable as possible but Doctor Holmes did not give them any encouragement. C.A. and J.R. couldn't quite believe their mother was so ill. They filled her room with flowers. Maria and Leann shopped for pretty gowns and a robe. Claire smiled but could not speak. Other problems began to add to her failing health. Will was reluctant to accept the gravity of her condition; the others realized that she wouldn't get well.

When the Doctor told them the end was near, C.A. said he would stay the night with his mother. Will and J.R. would wait in the waiting room. Will predicted, "She will pass away at sunrise as her father did."

It was a long night for all of them. J.R. didn't want to be there at the end so he made himself useful by bringing coffee and doughnuts to the others. He had just started into the room with coffee for C.A. when he looked out the window and saw the rising sun and heard his mother's final breath. He almost dropped the coffee.

J.R. said sadly, "She's gone. I hadn't wanted to be in here at the end but I am glad I was. She would have wanted that."

C.A. put his arm around him and said, "Yes, it has been as she would have wanted it."

J.R. and C.A. came back into the waiting room; Will stood up when he saw them. C.A. said, "Dad, she is gone."

Will couldn't grasp the fact that Claire had passed away. For the past 68 years Claire had always been there for him and taken care of their needs. He felt numb; he didn't know how to proceed so he turned to his sons and said, "You and the girls will have to take care of things now. You will have to make the arrangements."

C.A. and J.R. were not any better prepared than Will. C.A. said "Maria and Leann will help plan her service."

Maria had helped her Aunt Lula make arrangements for relatives on several similar occasions. They started with the funeral home, and then called the minister. They decided all of Claire's dresses were too dark and they didn't care for what the funeral home had to offer. Maria said, "I know the perfect thing. Remember the dressing gown she liked so much? She always said she was 'saving it for special.' It has pretty lace and ribbons at the neckline; it is a soft pink. She would look lovely and at rest."

Leann agreed. "That would be perfect. They do a nice job on hair at the funeral home."

Maria said, "We should have the organist play Christian Endeavor before and after the main service. Claire's favorite songs were, "In the Garden, Beautiful Isle of Somewhere, and In the Sweet By and By. Her favorite scripture was Psalms 121. She liked red roses; they will look nice on top of the metallic grey casket. We can have visitation tomorrow night." When plans were finished, they were all sure that Claire would have been pleased.

Leann said, "Now how will we get through the next few days?"

Maria responded, "I think the best thing is to go out to the farm and just be quiet and be together." It went better than they thought; friends and family came by, staying a few minutes, many bringing food, and asking if they needed anything. It was an opportunity for them to find out what a difference Claire, in her quiet way, had made for so many.

The story that moved Maria the most was a young woman who said that when she joined the church she was feeling so alone. Her family was gone and she hadn't lived in Brandton long enough to have close friends. Claire had come to congratulate her and said, "I was a close friend to your grandparents. They would be so proud of you if they were here today to

192

see what a fine young lady you are. Anytime you need a friend, I am here."

Claire was a charter member of the Ladies Church Organization. One member said, "We will surely miss Claire, not for what she said, but for

 what she did. We could always depend on her. She has made more pies and cooked more chickens for our church dinners than anyone.

Claire's service was consoling. There was a gathering at the house, and the church, and then the cemetery. Someone else provided the roasted chicken for the meal the church served the family.

Will spent the night pondering the question of how he would manage without Claire. She was the one who always made sure everything was ready for their needs. He would miss her. He had never dreamed she would die first.

The children stayed a few days to help Will adjust. They returned dishes to neighbors who had brought food, wrote thank you notes, and went through Claire's things at the farm. They took most of Claire's clothes to a Nursing Home. The four of them discussed the question they had all been pondering, "What can we do for Dad?" Leann said, "When he stayed with us in Jeff before your Mom died, he thought he would be going home soon. Do you think he would be happy to come back home with us now?" They all agreed that he wouldn't.

"He will want to stay on the farm," C.A. said

"He can't stay by himself!" the rest of them replied.

The boys had the difficult task of finding a housekeeper for Will. Friends gave them names of several women but they didn't find anyone who was interested in the job. One lady surprised them with the comment, "I think he would be hard to please. Claire was always hurrying around trying to have things just right to please Will."

At last they found a lady who had just retired as an Avon representative. She agreed to come and cook one meal a day for Will. She wouldn't do laundry, but she would clean the house once a week. She had her own car and would do the marketing.

"Looks as if that is the best we can do for now. We will take the laundry or do it when we come down," was J.R.'s dispirited comment.

If Hazel doesn't work out, that place in town that has room and board might be the solution," commented C.A.

A few days later a letter came for Will from Meggie.

Dearest Will,

*   I was so sorry to hear about Claire's passing.   I shall never forget how kind she has always been to me. We are all alone now, except for our memories. My Edward passed on a long time ago and the others are gone, too. Dear Will don't dwell on the unhappy things that have happened in your life. Instead think about the happy times we had growing up. Think of Mama and Papa and the others and how close we were.   Think about the good years and the happy times you and Claire had together.   I know the boys and their families will be a great comfort to you.   Thank God for the many good years you have had."*

All my love,
Meggie

After he finished reading Meggie's letter, Will sat there and cried. He thought about Claire. Then he thought about Jessie. 'Nothing is like it should have been.'

Will was surprised at how lonely he was on the farm. He missed Claire! He had never thought he would feel that way. Through the years he had been too busy on the farm and, he had to admit, thinking about Jessie. He wondered if Claire had ever had any suspicion of his feelings for Jessie. Will said out loud, with no one listening, "Do you suppose she guessed why I wanted to marry her?" He suspected that she had. Many times he had cringed when Claire had said, 'Why, I beat the time of the prettiest girl around to get Will. I must have had something she didn't.' Thinking back, he remembered that Maria had once heard Claire say that and had said 'He

 knew a good thing when he saw it.' Claire had replied with her usual airy little laugh. 'It is a comforting thought that we had a good life. I was good to her. We were both proud of our sons. We were both proud of our grand-children. I am glad she lived to know our great grandchildren. I am glad that we can keep the farm in the family. Claire wanted the farm to stay in the family.'

Alas, Jessie

Hazel Elkins lasted just two weeks. She called J.R. saying, "I quit! Your dad complains too much about what I spend. He said I am a good cook but that I spent twice as much as Claire for groceries!"

J.R. told her he would bring her a check on Saturday.

The next Saturday, J.R. came down from Jefferson City. It took some persuading to convince Will to make the change to live in town.

"OK, I guess I can try it for awhile. I can always come back to the farm and check on things."

To Will's great surprise, once he made the move he enjoyed town life. He liked walking down to the Post Office in the mornings and visiting a while with the other older men.

C.A.'s and J.R.'s visited frequently. Each visit included a trip out to the farm so Will could be sure everything was taken care of to his satisfaction. Of course he usually found something that Young William would need to repair.

Will didn't realize what a target he was for the unmarried women. He had an outstanding farm and no children living at home; eligible on all counts. First thing Will knew, little old ladies were coming by the boarding house with all kinds of cakes, pies, candy, even fried chicken. He really enjoyed all the perks of living in town. It never occurred to him to wonder why he got so much attention but he was enjoying himself.

One younger woman, Ruby, noticed Will. She had been the mistress for several businessmen over the years and had no interest in Will for herself. But she had an Aunt Ola who could use a good farm. And Aunt Ola in turn could leave it to Ruby for helping with the courtship. Ruby had no way of knowing that a number of years before, the boys had their parents sign the place over to C.A. They all wanted to keep the farm in the family and C.A. would see to that and see that it was kept up.

Ruby arranged a family outing at a nearby State Park. There were several carloads of relatives involved in the outing, and Ruby arranged for Will and Aunt Ola to ride in the back seat of her car. She made sure there was a youngster in the seat as well so they would have to sit close together.

Nancy happened to be in town and saw them getting into Ruby's car. As soon as Nancy got home, she called C.A. "It looks like Ruby Munson and her Aunt Ola are making quite a play for your Dad!"

C.A. replied, "I doubt if he realizes what they have in mind for his future. We'll be watching to be sure Dad doesn't get hurt."

Then Betty, Will's landlady, told C.A. "Ruby Munson and her Aunt Ola are giving your Dad a big rush. You know what they say, 'there is no fool like an old fool'. Ruby has a thing going with some of the businessmen and isn't interested in your Dad but she wants your Dad interested in Aunt Ola. He acts like he's more interested in Ruby! Anyway, I just wanted you to know what I know."

C.A. assured her they were aware of the situation and would watch out for Will.

C.A. and J.R. held a consultation. J.R. said, "In due time Ruby and her Aunt Ola will find out who the place belongs to, and when they do, they will loose interest in Dad."

Fate stepped in before Ruby and her Aunt Ola dropped Will. A fine misty rain was falling and it was turning cooler. Will started downtown for his daily rounds. Betty, his landlady, called after him, "Mr. Kennedy, you shouldn't get wet with that cold you have."

"Oh, I won't be out long." Will hollered back.

As Will came back by the frozen food locker plant, he saw the hunters bringing in their deer to process, and he stopped to chat. As he became interested in the conversations, he didn't realize how much time had passed and how wet he had become. He was soaked by the time he got back to the rooming house. Betty gave him quite a scolding and then brought him some hot tea with honey in it.

By the next morning, Will's cold had gone into his chest. His breathing sounded labored and Betty was alarmed! She called J.R. and C.A. to come as soon as they could. They all agreed that Will needed to be in the hospital right away. They asked Betty to call Leann to have the family doctor waiting to admit Will to the hospital. J.R. broke the speed limit on straight stretches of highway in an effort to get to the hospital as quickly as possible.

Leann and the doctor had everything ready for Will when he arrived. After Doctor Kinsey checked Will over, he said, "This didn't just happen over night. How long have you had this cold?"

"I guess a little over a week," was Will's weak reply.

"Well, I am ordering you to stay in bed. Call the nurse when you need to go to the bathroom. We will give you our best medicines."

When J.R. went to do the paperwork for Will's admission, the head nurse said, "I see your father is from the same section of Missouri as my parents. Perhaps he's heard of them. My mother was a Randolph and my father a Schmidt. I am named for my mother, Jessie. My parents live in Texas now."

After Will went to sleep, J.R. and Leann went home. The nurse had said there was nothing more they could do.

Will awakened in the night and wanted to go to the bathroom. He remembered what the doctor had said about calling a nurse, but he was convinced he could still take care of himself. It took him longer to get over the railing on the side of the bed than he thought it would. By the time he overcame that obstacle, he didn't have time to make it to the bathroom. Then to make matters worse, he slipped and fell in the puddle he had made. To add to his humiliation, he couldn't get up from his fall. The nurses heard the commotion and came quickly. Even before the doctor arrived, they knew he must have broken his hip.

The nurse called J.R. and told him about the accident and Doctor Kinsey's verdict that his Dad had broken his hip. Until they got his lungs cleared up they couldn't set the hip. All they could do immediately was make him as comfortable as possible with medication and put sand bags around the injury.

When the head nurse Jessie, came to see Will later, he seemed restless. Nurse Jessie wasn't satisfied with his condition, so she called Dr. Kinsey again. Dr. Kinsey wasn't satisfied either.

"He isn't responding to the medication. That fall was just too much for him. Better send for the other son." Nurse Jessie volunteered to sit with Will until the family came.

Will was looking up at Nurse Jessie as C.A. and J.R. came in the room. "Oh, you came. Oh, the blue sky in your eyes," he said weakly. "I am so sorry I didn't have anything. Oh-o-o-o...alas, Jessie." He drifted back into unconsciousness.

Nurse Jessie went to C.A. and J.R. and said, "I am so sorry, but his chances don't look good." As she started to leave she said, "Isn't it a small world? As I was sitting here I thought of your parents and mine being from the same community. Who would have thought that after all these years their children's paths would cross here."

C.A. asked, "What do you remember your folks telling you of their growing up there?"

"I remember my mother saying how happy her teen years were. She said she was the 'Belle of the Parties', and was set to marry the most handsome man around when he dumped her for someone with a farm. She married Dad instead. She was glad when they moved to Texas a few years later, because she had to work so hard in Missouri."

After Nurse Jessie left, J.R. turned to C.A. "Are you thinking what I am thinking?"

C.A. replied, "Yes, I am. Nurse Jessie didn't quite understand Dad clearly but I did. Dad was the handsome fellow who dumped Nurse Jessie's mother!"

"Dad thought Nurse Jessie was his sweetheart from so many years ago. I wonder if Mom knew?"

"I don't think she did in the early years. When I was growing up I remember how she did everything she could to please Dad. He did everything to improve the farm and she either fixed what she could or made do for the house."

"You remember Mom telling us how she beat the time of the prettiest girl in the community to get Dad. She told it in such a taunting manner and gave a little laugh, then looked at Dad. He didn't look too pleased about her comment. I think she knew by then." Both men agreed their parents had dealt with circumstances the way they had to, and that the results turned out better than most, but ....Alas, Jessie.